eyewitness
stories

eyewitness
stories

FOUR REPORTS ON THE LIFE OF CHRIST

FRANK BALL

WINEPRESS WP PUBLISHING

WinePress Publishing (PO Box 428, Enumclaw, WA 98022) functions only
as book publisher. As such, the ultimate design, content, editorial accuracy,
and views expressed or implied in this work are those of the author.

ISBN 13: 978-1-57921-931-4
ISBN 10: 1-57921-931-4
Library of Congress Catalog Card Number: 2007935974

table of contents

Introduction ix

Matthew 1

Mark 69

Luke 113

John 187

References to Prophecy Fulfilled 241

Chronology of Events 245

Comments on Difficult Passages 257

- Matthew 2:1–18—We have seen the star signaling
  his birth and have come to worship him. 257
- Matthew 2:19–23; Luke 2:39–52—When Jesus was
  twelve, the family went to Jerusalem to celebrate
  the Passover festival, according to Jewish custom 258
- Matthew 4:1–11; Mark 1:12–13; Luke 4:1–13—
  Satan took [Jesus] to the Temple in Jerusalem and
  stood him on a high place, towering above the
  Kidron valley. "Since you are the Son of God, jump." 258
- Matthew 21:12; Mark 11:15; Luke 19:45;
  John 2:15—In the Temple's outer court, Jesus
  threw out the merchants who were buying and
  selling there. 259
- Matthew 4:19; Mark 1:17—Come, follow me,
  and I will make you fishers of men. 260
- Matthew 10:16—Listen, I am sending you like
  lambs into a pack of wolves. Therefore, you must
  be wise as snakes . . . harmless as doves. 261
- Matthew 8:5–13; Luke 7:2–10—A Roman officer sent
  respected Jewish leaders to Jesus, pleading for help. 261

- Matthew 11:28–30—Take my yoke upon you. The load is light..262
- Matthew 12:26–28; Luke 17:20—If Beelzebub is my power over evil spirits, by whom do your followers cast them out?..262
- Matthew 9:18–34; Mark 5:21–43; Luke 8:40–56— My little daughter is dying, but if you will come lay your hand on her, she will live..................................263
- Matthew 10:5—Do not go among the Gentiles or into any Samaritan city. 263
- Matthew 15:21–28; Mark 7:24–30—I was only sent to the lost sheep of Israel..263
- Matthew 17:14–21; Mark 9:14–29; Luke 9:37–43—If you had real faith the size of a mustard seed, you could tell this mountain to move and it could not stand still. 264
- John 8:2–11—Their question was intended to trap [Jesus] into saying something against either the Law or public opinion. 264
- Matthew 6:9–13; Luke 11:1–13—"When you pray," Jesus said, "say something like this."............................265
- Luke 11:9—Ask and you will receive, seek and you will find, knock and the door will be opened for you. 265
- Matthew 23:37–39; Luke 13:34–35—I have wanted to gather you to myself like a hen brings her chicks under her wings..266
- Matthew 19:24–26; Mark 10:25–27; Luke 18:25–27 —Jesus said, "Those who trust in riches will have a very difficult time entering the Kingdom." [The disciples said,] "If that is true, who can be saved?" 266
- Matthew 20:1–16; 22:1–14—Many are called, and few are chosen. 267

- Matthew 20:20–28; Mark 10:35–45—In your glorious kingdom . . . award the seats of honor on your right and left. 268
- Luke 19:1–9—Sir, I will give half my wealth to the poor. If I have defrauded anyone, I will pay back four times the amount. 268
- Matthew 20:29–34; Mark 10:46–52; Luke 18:35–43— Two blind men, including one named Bartimaeus (son of Timaeus), sat by the side of the road, begging. 268
- John 15:1–8—Whatever you ask will be done..............268
- Matthew 27:3–10—[Judas] flung the silver across the Temple floor, left, and hanged himself........................269
- Matthew 27:46; Mark 15:34—My God, my God, for this I was born. 269
- Matthew 28:1–15; Mark 16:1–11; Luke 24:1–12; John 20:1–18—Mary Magdalene . . . was the first to see Jesus after he rose from the dead...........................270
- Mark 16:12–13; Luke 24:13–35—Two of Jesus' followers left for Emmaus.....................................271
- John 20:21–23—The sins you forgive will be forgiven, and the sins you do not forgive will not be forgiven.........272

Introduction

> *"Now you are speaking plainly,"* the disciples said,
> *"without the confusing figures of speech."*
>
> (John 16:29)

In high school in the 1950s, I had to read *Romeo and Juliet* by William Shakespeare. "Romeo, Romeo, wherefore art thou?" Juliet said. I never questioned my understanding of her words, because the meaning seemed obvious. I imagined some kind of hide-and-seek where Juliet searched for her lover and wanted him to reveal where he was. For forty years, I had that misconception, until I discovered how our language had changed. Juliet was using the common greeting in Shakespeare's day that was the equivalent to saying, "Romeo, how are you doing?"

The Gospel writers penned a valuable message to readers in the first century, but that audience is no longer alive. Every new generation brings changes to the way we say things, differences that may be too subtle to notice but are there nevertheless. For many, the ancient speech of King James is still pleasant to their ears. However, the old language can be misleading. For the best understanding and to share the message with others, we need to hear the Gospel stories in plain speech, using today's English.

Eyewitness Stories: Four Reports on the Life of Christ avoids words that have acquired an inappropriate religious connotation. For example, in today's culture, *Lord* is often regarded as a title of worshipful admiration that obviously does not fit the greeting from people who wanted to kill Jesus. The word *sir* is much better. *Scribes* may be misunderstood to mean people who do no more than copy words, so *teachers of the Law* is more accurate. Many people don't understand "in my name" and treat the use of Jesus' name similar to "abracadabra" or "open sesame." Therefore, the "in my name" phrase is best described as "under my direction and authority."

Eyewitness Stories pays special attention to the context, making sure the meaning of each sentence has been correctly rendered in easy-to-understand language.

Matthew

Chapter 1

¹Matthew reports the ancestors of Jesus starting with Abraham, ²his son Isaac, and Isaac's son Jacob. ³After that, there was Judah and his son Perez (whose mother was Tamar). Perez's descendents were Hezron, Ram, ⁴Ram, Amminadab, Nahshon, Salmon, ⁵and Boaz (whose mother was Rahab). Boaz's descendants were Obed (whose mother was Ruth), Jesse, ⁶David, and Solomon (whose mother was Bathsheba, the widow of Uriah).

⁷Solomon's descendents were Rehoboam, Abijah, Asaph, ⁸Jehoshaphat, Jehoram, Uzziah, ⁹Jotham, Ahaz, Hezekiah, ¹⁰Manasseh, Amos, Josiah, ¹¹and Jehoiachin, who was born when the Jews were exiled to Babylon. ¹²Jehoiachin's descendents were Shealtiel, Zerubbabel, ¹³Abiud, Eliakim, Azor, ¹⁴Zadok, Akim, Eliud, ¹⁵Eleazar, Matthan, and Jacob. ¹⁶Joseph was Jacob's son and the husband of Mary, the mother of Jesus the Messiah.

¹⁷Fourteen generations are listed from Abraham to King David, fourteen from David's time to the Babylonian exile, and fourteen from the exile to the Messiah.

¹⁸The birth of Jesus the Messiah happened this way: His mother, Mary, was engaged to Joseph, but before the marriage, while still a virgin, she became pregnant by the power of the Holy Spirit.

¹⁹When Joseph discovered that his fiancée was pregnant, he did not want to subject her to public disgrace, so he decided to break their engagement quietly. ²⁰While still contemplating exactly what he would do, an angel appeared to him in a dream, saying, "Joseph, son of David, do not be afraid to get married. The child has been

conceived in Mary by the Holy Spirit. ²¹She will have a son, and you must name him Jesus because he will save his people from their sins."

²²All this happened to fulfill what God had spoken through the prophet Isaiah: ²³*Watch for this! A virgin will become pregnant and give birth to a son named Immanuel*, meaning "God with us." ²⁴Aroused from sleep, Joseph did as the angel had commanded. He took Mary to be his wife ²⁵but avoided intimacy with her until after the baby was born. And he named him Jesus.

Chapter 2

¹After Jesus was born, wise men came to Jerusalem from lands beyond the eastern horizon. ²"Where is the newborn king of the Jews?" they asked. "We have seen the star signaling his birth and have come to worship him."

³When King Herod heard about them, he and most of Jerusalem were mystified. ⁴He called a meeting of the chief priests and teachers of the Law and asked, "Where is the Anointed One supposed to be born?"

⁵"In Bethlehem in Judea," they told him. "This is what the prophet Micah wrote: ⁶*But you, Bethlehem near Ephrath, are only a small village among the people of Judah. Yet out of you will come one who will rule Israel, whose origin is from ancient times.*"

⁷Herod called a private meeting with the wise men to determine exactly when the star had first appeared. ⁸"Go to Bethlehem," he told them, "and diligently search for the child. When you find him, come tell me where he is so I may also worship him."

⁹After receiving the king's instructions, they knew where to go. ¹⁰On the way to Bethlehem, they were filled with joy as the star they had seen in the east appeared again and guided them to the place where the child was. ¹¹They entered the house and saw the

child with his mother, Mary. After bowing in worship, they opened their treasure chests and presented gifts of gold, frankincense, and myrrh. [12]Warned by God in a dream, they did not return to Herod but left for their own country by another route.

[13]After they had gone, an angel of God appeared to Joseph in a dream. "Get up," the angel said. "Herod will search for the child to kill him. Flee to Egypt with the child and his mother, and stay there until I tell you to return."

[14]While it was still night, Joseph got up, took the child and his mother, and left for Egypt. [15]This fulfilled Hosea's prophecy: *I called my son out of Egypt.*

[16]Herod was furious when he realized the wise men had tricked him. He sent soldiers to kill all the boys in Bethlehem and areas nearby—all who were two years old and under—in keeping with the time he had learned from the wise men's report. [17]His brutality fulfilled what Jeremiah had prophesied: [18]*A cry is heard in Ramah, mourning and bitter weeping. Rachel weeps for her children and will not be comforted, because they are gone.*

[19]After Herod's death, an angel of God appeared to Joseph in a dream, saying, [20]"Get up and take the child and his mother to Israel. Those who tried to kill the child are now dead."

[21]So Joseph left Egypt with his family and would have settled in Judea [22]but heard that Archelaus reigned in place of his father, Herod. Afraid to go there and warned in a dream, Joseph took Mary and Jesus [23]to Nazareth, a village in the Galilean hills. That fulfilled what the prophets had written: *He will be called a Nazarene.*

Chapter 3

[1]The word of God came to John the Baptizer in the Judean wilderness. [2]"Repent," he said, "for the Kingdom of Heaven is near."

³Long ago, the prophet Isaiah referred to John when he wrote: *Listen! Someone is shouting, "Clear a path in the wilderness, for the Lord our God is coming. Fill the valleys and flatten the mountains. Straighten the curves and smooth the rough places."*

⁴He wore camel's hair clothing with a leather belt around his waist and lived on a diet of locusts and wild honey.

⁵People came from Jerusalem, all of Judea, and the Jordan valley ⁶to see and hear John. They confessed their sins and were baptized in the Jordan River.

⁷When John saw many Pharisees and Sadducees coming, he said, "You bunch of snakes. Who warned you to flee God's judgment? ⁸The way you live proves whether you have left your sins and turned to God. ⁹Do not say to one another, 'We are all right because we are Abraham's descendents.' That does not mean anything. God can make these stones into children of Abraham. ¹⁰His ax is raised, ready to sever the roots of every tree that does not produce good fruit. You will be chopped down and thrown into the fire!

¹¹"One is coming after me," he cried, "who is so great I am not worthy to carry his sandals. I baptize with water, but he will baptize you with the Holy Spirit. ¹²He holds his threshing fork and will thoroughly clean his floor. He will gather the wheat into his barn but burn the chaff with unquenchable fire."

¹³From Galilee, Jesus came to be baptized of John.

¹⁴John objected, saying, "I should be baptized by you. Why are you coming to me?"

¹⁵"This is what should be done," Jesus said. "We must do all that God requires of us."

So John consented and baptized him.

¹⁶As Jesus came up out of the water, the sky opened, and the Spirit of God descended like a dove, lighting upon him.

¹⁷A voice spoke from heaven: "You are my son, whom I love. I am well pleased with you."

Chapter 4

¹The Holy Spirit led Jesus into the wilderness to be tempted by Satan. ²For forty days, Jesus fasted, eating nothing at all. Afterward, it was time to eat.

³The tempter came and said, "Since you are the Son of God, command these stones to become bread."

⁴Jesus refused, quoting from Deuteronomy: *"People do not live by bread only but by everything God says."*

⁵After that, Satan took him to the Temple in Jerusalem and stood him on a high place.

⁶"Since you are the Son of God, jump. For it is written in the Psalms: *God will command his angels to protect you. They will hold you in their hands lest you strike your foot against a stone."*

⁷"It is also written," Jesus said, quoting from another Deuteronomy passage, *"You must not test the Lord your God."*

⁸Once more, Satan took him to a high mountain and showed him the magnificence of the kingdoms of this world. ⁹"I will give you all of this," he said, "if you will bow and worship me."

¹⁰Again, Jesus refused. "Get out of here, Satan. The scriptures say: *Love the Lord your God and serve only him."*

¹¹Then Satan left, and angels came and ministered to Jesus.

¹²After Jesus heard that John had been put in prison, he left Judea and went to Galilee.

¹³Jesus left Nazareth and settled in Capernaum by the Sea of Galilee, a town in the area of Zebulun and Naphtali. ¹⁴This fulfilled the prophecy that Isaiah wrote: ¹⁵*Darkness will not last forever. The insignificant land of Zebulun and Naphtali, between the Jordan River and the Mediterranean Sea, will be a glory to the nation.* ¹⁶*People who walk in*

darkness will see a bright light. Upon those who live under dark shadows of death, the light will shine. ¹⁷After that, Jesus began to preach, "Repent of your sins and turn to God, for the Kingdom of Heaven is near."

¹⁸As Jesus walked along the seashore of Galilee, he saw Simon called Peter and his brother Andrew casting a net into the water, for they were fishermen. ¹⁹"Come, follow me," Jesus said, "and I will make you fishers of men."

²⁰At once, they left their nets and followed him.

²¹A little farther up the shore, he saw James and his brother John in a boat with their father, Zebedee, mending their nets. ²²As soon as he called out to them, they left their boat and followed him.

²³Throughout Galilee, Jesus taught in the synagogues, preached the good news of the Kingdom, and healed people who had every kind of disease and sickness. ²⁴News spread all the way through Syria. Soon, people brought those who suffered from various diseases, seizures, or paralysis, and were tormented by evil spirits. He healed them all. ²⁵Great multitudes from Galilee, the Decapolis, Jerusalem, Judea, and from beyond Jordan followed him wherever he went.

Chapter 5

¹When Jesus saw a crowd gathering, he went up on the hillside, and his disciples came to him. ²He taught them, saying, ³"Blessed are the poor in spirit, those who recognize their need for God, for the Kingdom of Heaven belongs to them. ⁴Blessed are the mourners, those who are grieving, for God will bring comfort, joy, and laughter to their aching hearts. ⁵Blessed are the humble, those who are content with their identity, for they will inherit the land.

⁶"Blessed are the righteous, those who hunger and thirst to please God, for they will find true satisfaction. ⁷Blessed are the merciful, those who care for others, for they will receive mercy. ⁸Blessed

are the pure in heart, those who are inwardly clean, for they will see God. ⁹Blessed are the peacemakers, those who respond to an offense with kindness, for they will be called God's children.

¹⁰"Blessed are the persecuted, those who suffer because of righteousness, for theirs is the Kingdom of Heaven. ¹¹Blessed are the hated, those who are rejected, insulted, and falsely accused because of me. ¹²In their day of abuse, they will rejoice because their reward in heaven is great. The ancient prophets were treated the same way.

¹³"You are like the salt of the earth," Jesus said. "But if salt no longer tastes like salt, where is its seasoning value? It's worthless, so it's thrown out and people walk on it.

¹⁴"You are here to give light to the whole world. A city built on a hilltop cannot be hidden. ¹⁵People do not light a lamp and hide it under a bowl. It is placed on a stand to give light to everyone in the house. ¹⁶In the same way, you should let your kindness shine before men so they may see your good deeds and praise your Father in heaven.

¹⁷"Do not think I am here to abolish the Law or the words of the prophets. I came to fulfill their purpose. ¹⁸The truth is, until heaven and earth disappear, the smallest letter or the least meaningful pen stroke will not go away until its purpose is achieved.

¹⁹"Anyone who regards one of the commandments as unimportant and leads others to agree is the lowest of the lowly. But those who obey God's Law set an example for others and will rank high in the Kingdom of Heaven. ²⁰I am telling you, unless your righteousness is greater than the righteousness of the Pharisees and teachers of the Law, there is no way you will enter the Kingdom.

²¹"Since ancient times, you have heard it said, 'Do not commit murder,' and, 'A murderer must be brought to trial.' ²²But I tell you, anyone who is angry with his brother will stand trial. For

slander, someone may be brought to court, but anyone who calls another person stupid is in danger of hell's fire.

²³"So if you are praying at the altar and remember a grudge against another person, ²⁴leave your offering and seek reconciliation. Then come and offer your gift.

²⁵"When you are headed for court, settle your obligations quickly, or your accuser may take you to the judge, who will tell the officer to throw you into prison. ²⁶If that happens, you will not get out until you have paid the last penny owed.

²⁷"You have heard it said, 'Do not commit adultery.' ²⁸But I say that anyone with a lustful look has already committed adultery in his or her heart.

²⁹"If your right eye leads you to sin, gouge it out and throw it away. It is better to lose one eye than to have your whole body thrown into hell.

³⁰"If your right hand causes you to sin, it would be better to cut off your hand than to have your whole body go to hell.

³¹"You have been taught that a man who divorces his wife must give her a certificate of divorce. ³²But I say that anyone who divorces his wife, except for being unfaithful, causes her to become an adulteress, and anyone who marries a divorced woman commits adultery.

³³"For ages, you have heard it said, 'Do not swear falsely, but keep the vows you make to God.' ³⁴I say you should not swear at all, not by heaven, because it is God's throne, ³⁵not by earth, because it is his footstool, and not by Jerusalem, because it is the city of the great King. ³⁶"Do not swear by your head, because you cannot make even one hair white or black. ³⁷Simply mean what you say, your 'yes' meaning 'yes' and your 'no' meaning 'no.' Anything more is of the devil.

³⁸"You have heard it said, 'An eye for an eye and a tooth for a tooth,' ³⁹but I say you should not try to get even. If people slap you on the cheek, do not retaliate, but allow them to slap the other cheek. ⁴⁰If someone wants your shirt, be willing to give up your coat as well. ⁴¹If a soldier demands you carry his pack for one mile, carry it for two. ⁴²Give to everyone who asks, and do not refuse those who want to borrow something.

⁴³"People usually say, 'Love your neighbor, and hate your enemy,' ⁴⁴but I say you should show kindness to your enemies, doing good to those who persecute you. ⁴⁵Your Father in heaven causes the sun to rise on the evil as well as the good and sends rain on both the righteous and unrighteous. You should show kindness as he does. ⁴⁶What is commendable about loving only those who love you? Even greedy tax collectors and other sinners do that. ⁴⁷If you warmly greet only your brothers, you accomplish no more than the pagans. ⁴⁸Show mercy to others, just as your Father has shown mercy to you."

Chapter 6

¹"Be careful not to do your good deeds publicly so others will admire you. If you do, you will have no reward from your Father in heaven. ²When you give to the needy, do not call attention to yourself, as the hypocrites do in the synagogues and streets. They want people to praise them. Without a doubt, they have received all the reward they will ever get. ³Instead, when you help someone, do it quietly, without fanfare. ⁴Then your Father will see what you have done in secret and will reward you.

⁵"Do not be like the hypocrites, who love to stand and pray in the synagogues and on the street corners so people will see them. I assure you, they already have their reward. ⁶Go to your room, close the door, and pray to your Father without being seen. Then your Father will see what you have done in secret and will reward you.

[7]"When you pray, do not repeat empty words like the pagans, who think they will be heard because of their incessant babbling. [8]Do not be like them, because your Father knows what you need before you ask.

[9]"Pray like this: 'Our Father in heaven, may your name be honored. [10]May your Kingdom come and your will be done, on earth as it is in heaven. [11]Give us the bread we need for today. [12]Forgive our wrongs as we forgive the wrongs of others. [13]Keep us from temptation and protect us from evil. For yours is the Kingdom and the power and the glory forever. Amen.'

[14]"If you forgive others for the wrongs they have done, your heavenly Father will forgive you. [15]But if you refuse to forgive them, he will not forgive you.

[16]"Do not make your fasting obvious like the hypocrites, who look hungry and miserable so people will admire them for their sacrifice. I am telling you, they have received their reward. [17]Instead, comb your hair and wash your face [18]so no one will know. Your Father will see what was done in secret and will reward you.

[19]"Do not store up treasure for yourselves on the earth, where moths and rust can eat it up and thieves break in and steal. [20]Instead, store your treasure in heaven, where it is safe from moths and rust and thieves. [21]Wherever your treasure is, there your heart will be also.

[22]"Your eyes are like a lamp for the body. If your eyes are good, your whole body will be full of light. [23]But if your eyes are bad, darkness fills your body. If the light you think you have is really darkness, how terrible is that darkness!

[24]"You cannot be the slave of two masters. You will either hate the one and love the other or be devoted to the one and despise the other. You cannot serve both God and earthly treasure. [25]That is why you should not worry about your life, whether you have

enough food and drink or clothes to wear. Isn't life more important than food and the body more important than clothes?

²⁶"Look at the birds. They do not plant seeds, gather a harvest, or store grain in barns. Yet your heavenly Father feeds them. Aren't you far more valuable to him than they are? ²⁷Can all of your worrying increase your lifespan? ²⁸Why worry about clothes? Look how the wildflowers grow in the fields. They do not spin yarn or weave fabric. ²⁹Yet Solomon in his greatest splendor was never dressed like one of them. ³⁰If God clothes the wildflowers that are here now and gone tomorrow, don't you suppose he will care for you? Why do you have such weak faith?

³¹"Do not trouble yourselves with questions like 'What shall we eat?' or 'What shall we drink?' or 'What shall we wear?' ³²People who do not know God seek such things, but your heavenly Father already knows what you need. ³³Seek first his Kingdom and his righteousness, and he will give you everything you need.

³⁴"Do not worry about tomorrow, for tomorrow will have its own worries. Today's problems are enough for today."

Chapter 7

¹"Do not judge, and you will not be judged. ²In the way you judge others, you will be judged. The standard you apply in condemning others will be the standard used against you.

³"Why do you worry about the sawdust in your brother's eye but never notice the board in your own eye? ⁴How can you say, 'Brother, let me take the speck out of your eye,' and not admit the existence of something much larger in your own eye? ⁵Hypocrite! First take the large object from your eye. Then you can see clearly to remove the small piece from your brother's eye.

11

⁶"Do not give something holy to dogs. They will turn and attack, tearing you to pieces. Do not toss your pearls to pigs. They will only trample them under their feet.

⁷"Ask and you will receive. Seek and you will find. Knock and the door will be opened to you. ⁸For everyone who asks receives. He who seeks will find, and the door will be opened to those who knock.

⁹"Would any of you give a stone to a son who asks for bread? ¹⁰Would you give him a snake if he asked for fish? ¹¹Bad as you are, you know how to give good gifts to your children. How much more will your heavenly Father give only what is good to those who ask him.

¹²"Do what you would have others do to you, for this is the intent of everything taught in the Law and the prophets.

¹³"Enter through the small gate. For many take the wide gate and broad road that lead to destruction. ¹⁴Only a few find the small gate and narrow road that lead to life.

¹⁵"Watch out for false prophets who come disguised as sheep but inwardly are vicious wolves. ¹⁶Recognize them by their actions. No one picks grapes from thorn bushes or figs from briers. ¹⁷Good trees produce good fruit, and bad trees produce bad fruit. ¹⁸A good tree cannot produce bad fruit, and a bad tree cannot produce good fruit. ¹⁹Every tree that does not produce good fruit is cut down and burned. ²⁰Each tree is identified by its own fruit.

²¹"Not everyone who calls me master will enter the Kingdom of Heaven but only those who do the will of my heavenly Father. ²²On Judgment Day, many will say, 'Lord, didn't we prophesy, cast out evil spirits, and do many wonderful deeds in your name?' ²³Then I will tell them, 'I never knew you. Get away from me, you disobedient lawbreakers.'

[24]"Everyone who not only hears my words but also puts them into practice is like a wise man who dug deep and laid the foundation of his house on solid rock. [25]When a storm brought torrential rain, flooded streams, and hurricane-force winds, his house did not collapse, because it was well built on an unshakable foundation.

[26]"Anyone who hears my words but never acts on them is like a foolish man who built his house on sand, without a foundation. [27]The rain fell, causing the streams to rise. As soon as the high winds came, the house fell with a great crash and was completely destroyed."

[28]When Jesus finished teaching, the crowds were amazed [29]because he spoke with authority, nothing like the teachers of the Law.

Chapter 8

[1]When Jesus came down from the mountain, a huge crowd followed him.

[2]A leper kneeled before him, begging, "Sir, you could make me well if you wanted to."

[3]"I want to." Jesus touched him. "Be cleansed."

Immediately, all signs of the leprosy disappeared.

[4]"Do not tell anyone about this. Show yourself to the priest and offer the sacrifices commanded by Moses. Your healing will become public record so you will no longer be regarded as a leper."

[5]At Capernaum, a Roman officer sent a message to Jesus, pleading for help. [6]"Sir, my young servant lies at home, paralyzed with intense pain."

[7]"I will go and heal the servant," Jesus said.

[8]But the officer felt unworthy for Jesus to come. "I am not important enough to have you enter my house. Just give the order, and my servant will be healed. [9]For I also am a man under authority. At my

command under Caesar, my soldiers come and go and do exactly what I say."

[10]Jesus marveled at the message. To those following him, he said, "In all of Israel, I have never seen such faith. [11]I tell you, outsiders will come from everywhere to dine with Abraham, Isaac, and Jacob in the Kingdom of Heaven, [12]but many Israelites will be on the outside in the darkness, where there will be bitterness and weeping."

[13]He turned to the messengers. "You can go home now," he said. "As you have believed, so it will be."

At that moment, the servant was healed.

[14]When Jesus went to Peter's home, he saw Peter's mother-in-law sick in bed with a burning fever. [15]He went to her bedside and took her by the hand, and the fever left. At once, she got up and began to prepare dinner for them.

[16]That evening, people brought many who were possessed by an evil spirit. With a few simple words, he commanded the evil spirits to leave and healed those who were sick. [17]His actions fulfilled what the prophet Isaiah wrote long ago: *Truly, he has taken our infirmities and carried our pain.*

[18]Jesus saw how large a crowd had gathered around him and told his disciples to take him to the other side of the lake.

[19]A teacher of the Law said to him, "Teacher, wherever you go I will follow."

[20]"Foxes have dens, and birds have nests," Jesus said, "but the Son of Man has no home where he can lay his head."

[21]Another would-be follower said, "Sir, let me first go and care for my father until he dies."

[22]Jesus replied, "Follow me, and let the dead bury their dead."

[23]Then he climbed into a boat with his twelve disciples. [24]While he slept, a violent wind struck the lake and sent large waves crashing over the side.

[25]His disciples woke him, crying, "Sir, help us or we are going to drown!"

[26]"Why are you so afraid? You have such weak faith." Standing, Jesus ordered the wind and waves to be still.

Suddenly, the wind died and the waters became calm.

[27]The disciples looked at one another with amazement. "What sort of man is this? Even the wind and the waves obey him!"

[28]After crossing the lake, Jesus came to the region of the Gadarenes, where two men possessed by evil spirits met him. They lived among the tombs and were so fierce that no man dared pass their way.

[29]"What do you want with us," they screamed, "Jesus, Son of God? Have you come to torment us before the appointed time?"

[30]In the distance, a large herd of pigs was feeding.

[31]"If you force us out," the spirits begged, "send us into the herd of pigs."

[32]"Go!" Jesus commanded. So the evil spirits came out of the men and went into the pigs. Suddenly, the whole herd stampeded down the steep bank, plunged into the water, and drowned.

[33]The herdsmen ran into the town and told what had happened, how the men had been delivered and the pigs were lost. [34]So all the townspeople went out to see Jesus and begged him to leave their country.

Chapter 9

[1]Jesus took a boat across the Sea of Galilee to Capernaum.

[2]People carried a paralyzed man on a mat. Impressed by their faith, Jesus said, "Do not worry, my friend. Your sins are forgiven."

[3]Some of the teachers of the Law murmured among themselves, "What is he saying? That is blasphemy. Only God can forgive sins."

[4]Immediately, Jesus recognized their reaction. "Why are you thinking I've done something wrong? [5]Which is easier to say, 'Your

sins are forgiven,' or, 'Stand and walk'? [6]So you may know the Son of Man has authority on earth to forgive sins . . ." He turned to the paralyzed man. "Get up. Take your mat and go home."

[7]Without hesitation, the man stood and walked to his own house.

[8]Everyone marveled and glorified God for sending a man with such authority.

[9]As Jesus walked along, he saw the tax collector, Matthew, sitting at the place where people paid taxes. "Follow me," he said, and Matthew got up and followed.

[10]Later, Matthew had a big feast for Jesus at his house. Many tax collectors and other outcasts were among the dinner guests who ate with Jesus and his disciples. [11]When the Pharisees saw Jesus eating with them, they asked his disciples, "Why does he eat with such people?"

[12]Jesus heard them and answered, "Healthy people do not need a doctor. The sick do. [13]Go learn what the prophet meant when he said, *I wanted you to show love, not make sacrifices.* I have not come to invite to repentance those who think they are righteous. I have come for those who know they are sinners."

[14]One day, the followers of John the Baptizer asked Jesus, "Why do we and the Pharisees fast, but your disciples never do?"

[15]Jesus answered, "At a wedding, the friends of the bridegroom do not go without eating while he is still with them. But the day will come when he will be gone. Then they will fast."

[16]"No one uses a piece of new cloth to patch old clothes. The patch would shrink, pull away from the old, and make the tear worse. [17]Men do not pour new wine into old skins. If they did, the wineskin would burst, ruining both the wine and the wineskin. New wine is always kept in fresh skins so both are preserved."

[18]While Jesus taught, an official came and knelt before him. "My daughter has just died, but if you will come lay your hand on her, she will live."

[19]So Jesus and his disciples followed him.

[20]On the way, a woman who had suffered twelve years from constant bleeding walked up behind Jesus and touched the fringe of his robe. [21]She had thought, *If I can just touch his clothes, I will be healed.*

[22]Jesus turned and saw the woman. "Be joyful, daughter, because your faith has made you well." From then on, the woman's health was restored.

[23]At the house, Jesus saw musicians and mourners crying their funeral dirge. [24]"You can leave," he said to the crowd. "The girl is not dead, only sleeping."

They laughed and said he was crazy, because they knew she was dead.

[25]After the people had been sent outside, Jesus went in and took the girl by the hand, and she stood up.

[26]Report of this miracle spread throughout the area.

[27]When Jesus left, two blind men followed him, crying out, "Son of David, have mercy on us."

[28]He entered the house and watched the blind men make their way to him. "Do you believe I can make you see?"

"Yes," they answered. "We do."

[29]He touched their eyes. "Let it be according to your faith."

[30]Immediately, they could see.

In a demanding tone, Jesus said, "Do not tell anyone about this."

[31]But as soon as they were out the door, they spread the news throughout the area.

[32]As the blind men left, people brought to Jesus a man who could not speak because of an evil spirit. [33]After Jesus cast out the evil spirit, the man began to speak.

In amazement, the crowd said, "We've never seen anything like this in Israel."

³⁴But the Pharisees said, "He casts out devils by the power of Satan."

³⁵Jesus traveled through all the towns and small communities, teaching in the synagogues and preaching the good news of the Kingdom. He healed all kinds of sicknesses and infirmities.

³⁶As he looked at the large crowd, he was moved with compassion because he saw them as helpless and confused, like sheep that had no shepherd. ³⁷He turned to his followers. "The harvest is huge, but there are not many workers. ³⁸Pray for the lord of the harvest to send more workers into the fields."

Chapter 10

¹He called the twelve disciples and gave them authority to cast out evil spirits and heal all kinds of sicknesses and infirmities. ²Their names were Simon Peter and his brother Andrew, James and his brother John, sons of Zebedee, ³Philip, Bartholomew, Thomas, Matthew the tax collector, James son of Alphaeus, Lebbaeus known as Thaddaeus, ⁴Simon the zealous, and Judas Iscariot, who later betrayed Jesus.

⁵These were his instructions: "Do not go among the Gentiles or into any Samaritan city. ⁶Concentrate on the lost sheep of Israel. ⁷Wherever you go, preach the good news that the Kingdom of Heaven is near. ⁸Heal the sick, cleanse the lepers, cast out evil spirits, and raise the dead. Give as freely as you have received.

⁹"Do not take any money, ¹⁰a bag with extra clothes and sandals, or a walking stick. Let your work earn your support as you go.

¹¹"When you enter a town or small community, look for a godly man who will let you stay in his home until you leave for the next town. ¹²As you enter a home, greet the people with kindness. ¹³If

the residents welcome you, offer your blessings, but if not, then quietly withdraw.

[14]"When people do not welcome you or listen to your words, shake off the offense like dust from your feet and leave that house or town for another. [15]I assure you, on Judgment Day, the people of Sodom and Gomorrah will be better off than that place.

[16]"Listen, I am sending you like lambs into a pack of wolves. Therefore, you must be wise as snakes, slipping in unnoticed, and harmless as doves, fleeing when threatened. [17]Watch out, because people will take you before the local judges and beat you up in their synagogues. [18]Because of me, you will stand trial before governors and kings, giving testimony to the world about me. [19]When you are arrested, do not worry about what to say. Whenever you must speak, you will be given the right words to say. [20]You will not be the one speaking. The Spirit of your Father will speak through you.

[21]"Brothers will turn against brothers, fathers against children, and children against parents, causing them to be put to death. [22]Because of me, everyone will hate you, but those who keep their faith to the end will be saved. [23]When people persecute you in one town, flee to another. Believe me, you will not have reached all the cities of Israel before the Son of Man will come.

[24]"A student is not better than his teacher. A slave is not above his master. [25]What is good enough for the teacher and master is good enough for the student and slave. If the master is called Beelzebub, it is even more likely that people will speak evil of his household. [26]Do not be afraid of those people, because everything hidden will one day be revealed. All secrets will be brought to light.

[27]"What I whisper to you in the darkness, you must shout in broad daylight. What your ears have heard, preach from the housetops. [28]Do not fear people who can kill your body but cannot harm your soul. Fear only God, who can destroy both body and soul in hell.

29The price of two sparrows is not very much, but one cannot die without your Father's knowledge. 30He even knows the number of hairs on your head. 31Don't worry. You are worth more than many sparrows.

32"If anyone publicly acknowledges me before men, I will publicly acknowledge him before my Father in heaven. 33But anyone who denies me before men I will deny before my Father in heaven.

34"Do not assume that I came to bring peace on earth. Instead of peace, I bring a sword. 35I have come to set a man against his father, a daughter against her mother, and a daughter-in-law against her mother-in-law. 36A man's enemies will come from his own home.

37"If you love your father, mother, son, or daughter more than you love me, you are not worthy of being my disciple. 38Unless you are willing to sacrifice your own life and do what I ask, you are not worthy of being my disciple. 39If you try to save your life, you will lose it. But if you lose your life for my sake, you will discover real life.

40"Those who accept you are accepting me, and those who accept me are accepting the Father, who sent me. 41Those who accept God's messenger for who he is will experience the messenger's reward. Those who accept a righteous man for who he is will experience the righteous man's reward.

42"Those who give something as insignificant as a cup of cold water to the least of my disciples, because you are my disciples, are sure to be rewarded."

Chapter 11

1As soon as Jesus finished instructing his twelve disciples, he left to teach and preach in the towns of Galilee.

²John the Baptizer was in prison but heard what the Messiah was doing. He sent two of his disciples ³with the question: "Are you the one to fulfill God's promise, or must we look for someone else?"

⁴"Go tell John what you have seen and heard," Jesus replied. ⁵"The blind see, the lame walk, and the lepers are cleansed. The deaf can hear, the dead are raised, and the needy receive words of hope. ⁶Tell him a man is blessed when he puts his faith in me."

⁷As the two left, Jesus asked the people about John. "What did you go into the wilderness to see? A reed blown over by the wind? ⁸Why did you go? Was it to see a man dressed in fine clothes? No, those people live in the royal palaces. ⁹What did you expect to see? A prophet? Yes, and I tell you, he is more remarkable than a prophet. ¹⁰He is the one the prophet Malachi talked about when he wrote: *See, I will send my messenger to prepare the way before me.*

¹¹"Believe me, John the Baptizer is greater than any other person ever born. Yet the lowliest one in the Kingdom of Heaven is greater than John. ¹²"Ever since the Messiah's coming was foretold, violent people have sought to take the Kingdom of Heaven by force. ¹³For the Law and the prophets anticipated John's coming, ¹⁴and if you can believe it, John is the 'Elijah' who must come before the Messiah. ¹⁵If you have ears, pay attention to what I am saying."

¹⁶Jesus asked, "What are the people of this generation like? They are like children in the marketplace, whining to get what they want. ¹⁷They say, 'We played our flutes, but you would not dance for us. We wailed our funeral songs, but you never shed a tear with us.' ¹⁸John the Baptizer did not party with the people. He chose not to eat or drink with others, and they said, 'He has an evil spirit.' ¹⁹When the Son of Man came, he ate bread and drank wine. They condemned him as well, calling him a drunkard and a glutton, a friend of dishonest tax collectors and other sinners. However, the results show the actions to be wise."

²⁰Jesus reprimanded the people who lived in the towns where he had done many miracles, because they had refused to repent. ²¹"How terrible it will be for you, Korazin! And for you, Bethsaida! If the people of Tyre and Sidon had seen the miracles you saw me do in your towns, they would have turned to God long ago in sackcloth and ashes. ²²You can be sure, on Judgment Day, they will fare better than you. ²³And you in Capernaum who think you are so high and mighty, God will bring you to the lowest depths. For if the people of Sodom had seen the miracles I did for you, that city would still be standing today. ²⁴You can be sure, on Judgment Day, they will fare better than you."

²⁵Suddenly, he looked upward and said, "I thank you, Father, ruler of heaven and earth, because you have revealed to ordinary people what you have hidden from those who think they are educated and wise. ²⁶Surely, Father, it pleases you to see it work in this way."

²⁷To the people, Jesus said, "The Father has entrusted everything to me. No one knows the Son like the Father, and no one knows the Father except the Son and those to whom the Son reveals him. ²⁸Come to me, all who are overburdened and weary. Like the lead ox on a team, I will help pull your heavy load. ²⁹Take my yoke upon you, and learn to walk my way, for I am gentle and humble of heart. In me, you will find rest for your souls ³⁰because my yoke fits and your share of the load is light."

Chapter 12

¹On a Sabbath day, Jesus went through the grain fields. His disciples were hungry, so they picked some heads of grain. They rubbed off the husks with their hands and ate the kernels. ²When the Pharisees saw them, they said to Jesus, "Look! Your disciples are doing work that is not permitted on the Sabbath."

³"Haven't you read," Jesus said, "what David and his men did when they were hungry? ⁴He entered the house of God and ate the sacred bread that only the priests were allowed to eat. He also gave loaves to his men. ⁵Haven't you read in the Law that the Temple priests desecrate the Sabbath but are innocent? ⁶I tell you, one greater than the Temple is here. ⁷If you knew what the prophet meant when he said, *I wanted you to show love, not make sacrifices*, you would not condemn these innocent men. ⁸The Son of Man is Lord even of the Sabbath."

⁹Jesus left and entered the synagogue, ¹⁰where there was a man with a crippled hand.

The Pharisees were looking for a reason to accuse Jesus, so they asked, "Is it lawful to heal on the Sabbath?"

¹¹He answered, "If you had a lamb that fell into a pit on the Sabbath, wouldn't you work to pull it out? Of course you would. ¹²People are much more valuable than sheep. Therefore, it is lawful to do good on the Sabbath." ¹³He said to the man, "Stretch out your hand."

As the man reached out, his hand became completely restored, as healthy as the other.

¹⁴The Pharisees were furious and immediately plotted how they might kill Jesus.

¹⁵Aware of the threat from the Pharisees, Jesus left town and went to the lakeshore. A large crowd from Galilee and Judea followed them. He healed their sick ¹⁶but sternly ordered them not to tell who he was. ¹⁷This event fulfilled what the prophet Isaiah wrote long ago: ¹⁸*Here is my chosen servant, my beloved in whom I am well pleased. I have put my Spirit upon him to bring justice to the people.* ¹⁹*He will not argue or raise his voice in the streets.* ²⁰*He will not break off a weakened reed or put out a flickering lamp but will judge in truth. He will not quit until*

he has established justice throughout the earth. ²¹*Distant lands will place their hope in him.*

²²When people brought to Jesus a man who was blind and could not speak because of an evil spirit, Jesus healed him, so he could both see and talk.

²³The crowd was astonished, saying, "Could this be the Son of David?"

²⁴Pharisees heard what the people said. "No," they argued. "This man casts out evil spirits by the power of Beelzebub, the ruler of evil spirits."

²⁵Jesus knew what the people were pondering, so he said, "A kingdom working against itself will soon be destroyed. Any city or family who fights internally cannot last very long. ²⁶If Satan drives out Satan, he is warring against himself and his kingdom cannot survive. ²⁷If Beelzebub is my power over evil spirits, by whom do your followers cast them out? They prove you are using a double standard of judgment. ²⁸But if I cast out evil spirits by the Spirit of God, the Kingdom of God has come unto you. ²⁹How can a man force his way into a strong man's house and take his property? First he must bind the strong man. Then he can plunder his house.

³⁰"Anyone who is not with me is against me. If you are not gathering with me, you are scattering. ³¹Understand this: all kinds of sin and evil speaking may be forgiven, but speaking evil of the Holy Spirit cannot be forgiven. ³²You may speak against the Son of Man and be forgiven, but whoever speaks against the Holy Spirit will not be forgiven. Not now. Not ever.

³³"Either a tree is good, and its fruit is good, or the tree is bad, and its fruit is bad. A tree must be judged by its fruit. ³⁴You pit of snakes! If you are evil, how can you say anything good? As the heart overflows, the mouth speaks. ³⁵From the treasury of a good heart, a good person brings forth good things. From the treasury

of an evil heart, an evil person brings forth evil things. [36]You can be sure, on Judgment Day, people will have to account for every word carelessly spoken. [37]By your words, you will be either justified or condemned."

[38]At that time, some Pharisees and teachers of the Law said, "Teacher, show us a miraculous sign that will prove your authority."

[39]Jesus said, "Wicked and adulterous people demand miraculous signs, but no sign will come except the sign of the prophet Jonah. [40]Just as Jonah spent three days and nights in the fish's belly, so shall the Son of Man be in the heart of the earth for three days and nights. [41]The people of Nineveh give evidence to condemn this generation, because they repented at the preaching of Jonah. Behold, someone greater than Jonah is here, but you do not repent. [42]The Queen of Sheba will testify and condemn this generation, because she came from far away to hear the wisdom of Solomon. Now someone wiser than Solomon is here, but you refuse to listen.

[43]"When an evil spirit leaves a person, it wanders through barren places in search of rest but finds none. [44]It then says, 'I know. I will return to the person I left.' It finds its former home empty, swept clean, and ready to be occupied. [45]So it finds seven spirits more evil than itself, and they go to live there. That person is worse off than before. This is what will happen to the evil people of this generation."

[46]While Jesus talked to the crowd, his mother and brothers stood outside the crowded house, wanting to speak to him.

[47]Someone told him, "Your mother and brothers are outside. They want to talk with you."

[48]"Who is my mother?" he answered. "Who are my brothers?"

⁴⁹He pointed to his followers. "Here are my brothers and my mother. ⁵⁰Anyone who does the will of my Father in heaven is my brother, sister, and mother."

Chapter 13

¹Later that day, Jesus left the house and sat by the seashore. ²A large crowd gathered, so many that he boarded a boat, sat down, and from there taught the people who stood on the shore. ³He taught them with illustrations, saying, "A farmer went to sow his seeds in the field. ⁴As he scattered the seeds, some fell on the road, where they were eaten by the birds. ⁵Some fell on rocky ground, where the soil had little depth. The plants sprang up ⁶but had shallow roots, so they soon wilted under the scorching sun. ⁷Some seeds fell among thorny weeds that grew more quickly and choked out the tender plants. ⁸Other seeds fell on fertile soil and became healthy plants, producing a hundred, sixty, or thirty times the amount of seed sown. ⁹If you have ears, pay attention to what I am saying."

¹⁰His disciples came to him and asked, "Why do you teach with illustrations that are difficult to understand?"

¹¹Jesus said, "I have given you insights into the mysteries of the Kingdom of Heaven, but others have only the stories. ¹²Those who have a desire to hear will be given an abundance of knowledge, but those who dislike the truth will lose what little understanding they have. ¹³I teach with stories because some people with open eyes choose to see nothing. They listen with their ears but do not want to understand. ¹⁴In them, the prophet Isaiah's words are fulfilled: *You listen but do not understand. You see but have no recognition. ¹⁵Harden the hearts of these people and close their ears and cover their eyes so they will not see with their eyes, hear with their ears, and understand with their hearts and be forced to turn to me and be healed.*

[16]"How fortunate you are to have eyes that see and ears that hear. [17]I assure you, many prophets and righteous people have wanted to see what you are seeing. They wanted to hear what you are hearing, but they could not.

[18]"Hear the meaning of the farmer sowing seeds. [19]The seeds that fell on the road are people who hear the Kingdom message but do not understand. The evil one takes away the seed that was planted in their hearts. [20]The seeds that fell on rocky ground are those who hear the message and eagerly accept it, [21]but their roots are shallow. As soon as the message causes them to experience trouble or persecution, they forsake their faith. [22]The seeds that fell among thorny weeds are people who allow the worries of this life and the enticement of wealth to choke the message, so no fruit is produced. [23]The seeds that fell on fertile soil are the people who hear, understand, and act on God's word, yielding a hundred, sixty, or thirty times what was sown."

[24]Jesus gave this illustration: "The Kingdom of Heaven is like a farmer who sowed good wheat in his field. [25]While everyone slept, his adversary sowed weeds among the wheat and slipped away, unseen. [26]As the wheat grew and developed its heads of grain, the weeds also grew.

[27]"The workers said to the farmer, 'Didn't you sow good seed in your field? Where did the weeds come from?'

[28]"'An enemy has done this.'

"'Do you want us to pull the weeds?' they asked.

[29]"'No. While you are pulling the weeds you might uproot some of the wheat. [30]Let them both grow until harvest time. Then I will tell the reapers to bundle the weeds, burn them, and bring the wheat into my barn.'"

[31]In another illustration, Jesus said, "The Kingdom of Heaven is like a grain of mustard seed that a farmer planted in his field.

³²Although it is the tiniest of all seeds, it became the largest plant in the field, a tree where birds can perch in its branches."

³³Jesus added this analogy: "The Kingdom of Heaven is like a little yeast that a woman kneaded into three measures of flour. The yeast made the whole batch of dough rise."

³⁴When speaking to the crowd, Jesus always used illustrations like these. No one heard him speak without some kind of story. ³⁵This fulfilled what the psalmist prophesied: *I will open my mouth with a parable and explain mysteries kept secret from the beginning.*

³⁶After sending the crowd away, Jesus went into the house. There his disciples said, "Explain what you meant about the weeds sown in the field."

³⁷Jesus said, "The farmer who sowed the good seed is the Son of Man. ³⁸The field is the world, and the good seeds are the people of the Kingdom. The weeds are the people who belong to the evil one. ³⁹The enemy who sowed the weeds is the devil. The harvest is the end of the age. And the reapers are the angels. ⁴⁰Just as the weeds are bundled and burned, so will it be with people at the end of this age. ⁴¹The Son of Man will send his angels to separate from his Kingdom those who do evil and draw others into sin. ⁴²The angels will throw the evildoers into a fiery furnace, where people will cry and grit their teeth in pain. ⁴³Then the righteous will shine like the sun in the Kingdom of their Father. If you have ears, pay attention to what I am saying.

⁴⁴"The Kingdom of Heaven is like hidden treasure buried in a field. When a man found the treasure, he was overcome with joy. He buried the treasure, sold everything he owned, and bought the field.

⁴⁵"Again, the Kingdom of Heaven is like a merchant seeking costly pearls. ⁴⁶When he found one pearl of exceptional value, he sold everything he owned and bought it.

⁴⁷"Also, the Kingdom of Heaven is like a net that was cast into the sea and caught all kinds of fish. ⁴⁸Men dragged the full net onto the shore, sat down, and gathered the good fish into containers. They threw the bad fish away. ⁴⁹That is how it will be at the end of this age. The angels will come and separate the evil people from the righteous ⁵⁰and will throw the evil ones into a fiery furnace, where they will cry and grit their teeth in pain.

⁵¹"Have you understood what I have said?"

"Yes," they said. "We understand."

⁵²"Every teacher of the Law who becomes a disciple in the Kingdom of Heaven is like a homeowner who brings both old and new things from his storehouse of treasures."

⁵³After teaching the people, Jesus left.

⁵⁴Jesus went to his hometown, Nazareth, and taught in the synagogue there.

People were amazed at his teaching, saying, "Where did he get such wisdom and the power to do miracles? ⁵⁵Isn't he the carpenter's son? We know his mother, Mary, and his brothers, James, Joseph, Simon, and Judas. ⁵⁶His sisters, don't they live here in town? How did this man become so different that he can do these things?" ⁵⁷They did not trust his actions or what he said.

Jesus said to them, "A prophet has honor everywhere except in his own country and in his own household."

⁵⁸Because of their unbelief, he did very few miracles there.

Chapter 14

¹When Herod, ruler of Galilee, received reports about Jesus, ²he said to his aides, "He must have the spirit of John the Baptizer who has returned from the dead. That is why he has the power to do such miracles." ³Earlier, Herod had taken Herodias, his brother Philip's wife, to be his wife. He had John arrested, bound in chains, and put

in prison ⁴for saying to him, "Under God's law, you have no right to be married to her." ⁵He would have put him to death, but he feared all the people who thought John was a prophet.

⁶During Herod's birthday feast, Herodias's daughter danced before his guests in a way that immensely pleased him, ⁷so much so that he swore to give her anything she wanted.

⁸She answered with what her mother had told her to say. "Bring me John the Baptizer's head on a platter."

⁹This grieved the king, but because he had sworn an oath before his guests, he gave the order ¹⁰to have John beheaded in prison. ¹¹The head was given to her on a platter, and she took it to her mother.

¹²John's disciples claimed the body, buried him, and then went and told Jesus what had happened.

¹³When Jesus heard about John the Baptizer's death, he left by boat to a desolate place where he could be alone. But when the people heard where he was going, they left their towns and followed on foot. ¹⁴At the seashore, Jesus saw the huge crowd waiting for him. He was moved with compassion and healed their sick.

¹⁵As evening grew near, the disciples said to Jesus, "We are far from town, and it is getting late. Send the people away so they can go to the towns and buy food."

¹⁶Jesus said, "They do not have to leave. Why don't you feed them?"

¹⁷"With what?" they said. "All we have are five loaves and two fish."

¹⁸"Bring the bread and fish to me." ¹⁹After telling the crowd to sit on the grass, he took the five loaves and two fish, looked toward heaven, and gave thanks. He broke the loaves and fish and handed them to his disciples, who distributed the pieces to the people.

²⁰They all ate as much as they wanted, and the disciples gathered twelve baskets full of leftover bread and fish. ²¹Besides the women and children, about five thousand men were fed.

²²After the five thousand had been fed, Jesus told his disciples to get into their boat and go to the other side while he dismissed the crowd. ²³When the people had gone, he went up the mountain to pray. In the evening, he was there alone.

²⁴The boat, now well out to sea, was being shoved back by high waves and a strong headwind. ²⁵In the fourth watch of the night, between three and six o'clock in the morning, Jesus walked toward them on the water.

²⁶When they saw him, the disciples were terrified. "It's a ghost!" they cried.

²⁷"It's all right. I am Jesus. You do not need to be afraid."

²⁸Simon Peter said, "Sir, if it is really you, tell me to come walking on the water."

²⁹"Come!" Jesus said.

So Peter got out of the boat and walked on the water toward Jesus. ³⁰When he felt the strong wind and saw the high waves, he was frightened and began to sink. "Sir, save me!"

³¹At once, Jesus grabbed him. "You of weak faith, why did you doubt?"

³²As soon as they climbed into the boat, the wind calmed.

³³Utterly amazed and worshipful, the disciples said, "Truly you are the Son of God."

³⁴After crossing the lake, Jesus and the disciples came to shore near Gennesaret. ³⁵People recognized him and news of his arrival spread throughout the region, so all the sick were brought to him. ³⁶Some of them begged to touch the fringe of his robe. Those who touched his robe were healed.

Chapter 15

¹Pharisees and teachers of the Law who had come from Jerusalem asked Jesus, ²"Why do your disciples violate the rules of behavior that were established by our ancestors? When they eat bread, they do not wash their hands."

³Jesus answered, "Why do you violate God's commandments by following your own tradition? ⁴God says, 'Honor your father and mother,' and, 'Anyone who curses father or mother must be put to death.' ⁵By your rules, it is all right for a man to say to his parents, 'I have dedicated all my possessions to God. ⁶I am sorry, but the Law will not allow me to help with your need.' With your tradition, you nullify God's commandment.

⁷"Hypocrites! You only pretend to be righteous. You fulfill what Isaiah said about you: ⁸*These people express love with their mouths and their lips offer praise, but their hearts are somewhere else. ⁹Their reverence for me is nothing but a ritual.*"

¹⁰Jesus called the people closer. "Listen, and understand what I am saying. ¹¹You are not defiled by what goes into your mouth. It is what comes out that makes you unclean."

¹²Later, his disciples asked him, "Did you know you offended the Pharisees with your words?"

¹³"Every plant that was not planted by my heavenly Father will be pulled up with its roots," Jesus said. ¹⁴"Let them go their own way. They are blind leaders of the blind. When blind people follow blind leaders, they both fall into the ditch."

¹⁵Simon Peter said, "How is it that people are not defiled by what they eat? Explain your analogy to us."

¹⁶"You still do not understand? ¹⁷You should know that anything you eat simply passes through the stomach and out. ¹⁸But what comes out of a person's mouth is from the heart, revealing the filth

that exists inside. [19]From the heart come evil thoughts, murder, adultery, erotic sexual acts, theft, lies, and cursing. [20]These things make a person unclean. It is not from eating without washing your hands."

[21]Leaving Gennesaret, Jesus went to a region near Tyre and Sidon.

[22]A Canaanite woman who lived in the area came, crying, "Sir, Son of David, my daughter is cruelly tormented by an evil spirit."

[23]Jesus did not say a word.

His disciples came and begged, "Send her away. Now she is crying after us."

[24]"I was only sent to the lost sheep of Israel," Jesus said.

[25]The woman knelt at his feet. "Sir, I beg you. Please help me!"

[26]"It is not right to take the children's bread and throw it to the dogs."

[27]"That is true, sir. But even dogs eat the scraps that fall from the master's table."

[28]"Woman, you have great faith. Let it be done exactly as you have asked." At that moment, her daughter was healed.

[29]After Jesus left the vicinity of Tyre, he walked back toward the Sea of Galilee. He went up on the mountainside and sat down.

[30]A large crowd gathered. People brought to the feet of Jesus the crippled, blind, mute, disabled, and those who suffered many other afflictions. And he healed them. [31]The people were amazed when they saw the mute able to speak and disabled people made whole. The crippled walked, and the blind could see. So they praised the God of Israel.

[32]Jesus called his disciples. "I feel sorry for all these people who have been with me for three days and have nothing left to eat. I do not want to send them away hungry, or they might faint on their way home."

³³The disciples said, "In a desolate place like this, where can we get enough food to feed so many?"

³⁴"How many loaves do you have?"

"Seven," they said. "And a few small fish."

³⁵Jesus told the people to sit on the ground. ³⁶He took the loaves and fish, gave thanks, and broke them. He gave the pieces to the disciples, who distributed them to the crowd. ³⁷After all had eaten as much as they wanted, the disciples gathered seven full baskets of leftover pieces.

³⁸Four thousand men were fed, plus women and children.

³⁹After Jesus had sent the people home, he got into a boat and went to the area of Magadan.

Chapter 16

¹Some Pharisees and Sadducees came to test his claim that he had been sent by God. So they asked him to show them a miraculous sign from heaven.

²Jesus said, "In the evening, you say, 'The sky is red, so we will have clear weather.' ³In the morning, you look at the dark sky and say, 'It is going to rain.' You hypocrites! You can look at the sky and predict the weather, but you cannot interpret the signs of the times. ⁴Only an evil, unfaithful generation would demand a miraculous sign. I will give you no proof except for the sign of the prophet Jonah."

He turned away and left.

⁵When Jesus' disciples reached the other side of the lake, they realized they had forgotten to bring bread.

⁶"Watch out!" Jesus said. "Be careful to avoid the yeast of the Pharisees and Sadducees."

⁷They reasoned among themselves what Jesus meant. "He must have said this because we failed to bring any bread."

[8]Jesus knew what they were saying. "How little trust you have in me. Why do you think it's a problem that we have no bread? [9]Do you not yet understand? Don't you remember the five loaves that fed five thousand and how many baskets of leftovers you had? [10]Or the seven loaves that fed four thousand and how many baskets were left? [11]You should know that I was not talking about bread. I am telling you to watch out for the leaven of the Pharisees and Sadducees."

[12]Then they understood that he was not talking about bread, but the danger of the teachings of the Pharisees and Sadducees.

[13]As Jesus came into the area near Caesarea Philippi, he asked his disciples, "Who do people say that I, the Son of Man, am?"

[14]They said, "Some say you are John the Baptizer. Others say you are Elijah, Jeremiah, or one of the other prophets."

[15]"Who do you say that I am?"

[16]Simon Peter answered, "You are the Anointed One, the Messiah, the son of the living God!"

[17]"Very good, Simon, son of Jonah. You did not become convinced because of someone's teaching, but my Father in heaven revealed it to you. [18]Now I am telling you that you are Peter. Upon this rock, I will build my church, and the powers of hell will not prevail against it. [19]I will give you the keys of the Kingdom of Heaven, so the things on earth will be either bound or set free according to what is in heaven."

[20]He gave a stern warning: "Do not tell anyone that I am the Messiah."

[21]From that time, Jesus began to explain to his disciples his need to go to Jerusalem and endure great suffering at the hand of government officials, chief priests, and teachers of the Law. "I will be killed," he said, "but three days later I will rise to life."

[22]Simon Peter took Jesus aside and privately reprimanded him for saying such things. "Master, this is not possible. God would never allow this to happen to you!"

[23]Jesus looked at Peter. "Do not stand in my way, adversary. You are a hindrance to me because you do not understand the plan of God. You see only from a human point of view."

[24]Then he taught his disciples. "If anyone wants to follow me, he must sacrifice his selfish desires. Take up your cross, and then you can follow me. [25]If you try to save your life for yourself, you will lose it. But if you lose your life for my sake, you will find it. [26]What have you gained if you own the whole world but lose your life? Nothing has sufficient value that you should want to exchange it for your life. [27]One day, the Son of Man will come in his Father's glory with his angels and will judge the people according to their deeds. [28]I guarantee, some of you standing here will not die before they see the Son of Man coming in his Kingdom."

Chapter 17

[1]Six days after Jesus told the disciples about his need to die, he took Simon Peter and the two brothers, James and John, to be alone, high up on the mountain. [2]The three saw his whole appearance change. His face shone bright as the sun, and his clothes became dazzling white. [3]Suddenly, Moses and Elijah appeared and talked with him.

[4]Peter said, "Sir, it is wonderful to be here. If you want, we can build three shrines here—for you, Moses, and Elijah."

[5]While Peter was still speaking, a brilliant cloud overshadowed them. A voice came from the cloud. "This is my dearly loved son, in whom I am well pleased. Listen to him!"

[6]When the disciples heard the voice, they fell facedown on the ground, terrified.

[7]Jesus came and touched them. "Get up and do not be afraid."

[8]When they looked around, no one was there except Jesus.

[9]As they came down the mountain, Jesus told them, "Do not tell anyone what you saw, not until after the Son of Man has risen from the dead."

[10]The disciples asked Jesus, "Why do the teachers of the Law say Elijah must come before the Messiah comes?"

[11]"They are right," Jesus said. "Elijah comes first, to prepare for the Messiah's coming. [12]The truth is, Elijah has already come, but people did not recognize who he was. Instead, they chose to abuse him. In the same way, they will cause the Son of Man to suffer."

[13]Then they understood that he was talking about John the Baptizer.

[14]When they arrived where a large crowd was waiting, a man came and knelt before Jesus.

[15]"Sir, have mercy on my son because he is out of his mind and suffers terribly. He often falls into the fire or into the water. [16]I brought him to your disciples, but they could not heal him."

[17]Jesus said, "How long must I be with this faithless and corrupt generation? How long must I put up with you? Bring your son to me."

[18]Jesus spoke against the evil spirit, and it came out of the boy and left. From that moment, the boy was well.

[19]Later, the disciples talked to Jesus privately. "Why couldn't we cast out the evil spirit?"

[20]"Your faith did not work because it had no God connection. The truth is, if you had real faith the size of a mustard seed, you could tell this mountain to move and it could not stand still. Nothing would be impossible. [21]That is why you need to fast and pray."

[22]While they were still in Galilee, Jesus told his disciples, "The Son of Man will soon be betrayed into the hands of men [23]who will kill him. On the third day, he will rise to life again."

The disciples were deeply grieved.

²⁴When Jesus and the disciples arrived in Capernaum, collectors of the Temple tax asked Simon Peter, "Doesn't your teacher pay the Temple tax?"

²⁵"Yes, of course he does."

When Peter arrived at the house, Jesus spoke to him before he could ask if he had answered correctly. "Tell me what you think. When kings collect taxes, who pays, their sons or strangers?"

²⁶"The strangers."

"Then the sons are exempt. ²⁷However, there is no need to offend the tax collectors. Go to the lakeshore and drop a baited hook. As soon as you catch a fish, open its mouth. There you will find a coin. Take it and pay the taxes for both of us."

Chapter 18

¹At that time, the disciples asked Jesus, "Who will be the greatest in the Kingdom of Heaven?"

²Jesus called a little boy to stand in front of them. ³"I tell you for sure, unless you change and become like little children, you will never enter the Kingdom of Heaven. ⁴The greatest in the Kingdom are those who humble themselves like this little one. ⁵Anyone who welcomes such a child in my name is welcoming me. ⁶But if you cause one who believes in me to stumble, it would be better to have a millstone tied around your neck, be thrown into the sea, and drown in its depths. ⁷How terrible it will be for the world because of its offenses! Such things must come, but it will be terrible for the one who causes them.

⁸"If your hand or foot causes you to sin, cut it off and throw it away. You are better off maimed or lame than to keep both hands and feet and be thrown into eternal fire. ⁹If your eye causes you to

sin, gouge it out and throw it away. You are better off blind in one eye than to keep both eyes and be thrown into a fiery hell. [10]"Be careful not to disregard a child. I tell you, their angels are always in my Father's presence in heaven. [11]For the Son of Man came to save those who are lost. [12]What do you think? If a man has a hundred sheep and one wanders away, won't he leave the ninety-nine on the hillside to find the one that is lost? [13]Without a doubt, when he finds the stray, he will rejoice more for that one than for the ninety-nine that never wandered. [14]Likewise, your Father in heaven does not want even one of these little ones to perish.

[15]"If another believer does you wrong, privately point out the offense. If the person listens, you have gained a friend. [16]But if you are rejected, take one or two people with you so the facts may be established by two or three witnesses. [17]If the believer still refuses to listen, take the matter to the church. If he or she will not accept the church's judgment, treat that person as an unbeliever and foreigner.

[18]"Believe what I say. The things on earth must be either bound or set free according to what is in heaven. [19]Also, I need to say, if two of my followers here on earth agree in prayer, it will be done by my Father in heaven [20]because I am present whenever two or three are gathered under my direction and authority."

[21]Simon Peter asked Jesus, "How often should I forgive someone who has wronged me? Seven times?"

[22]"No, that is not enough. Until seventy-seven times, you should keep forgiving.

[23]"The Kingdom of Heaven is like a king who decided to collect the debts owed by his subjects. [24]In the accounting, a man owing a million dollars was brought to him. [25]Since he was unable to pay, the king ordered that he and his family and all his possessions be sold for payment of the debt.

²⁶"The man fell to his knees before the king and begged, 'Be patient with me, and I will pay all I owe.'

²⁷"The king was moved with compassion, released the man, and cancelled the debt.

²⁸"Later, that man met a debtor who owed him a hundred dollars, grabbed him by the throat, and demanded immediate payment. ²⁹The debtor begged, 'Be patient with me, and I will pay all I owe.' ³⁰But the man refused to wait and had the debtor thrown into prison until the debt was fully paid.

³¹"Others were disturbed by what they saw happen and told the king.

³²"The king summoned the man to appear before him. 'You are a wicked man! You begged me to be patient, and I cancelled all your debt. ³³Shouldn't you have had compassion for your debtor as I had for you?' ³⁴The king was furious, so he sent the man to prison until the million dollars was fully paid.

³⁵"My heavenly Father will deal with you in the same way if you fail to forgive others for the wrongs they have done to you."

Chapter 19

¹When Jesus had finished teaching these things, he left Galilee and went to the area of Judea on the east side of the Jordan River. ²Large crowds followed him, and he healed their sick.

³The Pharisees came to trap Jesus into saying something they could use against him, so they said, "Is it lawful for a man to divorce his wife for any reason whatever?"

⁴"Haven't you read the scripture?" Jesus asked. "From the beginning, God made them male and female. ⁵That is why a man leaves his father and mother, is united with his wife, and the two become one. ⁶Since they are no longer two but one, and God has joined them, no one should separate them."

⁷"If that is true, why did Moses command a man to write his wife a bill of divorce and send her away from his house?"

⁸"Because of your hard hearts, Moses allowed you to divorce your wives, but that was not God's plan from the beginning. ⁹I say, for any reason other than sexual unfaithfulness, any man who divorces his wife and marries someone else commits adultery. And anyone who marries a divorced woman commits adultery."

¹⁰Jesus' disciples said, "If that is the only reason a man can divorce his wife, it is better to never marry."

¹¹Jesus said, "Not everyone can accept what God intends for marriage and for being single. ¹²Some have never had a desire to marry, and others choose to remain single for the sake of the Kingdom of Heaven. You should only wear the marriage garment if it fits."

¹³Parents brought their children so Jesus could lay his hands on them and pray, but the disciples rebuked them.

¹⁴"Don't stop them," Jesus said. "Allow the little ones to come to me. Of such is the Kingdom of Heaven." ¹⁵So he laid his hands on them and blessed them before he left.

¹⁶A man came to Jesus and asked, "Most excellent Teacher, what good deed must I do to have eternal life?"

¹⁷"Why do you call me most excellent?" Jesus said. "No one is most excellent except God. If you want to enter that life, keep the commandments."

¹⁸"Which ones?"

Jesus replied, "Do not murder, commit adultery, steal, or give false testimony. ¹⁹Honor your parents, and love your neighbor as much as yourself."

²⁰"I've done all that since I was young. What else must I do?"

²¹"If you want to be perfect, go and sell everything you own, and give the money to the poor. You will have treasure in heaven and can follow me."

²²After hearing this, the young man walked away sad, because he was very wealthy.

²³Jesus said to his disciples, "I tell you the truth, it is nearly impossible for a rich man to enter the Kingdom of Heaven. ²⁴It is harder for a man of great wealth to enter the Kingdom than for a camel to get through a needle's eye."

²⁵The disciples could not believe what Jesus was saying. "If that is true, then who in the world can be saved?"

²⁶Jesus looked intently at them. "With men, it is impossible. But with God, all things are possible."

²⁷Simon Peter said to him, "We have left everything to follow you. What does that do for us?"

²⁸"There will be a time when the Son of Man sits on his glorious throne, and you will sit on twelve thrones to judge the tribes of Israel. ²⁹Those who have sacrificed their homes, relatives, or possessions for my sake will receive a hundred times more and will have eternal life. ³⁰Many who have the seat of lowest honor here will have the highest there. And many who have the seat of highest honor here will have the lowest there."

Chapter 20

¹"The Kingdom of Heaven is like a business owner who went early in the morning to hire workers for his vineyard. ²After reaching an agreement to pay a day's wages, he sent them into his vineyard.

³"Around nine o'clock, he saw people in the marketplace doing nothing. ⁴'Go work in my vineyard,' he told them, 'and I will pay you a fair wage.' So they went.

⁵"At noon and at three o'clock in the afternoon, he did the same thing.

⁶"Later, at almost five o'clock, he saw others standing around. 'Why have you been standing here all day, doing nothing?' he asked.

⁷"'Because no one has hired us.'

"'Then go work in my vineyard, and I will pay you whatever is right.'

⁸"In the evening, the owner said to his manager, 'Call the workers and give them their pay, starting with those hired last.'

⁹"Those who were hired at five o'clock received a day's wages.

¹⁰"When those who were first hired came, they expected to receive more but were only given a day's pay, ¹¹so they complained to the owner. ¹²'The men you hired last have only worked an hour, but you gave them as much as you paid us for working in the heat all day.'

¹³"The owner said, 'Men, I've done you no wrong. Didn't you agree to work for one day's pay? ¹⁴Take your money and go. If I want to give the last workers as much as I gave you, ¹⁵I have the right to do so. It's my money. Do you think I am evil because I've chosen to be generous?'

¹⁶"So it is with the Kingdom of Heaven. Those who were thought to be least important are first, and the first are last. Many are called, and few are chosen."

¹⁷While going up to Jerusalem, Jesus took the twelve disciples aside and said to them privately, ¹⁸"Soon, the Son of Man will be handed over to the chief priests and teachers of the Law, who will sentence him to die. ¹⁹They will deliver him to the Romans to be mocked, whipped, and crucified. But on the third day, he will rise again."

²⁰Zebedee's wife went to Jesus with her sons. She knelt before him and asked if he would do her a favor.

²¹"What do you want?" Jesus asked.

"In your glorious Kingdom," she said, "award the seats of honor on your right and left to my two sons."

²²"You have no idea what you are asking." To the sons, he said, "Are you able to drink the cup that I am about to drink?"

They answered, "Yes, we are."

²³"Indeed you will drink from my cup, but the places on my right and left are not mine to give. They are reserved for the ones for whom they have been prepared by my Father."

²⁴When the other ten disciples heard what had happened, they were angry with the two brothers.

²⁵So Jesus called them together. "You know that the most honored among the Gentiles exercise dominion over others. Great rulers command unquestioned service. ²⁶But you will not be like kings. Your greatness will depend on how well you serve others. ²⁷If you want the highest place of honor, you must be the best servant, ²⁸just like the Son of Man, who has come to serve and sacrifice his life for many."

²⁹As Jesus and the disciples left Jericho, a large crowd followed.

³⁰Sitting on the side of the road, two blind men heard that Jesus was coming toward them. "Sir, Son of David," they cried, "have mercy on us." ³¹When the crowd rebuked them, telling them to keep quiet, they shouted even louder, "Sir, Son of David, have mercy on us!"

³²So Jesus stopped and called for them. "What do you want me to do for you?"

³³"Heal our eyes, sir, so we can see."

³⁴Having compassion for them, he touched their eyes. Immediately, their eyes were healed and they joined those who followed him.

Chapter 21

¹As Jesus and the disciples approached Jerusalem, they stopped near Bethphage at the Mount of Olives. Jesus sent two disciples, ²saying, "Go into the village. As soon as you enter, you will see a donkey tethered with its colt. Untie them and bring them to me. ³If someone asks what you are doing, say, 'The Master needs them,' and he will allow you to take them without hesitation."

⁴This event fulfilled the words of Zechariah: ⁵*People of Zion, rejoice. Shout for joy, people of Jerusalem. Look! The king is coming. He is a righteous and victorious savior, yet humble, riding upon a colt, a donkey's foal.*

⁶So the disciples did as they were told ⁷and brought the donkey with its colt. With their coats laid upon the colt's back, Jesus rode toward Jerusalem.

⁸A huge crowd gathered along the road and spread their garments before him. Some cut palm branches to lay a carpet in his path. ⁹Some walked ahead of Jesus while others followed, shouting, "Great glory to the Son of David. Blessed is the one who comes in God's name. Praise God in the highest heaven."

¹⁰Jesus' entry into Jerusalem stirred up the whole city. "Who is this?" people asked.

¹¹Those in the crowd who had been following him answered, "The prophet Jesus, from Nazareth in Galilee."

¹²In the Temple's outer court, Jesus threw out the merchants who were buying and selling there. He overthrew the moneychangers' tables and knocked over the cages of those selling doves. ¹³He said to the people, "The scriptures say, 'My Temple will be called a house of prayer for all nations,' but you have turned it into a hangout for robbers."

¹⁴When the blind and lame came to the Temple, Jesus healed them.

¹⁵The chief priests and teachers of the Law were very upset when they saw the wondrous miracles and heard the children crying, "Hail to the Son of David!" ¹⁶They said to Jesus, "Do you hear what these children are saying?"

"Yes, I do," Jesus said. "Haven't you read the scriptures? *From the mouths of infants and children, you have raised up a strong voice to refute your enemies, silencing the adverse words of all who oppose you.*"

¹⁷He left the city and spent the night in Bethany.

¹⁸On his way to Jerusalem the next morning, he was hungry ¹⁹and walked over to a fig tree beside the road, but found no fruit, only leaves. "Let no fruit grow on you," he said to the tree. Before long, it withered.

²⁰The disciples were amazed. "Why did the tree suddenly die?"

²¹"Know this for certain. If you have unwavering faith, you will not only do things like this, but you will say to this mountain, 'Rise and be thrown into the sea,' and it will obey. ²²When faith connects your prayer with what God wants to do, you will see it happen."

²³The chief priests and Jewish leaders came to Jesus when he was teaching in the Temple. "What right do you have to do these things? Who gave you the authority?"

²⁴"Let me ask you a question. If you can give me the answer, I will tell you by what authority I do these things. ²⁵From where did John receive his authority to baptize? Was it from God or men?"

They discussed the question among themselves. "If we say, 'From God,' he will ask why we did not believe him. ²⁶But if we say, 'From men,' we turn the people against us because they all regard John as a prophet." ²⁷So they said to Jesus, "We don't know."

"Then I won't tell you by what authority I do these things. ²⁸Tell me what you think. A man told the older of two sons to go work in his vineyard. ²⁹The son said, 'No. I have other things to do.' Later, he changed his mind and went. ³⁰The man made the same request of the younger son, who said, 'Yes, sir. I will.' But he did not go. [31]Which of the two did what his father wanted?"

"Obviously, the older son."

"I guarantee," Jesus said, "that tax collectors and prostitutes will reach the Kingdom of God ahead of you. [32]John showed you the way of righteousness. You did not believe him, but the tax collectors and prostitutes did. And later, after seeing all this, you still won't change your mind and believe.

[33]"Now listen to this illustration," Jesus said. "A landowner planted a vineyard, put a fence around it, dug a winepress, and built a watchtower. He left the vineyard under the care of sharecroppers and went to another country. [34]At harvest season, he sent his servants to collect his share from the vineyard. [35]The sharecroppers grabbed and beat up one servant, killed another, and stoned a third. [36]Again, the landowner sent servants, but the sharecroppers mistreated them in the same way. [37]Finally, he sent his son, saying, 'They will respect my son.' [38]When the sharecroppers saw him coming, they said to themselves, 'He is the heir. If we kill him, we can have his inheritance.' [39]So they grabbed him, dragged him out of the vineyard, and killed him. [40]What do you think the landowner will do to those sharecroppers when he returns?"

[41]"He will destroy those wicked men with a horrible death and find others who will give him his share of the harvest."

[42]"Haven't you read the scripture? *The stone that the builders rejected has become the cornerstone. God has done this, and it is a wonderful sight to behold.* [43]So I am telling you, the Kingdom of God will be taken from you and will be given to a fruitful people. [44]Those who fall on this stone will be broken, but those on whom this stone falls will be crushed."

[45]After the Pharisees and chief priests heard his illustrations, they realized that he was talking about them. [46]They wanted to arrest him

but could not because they feared the many people who believed Jesus was a prophet.

Chapter 22

¹Again, Jesus taught using illustrations.

²"The Kingdom of Heaven is like a king who prepared a wedding feast for his son. ³He sent servants to invite everyone on the guest list, but no one would come. ⁴So he sent other servants, saying, 'Tell everyone on the list that preparations are complete. The fattened calves and bulls have been butchered, and the table is set. Come to the wedding.' ⁵But the people were not impressed. They pursued their own interests on their farms and in other places of business. ⁶Those who remained grabbed the servants, abused them, and finally killed them. ⁷When the king heard what had happened, he was furious. He sent his soldiers to destroy the murderers and burn their city to the ground. ⁸He said to his servants, 'The wedding feast is ready, but the people we invited did not deserve the honor. ⁹Go down the streets and invite everyone you can find.' ¹⁰The servants brought in all the people from the streets, paying no attention to how good or bad they looked, and filled the place with willing guests. ¹¹When the king came to meet the guests, he saw a man who was not appropriately dressed. ¹²'How is it that you are here without a garment suitable for a wedding?' The man did not know what to say. ¹³'Tie him hand and foot,' the king said, 'and throw him into the darkness outside, where there will be bitterness and weeping.'

¹⁴"Many are called, and few are chosen."

¹⁵The Pharisees gathered to plot how they might trap Jesus into saying something that could be used against him. ¹⁶They sent some of their group and people loyal to Herod to say, "Teacher, we know you are sincere and completely honest. You teach the truth about

God's ways without concern for what people think. ¹⁷So tell us what you believe. Is it right to pay taxes to Caesar?"

¹⁸Jesus recognized their evil scheming. "You hypocrites! Why are you testing me? ¹⁹Bring me a coin used to pay the tax."

They handed him a Roman coin.

²⁰"Whose image and inscription is this?"

²¹"Caesar's," they said.

"Then pay to Caesar what belongs to him, and give God all that is God's."

²²Amazed at his answer, they walked away.

²³The same day, some Sadducees, who believed there was no resurrection, came to question Jesus. ²⁴"Teacher, Moses said, *If a brother dies with no children, the widow must not marry someone outside the family. The surviving brother should marry her and have children for him.* ²⁵Once, there were seven brothers and the oldest brother died without children, leaving his widow to his younger brother. ²⁶Likewise, the second brother had no children when he died. This continued until the barren wife had married all seven brothers. ²⁷Finally, the woman died, still childless. ²⁸On the day when the dead rise to life, whose wife will this woman be? All seven were married to her."

²⁹"Your logic is wrong," Jesus said, "because you do not know the scriptures, and you do not understand how God works. ³⁰In the resurrection, people will not marry but will be like the angels of heaven. ³¹Now, on the issue of rising from the dead, have not you read the scripture where God says, ³²*I am the God of Abraham, the God of Isaac, and the God of Jacob?* He is the God of the living, not of the dead."

³³The crowd was impressed with his teaching.

³⁴When the Pharisees heard that Jesus had silenced the Sadducees, they gathered together with Jesus. ³⁵One of them who had

exceptional knowledge of the Law tested him by asking, [36]"Teacher, what is the most important commandment in the Law?"

[37]"*You must love God with your whole heart, with all your being and all your strength.* [38]This is the first and most important of all commandments. [39]But the second commandment is equally important. *Love your neighbor as yourself.* [40]All the Law and the prophets are based on these two commandments."

[41]While the Pharisees were gathered around him, Jesus asked, [42]"What do you believe about the Messiah? Whose son is he?"

They answered, "He will be a descendant of King David."

[43]"Assuming that is true, how do you explain the fact that David, under the inspiration of the Holy Spirit, called the Messiah 'my Lord.' He said, [44]*God said unto my Lord, 'Sit here at my right hand until I have put all your enemies beneath your feet.'* [45]If David called him Lord, how can he be his son?"

[46]No one could answer him.

From then on, the Pharisees lost heart in asking questions.

Chapter 23

[1]Jesus said to the crowd and to his followers, [2]"The Pharisees and teachers of the Law are telling you what Moses says you should do. [3]You may do what they teach, but do not copy what they do, because they do not practice what they teach. [4]They place unbearably heavy burdens on others but will carry none of the weight themselves. [5]What they do is intended to gain admiration from the people. They put long tassels on their robes and wear big prayer boxes containing scriptures, making them large so they will be seen. [6]At feasts and in the synagogues, they love the seats of honor. [7]In the marketplaces, they seek respectful greetings and love to be called Teacher or Master.

[8]"Do not let people praise you as someone especially to be admired, because you are all brothers and sisters under one Master. [9]Do not recognize any human being as the one who gave you life because you have only one true Father, who is in heaven. [10]Do not let people praise you as their teacher, because you all have one teacher, who is the Messiah.

[11]"Whoever is the greatest among you must be everyone's servant. [12]Those who try to make themselves great will be humbled, and those who humble themselves will be exalted.

[13]"How terrible for you Pharisees and teachers of the Law. Hypocrites! You block the door to the Kingdom of Heaven, not entering yourselves and preventing others who would like to get in.

[14]"How terrible for you Pharisees and teachers of the Law. Hypocrites! Because you take advantage of widows while making long prayers to appear righteous, you will be punished most severely.

[15]"How terrible for you Pharisees and teachers of the Law. Hypocrites! You cross land and sea, looking for converts. And when you find them, you make them twice the children of hell that you are.

[16]"How terrible it will be for you blind leaders who say, 'Swearing an oath by the Temple means nothing, but those who swear by the gold in the Temple must keep their promises.' [17]You blind fools! Which is more important, the gold or the Temple that makes the gold sacred? [18]You say, 'Swearing by the altar means nothing, but those who swear by the gift on the altar must keep their promises.' [19]You blind fools! Which is more important, the gift or the altar that makes the gift sacred? [20]Swearing by the altar is swearing by it and everything on it. [21]Swearing by the Temple is swearing by it and

everything within. [22]Swearing by heaven is swearing by the throne of God and the one sitting there.

[23]"How terrible for you Pharisees and teachers of the Law. Hypocrites! You give a tenth of your mint, dill, and cumin, but you neglect the most important parts of the Law, like justice, mercy, and faithfulness. You should not do the one while neglecting the other. [24]You blind leaders! You choke on a gnat but swallow a camel.

[25]"How terrible for you Pharisees and teachers of the Law. Hypocrites! You wash the outside of cups and platters, but you leave the inside dirty, full of greed and wickedness. [26]You blind Pharisees. First clean the inside. Then the outside will also be clean.

[27]"How terrible for you Pharisees and teachers of the Law. Hypocrites! You are like whitewashed tombs that look great on the outside but are full of dead men's bones and rottenness. [28]In the same way, you appear to be righteous but are actually full of hypocrisy and wickedness.

[29]"How terrible for you Pharisees and teachers of the Law. Hypocrites! You build tombs for the prophets and raise monuments to the righteous. [30]You say, 'If we had lived back then, we would not have acted like our ancestors, killing the prophets.' [31]You testify against yourselves, that you are children of those who murdered the prophets. [32]Go ahead and complete the work your ancestors started. [33]You venomous snakes! How will you escape God's judgment?

[34]"Listen. I will send you prophets, philosophers, and teachers. You will stone some and crucify others. As they go from town to town, you will ridicule them in your synagogues and have them flogged. [35]From the murder of Abel in the beginning to Zechariah, who died between the altar and the Temple sanctuary, the righteous blood that has been shed on the earth [36]will be charged against this generation.

[37]"O Jerusalem, Jerusalem! You kill the prophets and those who have been sent to you. Many times, I have wanted to gather you to myself like a hen brings her chicks under her wings, but you were not willing. [38]Look! Your house is now empty. [39]You will not see me again until you say, 'Blessed is the one who comes in God's name.'"

Chapter 24

[1]As Jesus left the Temple, his disciples pointed out how impressive the Temple construction was.

[2]"Do you see all these buildings as something great?" Jesus asked. "I guarantee, their destruction will be so great, one stone will not be left standing on the other."

[3]Later, Jesus was sitting on the slopes of the Mount of Olives when his disciples came to him in private and said, "Tell us. When will all these things happen? What will signal your coming and the end of the world?"

[4]"Be careful," Jesus said. "Do not let anyone deceive you. [5]Many will claim to be the Messiah and will fool a multitude. [6]Do not panic when you hear about wars or battle threats. Such things must happen, but that does not mean the end has come. [7]Nation will war against nation and kingdom against kingdom. There will be famines and earthquakes in various places, [8]but that is only the beginning of the tragedies. [9]Men will hand you over to be flogged and even killed. Because of my name, you will be hated by people everywhere. [10]Many will forsake their faith and betray one another, each hating the other. [11]Many false prophets will come and lead large crowds astray. [12]Because evil will flourish, most people's love will grow cold. [13]But those who remain faithful until the end will be saved.

[14]"The good news of the Kingdom will be preached throughout the world for a testimony to all people. After that, the end will come. [15]When you see the abominations and desecration of the Holy Place as predicted by the prophet Daniel, [16]those in Judea should flee to the mountains. [17]People on their housetops should not take time to gather belongings from their houses. [18]A man in the field should not go back home for his coat. [19]How terrible it will be for pregnant women and nursing mothers. [20]Pray that you will not have to flee in winter or on a Sabbath, [21]because this will be the worst time of suffering that has ever been or ever will be. [22]Except those days be few, no one would survive, but the time will be shortened for the sake of God's people.

[23]"If anyone says, 'Look! Here is the Messiah,' or, 'There he is,' do not believe it. [24]False messiahs and ministers will perform such great signs and wonders that even God's people would be deceived, if that were possible. [25]Pay attention, because I've warned you ahead of time. [26]So if people say, 'He is in an obscure place or is hiding somewhere,' do not believe it. [27]When the Son of Man comes, his arrival will be as unmistakable as the lightning that flashes across the sky and is seen to the far east and west.

[28]"As the gathering of vultures shows where the carcass is, these signs indicate that the end is near. [29]Soon after those days of suffering, darkness will blanket the sky. The sun will hide and the moon will give no light. All the stars will disappear, and the powers of the universe will be shaken. [30]The Son of Man will appear in the sky, and the people of the earth will mourn. They will see him arrive in the clouds, with power and great glory. [31]With the mighty blast of a trumpet, he will send his angels to gather his people from everywhere on earth.

³²"From the fig tree, you can understand how it will be. When the branches bud and start to put on leaves, you know that summer is near. ³³In the same way, when you see these things come to pass, you will know the time is near. ³⁴When all these things have been fulfilled, this age will come to its close. ³⁵Heaven and earth will pass away, but my words will stand forever.

³⁶"No one knows the exact date and time, not even the angels in heaven. Only the Father knows. ³⁷The coming of the Son of Man will be like the days of Noah. ³⁸Before the flood, people were eating, drinking, and having a good time until the day Noah entered the ark. ³⁹They did not believe until the flood swept them away. It will be the same when the Son of Man comes.

⁴⁰"Two men will be working in the field. One will be taken, the other left behind. ⁴¹Two women will be grinding at the mill. One will be taken, the other left behind. ⁴²Always be watching, because you do not know when your Lord will come. ⁴³If a homeowner knew when a burglar would come, he would be prepared and would not allow him to break in. ⁴⁴Because you do not know when the Son of Man will arrive, you must always be ready.

⁴⁵"How does the faithful and wise servant behave, the one whom the owner would want to put in charge of his business of meeting the needs of others? ⁴⁶The good manager always focuses on business the same as if the owner were there, so he is found doing a good job when the owner arrives. ⁴⁷Truly, such a man will be put in charge of everything. ⁴⁸But if that servant is evil, he says to himself, 'The owner will not be back for a while.' ⁴⁹He takes advantage of others and spends his time partying. ⁵⁰The owner arrives when he is least expected, ⁵¹sees his hypocrisy, and terminates the servant without pay. The servant will be cast into the darkness, where there will be bitterness and weeping."

Chapter 25

[1]"The Kingdom of Heaven is like ten bridesmaids who took their lamps and went to meet the groom. [2]Five were wise, and five were foolish. [3]The foolish took only their lamps, [4]but the wise also carried flasks of oil. [5]After a long wait, the bridegroom still had not come. All ten became drowsy and fell asleep.

[6]"At midnight, someone shouted, 'Look! The groom is coming. Let's go meet him.'

[7]"The bridesmaids awakened and reached for their lamps.

[8]"The foolish said, 'Our lamps have gone out. Give us some of your oil.'

[9]"But the wise answered, 'No. We do not have enough for everyone. Go to the market and buy your own oil.'

[10]"While the foolish were shopping, the groom joined everyone who was ready and entered the wedding feast. The door was locked.

[11]"Later, the foolish bridesmaids came knocking. 'Sir, open the door for us.'

[12]"But the groom said, 'I am sorry. I do not know you.'

[13]"Likewise, you should always be prepared, because you do not know when the Son of Man will come.

[14]"The Kingdom of Heaven is like a man who was about to travel to a distant country. He called his servants and made them responsible for his money while he was gone. [15]According to their ability, he gave five bags of money to the first man, two bags to the second, and one bag to the third. Then he left.

[16]"The servant with five bags used the money in business transactions and made five more. [17]The servant with two bags also used the money in business and made two more. [18]But the servant with one bag dug a hole in the ground and hid the money.

[19]"After a long time, the man returned from his trip and asked his servants what they had done with his money.

[20]"The servant who had received five bags brought ten and said, 'Master, you gave me five bags, and I have gained five more.'

[21]"'Great job!' the man said. 'You are a good, trustworthy servant. Because you have been faithful with a little, I will now make you responsible for much more. Let's celebrate together.'

[22]"The servant who had received two bags brought four and said, 'Master, you gave me two bags, and I have gained two more.'

[23]"'Great job!' the man said. 'You are a good, trustworthy servant. Because you have been faithful with a little, I will now make you responsible for much more. Let's celebrate together.'

[24]"The servant who had received one bag said, 'Master, I knew how hard you are to please. You are like someone who expects a harvest but has planted no seeds. [25]I was afraid I might lose your money, so I hid your bag in the earth. Here is your money, still safe.'

[26]"'You are a wicked, lazy servant,' the man said. 'If you knew I expected an increase, and I expect a harvest where I've planted no seeds, [27]you should have invested with the moneychangers so I would have received my money with interest. [28]Take the bag and give it to the one who has ten. [29]People who put to good use what they have will gain more, but people who do nothing with what they have will lose what they have hidden. [30]Throw this good-for-nothing servant outside in the darkness, where there will be bitterness and weeping.'

[31]"When the Son of Man comes in splendor with all his angels, he will take his place upon his exalted throne. [32]All people will assemble before him, and he will separate them like a shepherd divides the sheep from the goats. [33]He will place the sheep on his right and the goats on his left.

³⁴"The King will say to those on his right, 'You who have been blessed by my Father, receive your inheritance, the Kingdom that was prepared for you from the creation of the world. ³⁵I was hungry, and you gave me food. I was thirsty, and you gave me drink. I was homeless, and you opened your home to me. ³⁶I needed clothes, and you gave me something to wear. I was sick, and you cared for me. I was in prison, and you came to visit me.'

³⁷"The righteous will say, 'Sir, when were you hungry and thirsty, and we gave you food and drink? ³⁸When did we see you homeless or in need of clothes? ³⁹When were you sick or in prison, and we came to visit you?'

⁴⁰"The King will answer, 'I assure you, whenever you helped one of my needy people, you did it to me.'

⁴¹"He will say to those on his left, 'Leave me, you who are condemned. Receive your inheritance in the eternal fire prepared for the devil and his angels. ⁴²I was hungry, and you gave me no food. I was thirsty, and you gave me nothing to drink. ⁴³I was homeless, and you would not open your home. I needed clothes, and you gave me nothing to wear. I was sick and in prison, but you never visited me.'

⁴⁴"They will ask, 'Sir, when were you hungry and thirsty, and we gave you no food and drink? When did we see you homeless or in need of clothes? When were you sick or in prison, and we did not visit you?'

⁴⁵"The King will answer, 'I assure you, whenever you failed to help one of my needy people, you failed to help me.'

⁴⁶"They will suffer eternal punishment, but the righteous will enjoy eternal life."

Chapter 26

¹When Jesus had finished his discourse, he said to his disciples, ²"As you know, Passover begins in two days. By then, the Son of Man will be betrayed and crucified."

³At that moment, the chief priests and Jewish leaders had convened at the palace of Caiaphas, the high priest, ⁴to plot how they would covertly capture Jesus and put him to death. ⁵"We must not do it during the feast," they agreed, "or we will cause a riot."

⁶At Bethany, Jesus was in the home of Simon the leper ⁷when a woman came with a jar made of fine gypsum filled with expensive perfume and poured it on Jesus' head as he sat at the table.

⁸The disciples were upset when they saw what she had done. "Why this waste?" they said. ⁹"That perfume could have been sold for a lot of money and given to the poor."

¹⁰Jesus knew what they were saying, so he said, "Why are you criticizing the woman for doing good for me? ¹¹You will always have the poor with you, but you will not always have me. ¹²In pouring the perfume, she has prepared my body for burial. ¹³I assure you, everywhere the good news is proclaimed throughout the world, this woman's deed will be remembered and told."

¹⁴Judas Iscariot, one of the twelve disciples, went to the chief priests ¹⁵and said, "How much will you pay me to deliver him to you?" So they reached an agreement to pay him thirty pieces of silver. ¹⁶After that, he looked for an opportunity to betray Jesus.

¹⁷On the first day of the Feast of Unleavened Bread, the disciples asked Jesus, "Where shall we prepare for you to eat the Passover meal?"

¹⁸"Go into the city and tell a certain man, 'The Teacher says, "My time is near. I will eat the Passover meal with my disciples at your house."'"

[19]The disciples did exactly as Jesus instructed and prepared the Passover meal.

[20]In the evening, Jesus sat with the twelve disciples at the table. [21]During the meal, he said, "I tell you the truth. One of you will turn against me."

[22]Everyone was deeply grieved and said, "Sir, you are not talking about me, are you?"

[23]"One who eats with me will betray me. [24]I, the Son of Man, must suffer according to the scriptures, but how terrible it will be for the man who turns against me. It would be better for him if he had not been born."

[25]"Teacher," Judas the betrayer said, "could I be the one?"

Jesus answered, "You have said so."

[26]While they ate, Jesus took the bread, blessed it, broke it, and passed it to the disciples. "Take this bread and eat. This is my body." [27]He held the cup, offered thanks, and passed it to the disciples. "Take this wine and drink, all of you. [28]This is my blood of the new agreement between God and his people, to be poured out so that many offenses may be pardoned. [29]I tell you, I will not drink wine again until I drink with you in my Father's Kingdom."

[30]After they had sung a hymn, they left for the Mount of Olives.

[31]"Tonight," Jesus said, "all of you will leave me, for the scripture says, *Strike the shepherd, and the sheep will be scattered.* [32]But after I have risen, I will reach Galilee before you do."

[33]Peter said, "Everyone else may abandon you, but I never will."

[34]"I guarantee," Jesus said, "before the rooster crows tonight, you will deny me three times."

[35]"Even if I have to die," Peter insisted, "I will not deny you."

The rest of the disciples said the same thing.

[36]When they arrived at Gethsemane, Jesus said to his disciples, "While I go over there to pray, you sit here." [37]He took with him

Peter and the two sons of Zebedee, James and John. He became grieved and was filled with distress. [38]"Stay here and watch with me," he said. "My heart is overcome with sorrow to the point of death."

[39]He went a little farther, fell on his face, and prayed, "My Father, if possible, let me escape this suffering. Nevertheless, I want your will, not mine."

[40]He returned to his disciples and found them asleep. "Can't you watch with me for an hour? [41]Stay alert and pray so you do not fall into temptation. The spirit is willing, but the body is weak."

[42]Again, Jesus left to pray. "My Father, if this cup of suffering cannot be emptied without my drinking it, let your will be done."

[43]Once more, he returned to find his disciples asleep. They could not keep their eyes open. [44]He left them for the third time and prayed the same words as before. [45]When he returned, he said, "How can you be at ease, sleeping? Look! It is time for the Son of Man to be handed over to wicked men. [46]Get up. Let's go! My betrayer is coming."

[47]While Jesus was still speaking, Judas, one of the twelve, arrived with a mob carrying swords and clubs, men sent by the chief priests and Jewish leaders. [48]To identify Jesus, the traitor had arranged a signal, saying, "The man I kiss is the one you want. Seize him."

[49]Without hesitation, Judas approached Jesus. "Hello, Teacher." He gave Jesus the customary kiss of greeting.

[50]"Friend," Jesus said, "what have you done?"

Men grabbed Jesus and held him captive.

[51]One of the disciples drew a sword and cut off the high priest's servant's ear.

[52]"Put away your sword," Jesus said to him. "Those who live by the sword will die by the sword. [53]Don't you know I could ask my Father, and he would immediately send twelve armies of angels?

⁵⁴But if I did, the scriptures could not be fulfilled that say this must happen."

⁵⁵Jesus looked at the mob surrounding him. "Am I a hardened criminal that you must capture me with swords and clubs? Every day, I taught in the Temple. Why didn't you arrest me there? ⁵⁶It has happened this way to fulfill the words of the prophets."

All the disciples abandoned him and escaped.

⁵⁷The arresting guards took Jesus to Caiaphas, the high priest, and a gathering of Jewish leaders and teachers of the Law.

⁵⁸Peter followed at a distance and entered the high priest's palace courtyard to see what would happen.

⁵⁹The chief priests and Jewish council brought in witnesses who were to give false testimony about Jesus so they could sentence him to die. ⁶⁰Although many false witnesses came, they could not get any two testimonies to agree. Finally, two men appeared before the council ⁶¹and said, "This man claimed he could destroy the Temple of God and rebuild it in three days."

⁶²The high priest stood and looked at Jesus. "Aren't you going to answer? What do you have to say about the charges brought against you?"

⁶³Jesus said nothing.

"By the authority of the living God, I command you to tell us if you are the Messiah, the Son of God."

⁶⁴"Yes," Jesus said, "you could say that. But I tell all of you, in the future you will see the Son of Man sitting on God's right hand and arriving on the clouds of the sky."

⁶⁵"Blasphemy!" The high priest ripped his clothes. "Why do we need more witnesses? With your own ears you have heard his blasphemy.

⁶⁶What is your verdict?"

"Guilty," they answered. "He should be put to death." [67]Then they spat at him, struck him with their fists, and slapped him in the face. [68]"Prophesy to us, Messiah," they scoffed. "Tell us who hit you."

[69]In the courtyard outside, a servant girl came to where Peter sat. "You are one of those who was with Jesus of Galilee."

[70]Before everyone around, Peter denied having been with Jesus. "It was not me," he said. "I do not know what you are talking about."

[71]As he left the courtyard and came near the entrance, another servant girl noticed him. "This man was with Jesus of Nazareth."

[72]With an oath, he denied any knowledge of Jesus. "I swear, I do not know that man."

[73]Later, some of those who stood near Peter said, "You must be one of them. Your accent is clearly Galilean."

[74]With cursing and swearing, Peter denied any connection with Jesus. "I tell you, I do not know this man." Immediately, a rooster crowed, [75]and he remembered what Jesus had said: "Before the rooster crows, you will deny me three times."

He went outside and broke down, crying.

Chapter 27

[1]At dawn, the chief priests and Jewish leaders again met to decide how to put Jesus to death. [2]They led Jesus away, his hands tied, and delivered him to Pontius Pilate, the governor.

[3]When Judas, the traitor, saw that Jesus had been condemned, he was sorry for his actions. So he took the thirty pieces of silver back to the chief priests and Jewish leaders. [4]"I have sinned," he said, "by betraying an innocent man."

"What does that have to do with us?" they asked. "That is your problem."

[5]He flung the silver across the Temple floor, left, and hanged himself.

⁶The chief priests gathered the pieces of silver but questioned what to do with them. "This is blood money, so we cannot put it in the Temple treasury." ⁷After further discussion, they used the money to buy the potter's field as a burial place for strangers. ⁸That is why the place became known as The Field of Blood. ⁹This fulfilled the words of Jeremiah the prophet: *They took the thirty pieces of silver, the value that Israel's people placed on him,* ¹⁰*and bought the potter's field as God commanded.*

¹¹Pilate questioned Jesus as he stood before him. "Are you the king of the Jews?"

Jesus said, "Yes, you could say that."

¹²When the chief priests and Jewish leaders brought accusations against him, he said nothing.

¹³"Haven't you heard all their accusations?" Pilate said.

¹⁴Jesus gave no response, not the slightest word, so the governor was greatly impressed.

¹⁵At every Passover feast, the governor would release one prisoner to the people, anyone they wanted. ¹⁶A notoriously bad criminal named Barabbas was in prison at the time, ¹⁷so when the people had gathered, Pilate asked them, "Which one do you want me to release to you—Barabbas, or Jesus, who is called the Messiah?" ¹⁸He knew the Jewish leaders had condemned Jesus because they envied his popularity with the people.

¹⁹While judging the case, he received a message from his wife that said, "Have nothing to do with that righteous man. Last night, I had a terrible nightmare about him."

²⁰The chief priests and leaders had persuaded the people to ask for the release of Barabbas and for Jesus to be crucified.

²¹Again, Pilate asked the crowd, "Which of the two shall I release to you?"

"Barabbas," they said.

[22]"What shall I do with Jesus the Messiah?"

They all shouted, "Crucify him!"

[23]"Why? What crime has he committed?"

But the crowd roared, "Crucify him!"

[24]When Pilate realized that his attempt to bring peace was near to causing a riot, he took a bowl of water and washed his hands before the people. "I am not to blame for this righteous person's death. This is your decision."

[25]"Let his death be our responsibility," the people said, "and our children's."

[26]So Pilate released Barabbas to the people and ordered the flogging and crucifixion of Jesus.

[27]The governor's soldiers took Jesus into their headquarters, where they assembled the entire regiment. [28]After stripping off his clothes, they dressed him in a scarlet robe, [29]placed a woven crown of thorns on his head, and put a staff in his right hand. They knelt before him and mocked him, saying, "Hail, king of the Jews." [30]They spat on him and used his staff to strike him on the head. [31]When they tired of mocking him, they removed the robe, dressed him in his own clothes, and took him to be crucified.

[32]On the way, they met Simon, a native of Cyrene, and forced him to carry Jesus' cross.

[33]At Golgotha, which means "skull," [34]they offered to Jesus wine mixed with a bitter drug. After tasting it, he refused the drink.

[35]After the soldiers nailed Jesus to the cross, they threw dice for the fair dividing of his clothes. [36]They sat down to keep guard over him. [37]Above his head, they had posted a sign to show the charge against him: "This is Jesus, king of the Jews."

[38]Two criminals were crucified with him, one on the right, the other on the left.

³⁹People who walked by insulted him and shook their heads. ⁴⁰"You said you could tear down the Temple and rebuild it in three days. If you have such power, save yourself. If you are the Son of God, come down from the cross."

⁴¹In a similar manner, the chief priests, teachers of the Law, and other Jewish leaders mocked him. ⁴²"He saved others," they said. "Let's see if he can save himself. If he is the king of Israel, let him come down from the cross. Then we will believe he is who he says he is. ⁴³He trusted God, so let God deliver him now if he cares anything about him. He said he was the Son of God."

⁴⁴The criminals who were crucified with him joined in the mockery.

⁴⁵From noon until three o'clock, darkness covered the land. ⁴⁶At three o'clock, Jesus screamed, *"Eloi, Eloi, lema sabachthani,"* which means "My God, my God, for this I was born."

⁴⁷Some of those standing there said, "He calls for Elijah."

⁴⁸One of them ran to fill a sponge with sour wine and lifted the sponge on the end of a branch so Jesus could drink.

⁴⁹The others said, "Wait. Let's see if Elijah will come to save him."

⁵⁰After Jesus screamed again, he quit breathing. ⁵¹The earth shook. Rocky cliffs broke apart. The Temple veil ripped in two, from top to bottom.

⁵²Tombs were opened, and many godly men and women rose from the dead. ⁵³After Jesus' resurrection, they left their graves, entered Jerusalem, and were seen by many people.

⁵⁴When the centurion and his guards felt the earthquake and saw all that had happened, they feared for their lives and said, "This man really was the Son of God."

⁵⁵Many women who had followed from Galilee to serve Jesus were watching from a distance. ⁵⁶Among them were Mary Magdalene,

Mary the mother of James and Joseph, and the mother of James and John, sons of Zebedee.

[57]In the late afternoon, Joseph, a rich man from Arimathea and a disciple of Jesus, [58]asked Pilate for the body of Jesus, and his request was granted. [59]He took the body, wrapped it in clean linen, [60]and laid it in his own unused tomb that was cut into the rock. He rolled a huge stone to close the entrance and left. [61]Mary Magdalene and the other Mary sat near the tomb.

[62]After sundown that ended the day of preparation, the chief priests and Pharisees went to see Pilate. [63]"Sir, while that deceiver was alive, he said, 'After three days, I will rise from the dead.' [64]Therefore, the tomb must be closely guarded or his disciples will steal his body and tell the people he has risen. If that happens, conditions will be worse than before."

[65]"You may have the guards," Pilate said. "Make it as secure as you can."

[66]So they sealed the tomb and posted guards.

Chapter 28

[1]After observing the Sabbath, Mary Magdalene and the other Mary headed to the tomb at the break of dawn on Sunday, the first day of the week.

[2]A great earthquake shook the ground. God's angel came from heaven, rolled the stone away from the tomb entrance, and sat on it. [3]His appearance was like lightning and his clothes were white as snow. [4]When the guards saw him, they trembled and became like dead men.

[5]The angel spoke to the women. "Do not be afraid. I know you are looking for Jesus, who was crucified. [6]He is not here, because he has risen as he said he would. Come and see where his body was. [7]Hurry now! Tell his disciples that he has risen from the dead. He

will go before you, and you will see him in Galilee as I have told you."

[8]With fear and amazement, they ran from the tomb to tell the disciples. [9]As they left, Jesus met and greeted them. They fell at his feet, reached out, and worshiped him.

[10]"Do not be afraid," Jesus said. "Tell my brothers to go to Galilee, where they will see me."

[11]While the women were on their way, the guards went into the city and told the chief priests what had happened.

[12]The priests met with other religious leaders to decide what to do. They gave a large amount of money to the guards [13]and told them, "Tell everyone that his disciples came during the night and stole the body while you were asleep. [14]If the governor hears that you have failed in your duty, we will speak to him and protect you from punishment."

[15]The guards took the money and did as they were told, so that story spread among the Jews.

[16]The eleven disciples went to the mountain in Galilee where Jesus had told them to go. [17]When they saw him, they worshiped him, but some had doubts.

[18]Jesus said to them, "I have been given all authority in heaven and on earth. [19]Therefore, go to all nations and make disciples, baptizing them in the name of the Father, Son, and Holy Spirit. [20]Teach them to obey all that I have commanded you. Remember, I will always be with you, even until the end of the world."

Mark

Chapter 1

¹The beginning of the good news about Jesus the Messiah, Son of God. ²It is written in the prophets, *Listen! I will send my messenger before you to prepare the way.* ³*Someone is shouting in the wilderness, "Clear a path, for the Lord our God is coming. Straighten the curves and smooth the rough places."*

⁴From the wilderness, John came preaching that people should repent and be forgiven by God for their sins. ⁵People came from Jerusalem, all of Judea, and the Jordan valley to see and hear John. They confessed their sins and were baptized in the river Jordan.

⁶He wore camel's hair clothing with a leather belt around his waist and lived on a diet of locusts and wild honey. ⁷"One is coming after me," he cried, "who is so great I am not worthy to stoop down and untie the straps of his sandals. ⁸I baptize with water, but he will baptize you with the Holy Spirit."

⁹Jesus left Nazareth in Galilee, came to the Jordan River, and was baptized by John. ¹⁰As Jesus came up out of the water, the sky opened, and the Spirit of God descended like a dove, lighting upon him.

¹¹A voice spoke from heaven: "You are my son, whom I love. I am well pleased with you."

¹²Immediately after his baptism, the Holy Spirit led him into the wilderness, ¹³where he was tempted by Satan. For forty days, Jesus lived among the wild animals, and angels cared for him.

[14]After John was put in prison, Jesus went to Galilee and preached the good news of the Kingdom of God. [15]"The time promised by God has finally come. Repent and believe the good news."

[16]As Jesus walked along the seashore of Galilee, he saw Simon and his brother Andrew casting a net into the water, for they were fishermen. [17]"Come, follow me," Jesus said, "and I will make you fishers of men." [18]At once, they left their nets and followed him.

[19]A little farther up the shore, he saw James and his brother John, Zebedee's sons, in a boat, mending their nets. [20]As soon as he called, they left their father and the hired servants and followed him.

[21]At Capernaum, Jesus entered the synagogue on the Sabbath and began to teach. [22]People were amazed. The authority with which he spoke was nothing like the teachers of the Law.

[23]A man possessed by an evil spirit screamed in torment. [24]"What do you want with us, Jesus of Nazareth?" he asked. "I know who you are, the Holy One sent from God. Have you come to destroy us?"

[25]"Silence!" Jesus commanded. "Come out of him."

[26]The evil spirit shrieked and violently shook the man before leaving.

[27]People were astonished and asked one another, "What is going on? What powerful new teaching is this? Even the evil spirits obey him." [28]The news quickly spread throughout the region of Galilee.

[29]After leaving the synagogue, Jesus went with James and John to the home of Simon Peter and Andrew, [30]where Peter's mother-in-law was sick in bed with a burning fever, and they told him about her. [31]Jesus went to her bedside, took her by the hand, and helped her sit up. At once, the fever left, and she began to prepare dinner for them.

[32]After sunset, people brought all the sick and possessed. [33]The whole town had gathered outside the door. [34]Jesus healed many who

suffered from various diseases. Because the evil spirits knew who he was, he did not allow them to speak but commanded them to go.

³⁵Before daylight the next morning, he left for a secluded place, where he prayed.

³⁶Later, Simon Peter and his companions went to find him. ³⁷When they found him, they said, "Everyone is looking for you."

³⁸"I must also preach in the other towns," Jesus said. "That is why I came." ³⁹So he continued to travel all over Galilee, preaching in the synagogues and delivering people from evil spirits.

⁴⁰A leper kneeled before Jesus, begging, "Sir, you could make me well if you wanted to."

⁴¹"I want to." Moved with compassion, Jesus touched him. "Be cleansed."

⁴²Immediately, all signs of the leprosy disappeared.

⁴³Jesus dismissed him with strict orders: ⁴⁴"Do not tell anyone about this. Show yourself to the priest and offer the sacrifices, taking two birds as commanded by Moses. Your healing will become public record so you will no longer be regarded as a leper."

⁴⁵Instead, the man went into the town and told everyone what had happened. As the report of Jesus' power rapidly spread, large crowds gathered to hear his teaching and ask for healing of their diseases. No longer could Jesus openly enter a town without being surrounded by large crowds. Even in the country, people from everywhere kept coming to him.

Chapter 2

¹A few days after Jesus arrived in Capernaum, people heard he had returned home. ²A crowd packed the room, so there was no space left, not even outside the door. As Jesus spoke God's word, ³four men carried a paralyzed man on a mat. ⁴They could not find a way into the house, so they went up onto the roof and lowered

him through an opening in the tiles, into the midst of the crowd and right in front of Jesus.

[5]Impressed by their faith, Jesus said, "My friend, your sins are forgiven."

[6]Some of the teachers of the Law murmured among themselves, [7]"What is he saying? That is blasphemy. Only God can forgive sins."

[8]Immediately, Jesus recognized their reaction. "Why are you thinking I've done something wrong? [9]Which is easier to say, 'Your sins are forgiven,' or, 'Stand and walk'? [10]So you may know the Son of Man has authority on earth to forgive sins . . ." He turned to the paralyzed man. [11]"Get up. Take your mat and go home."

[12]Without hesitation, the man stood, grabbed his mat, and walked through the amazed crowd to his own house. Everyone marveled and glorified God, saying, "We've never seen anything like this before."

[13]Again, Jesus went to the Sea of Galilee and taught the large crowd that gathered around him at the shore. [14]As he walked along, he saw Levi, son of Alphaeus, sitting at the place where people paid taxes. "Follow me," he said, and Levi got up and followed.

[15]Later, Matthew had a big feast for Jesus at his house. Many tax collectors and other outcasts who had become followers were among the dinner guests who ate with Jesus and his disciples.

[16]When the Pharisees and the teachers of the Law saw Jesus eating with them, they asked his disciples, "Why does he eat with such people?"

[17]Jesus heard them and answered, "Healthy people do not need a doctor. The sick do. I have not come to invite to repentance those who think they are righteous. I have come for those who know they are sinners."

[18]One day, when the Pharisees and followers of John the Baptizer were fasting, some people asked Jesus, "Why do the Pharisees and John's disciples fast, but your disciples never do?"

[19]Jesus answered, "At a wedding, the friends of the bridegroom do not go without eating while he is still with them. [20]But the day will come when he will be gone. Then they will fast.

[21]"No one uses a piece of new cloth to patch old clothes. The patch would shrink, pull away from the old, and make the tear worse.

[22]"Men do not pour new wine into old skins. If they did, the wineskin would burst, ruining both the wine and the wineskin. New wine is always kept in fresh skins so both are preserved."

[23]On a Sabbath day, Jesus went through the grain fields. His disciples picked some heads of grain.

[24]When the Pharisees saw them, they said to Jesus, "Look! Your disciples are doing work that is not permitted on the Sabbath."

[25]"Haven't you read," Jesus said, "what David and his men did when they were hungry? [26]When Abiathar was high priest, David entered the house of God and ate the sacred bread that only the priests were allowed to eat. He also gave loaves to his men. [27]The Sabbath was made to meet the needs of the people, not people to meet the requirements of the Sabbath. [28]The Son of Man is Lord even of the Sabbath."

Chapter 3

[1]Jesus entered the synagogue, where there was a man with a crippled hand.

[2]The Pharisees were looking for a reason to accuse Jesus, so they watched closely to see if he would heal the man.

[3]Jesus said to the man, "Come stand in front of everyone. [4]Is it lawful to do good or evil on the Sabbath, to save life or destroy it?"

The people did not say anything.

[5]Deeply grieved at the stubbornness of their hearts, he looked upon them with anger. He said to the man, "Stretch out your hand."

As the man reached out, his hand became completely restored, as healthy as the other.

⁶The Pharisees were furious and immediately met with the supporters of Herod to plot how they might kill Jesus.

⁷Jesus and his disciples left the town and went to the lakeshore. A large crowd from Galilee and Judea followed—⁸from Jerusalem, Idumaea, and places east of the Jordan River. They also came from Tyre and Sidon—a multitude who had heard reports of the great things Jesus was doing. ⁹To keep the crowd from crushing him, he instructed the disciples to get a small boat.

¹⁰After he had healed many people, others who were sick pressed in, wanting to touch him. ¹¹When those with evil spirits saw him, they fell to the ground and cried out, "You are the Son of God!" ¹²But he sternly ordered them not to tell who he was.

¹³One day, Jesus went up on a mountain and called those he wanted to be with him. ¹⁴He chose twelve men, whom he named apostles, to stay with him. He wanted to send them out to preach, ¹⁵heal diseases, and have authority over evil spirits. ¹⁶They were Simon, whom he named Peter, and ¹⁷James son of Zebedee and his brother John, who were given the name Boanerges, meaning Sons of Thunder. ¹⁸There were Andrew, Philip, Bartholomew, Matthew, Thomas, James son of Alphaeus, Simon the Zealot, Thaddaeus, ¹⁹and Judas Iscariot, who became a traitor.

²⁰When Jesus entered a house, so large a crowd gathered that he and his disciples were not even able to eat.

²¹When his family heard about this, they went to restrain him because people were saying, "He has lost touch with reality."

²²Teachers of the Law who had come from Jerusalem argued, "This man casts out evil spirits by the power of Beelzebub, the ruler of evil spirits."

²³So Jesus brought the people together and taught with these illustrations. "How can Satan cast out Satan? ²⁴A kingdom working against itself will soon be destroyed, ²⁵and any family who fights internally cannot last very long. ²⁶If Satan drives out Satan, he is warring against himself and his kingdom cannot survive.

²⁷"How can a man force his way into a strong man's house and take his property? First he must bind the strong man. Then he can plunder his house.

²⁸"Understand this: all kinds of sin and evil speaking may be forgiven, ²⁹but speaking evil of the Holy Spirit cannot be forgiven. Not now. Not ever." ³⁰He said this because they said, "He has an evil spirit."

³¹Jesus' mother and brothers arrived and stood outside the crowded house. They sent one person inside with a message for him to come to them. ³²Out of the crowd sitting around Jesus, someone said, "Your mother and your brothers are outside, asking for you."

³³"Who is my mother?" he answered. "Who are my brothers?" ³⁴He looked at those sitting around him. "Here are my brothers and my mother. ³⁵Anyone who does the will of God is my brother, sister, and mother."

Chapter 4

¹Again, Jesus taught by the seashore. A large crowd gathered, so many that he boarded a boat, sat down, and from there taught the people who stood on the shore.

²He taught them with illustrations, saying, ³"Listen! A farmer went to sow his seeds in the field. ⁴As he scattered the seeds, some fell on the road, where they were eaten by the birds. ⁵Some fell on rocky ground, where the soil had little depth. The plants sprang up ⁶but had shallow roots, so they soon wilted under the scorching sun. ⁷Some seeds fell among thorny weeds that grew more quickly

and choked out the tender plants, preventing growth of the grain. [8]Other seeds fell on fertile soil and became healthy plants, producing thirty, sixty, or a hundred times the amount of seed sown. [9]If you have ears, pay attention to what I am saying."

[10]Later, when Jesus was alone with the twelve and other followers, he was asked what the illustration meant.

[11]Jesus said, "I have given you insights into the mysteries of the Kingdom of Heaven, but others have only the stories. [12]With open eyes, they choose to see nothing. They listen with their ears but do not want to understand so they will not be forced to turn to me and be healed. [13]If you do not understand this illustration, you will not understand any other.

[14]"The farmer is a person who takes God's word to others. [15]The seeds that fell on the road are people who hear the Kingdom message but do not understand. Satan comes to take away the seed that was planted in their hearts. [16]The seeds that fell on rocky ground are those who hear the message and eagerly accept it, [17]but their roots are shallow. As soon as the message causes them to experience trouble or persecution, they forsake their faith. [18]The seeds that fell among thorny weeds are the people [19]who allow the worries of this life and the enticement of wealth and the desire for other things to choke the message, so no fruit is produced. [20]The seeds that fell on fertile soil are the people who hear, understand, and act on God's word, yielding thirty, sixty, or a hundred times what was sown."

[21]Jesus said, "Is a lighted candle ever put under a basket or couch? No, it is always placed where its light will shine. [22]Everything hidden will one day be revealed, and all secrets will be brought to light. [23]He who has ears, let him hear.

[24]"Believe me, the measure you give will be the measure you get. Even more knowledge will be given [25]to those who listen carefully.

But those who are not listening will lose what little understanding they have.

[26]"The Kingdom of God is like a farmer who sows seeds in his field. [27]All the time, whether he sleeps at night or works in the day, the seeds sprout and grow, but he does not understand how that happens. [28]Without the farmer's help, the earth produces the stalk and leaves. Then the full head of grain forms and ripens. [29]When the grain is ready, he wields his sickle because harvest time has come."

[30]Jesus also asked, "To what can we compare the Kingdom of God, or what story can we use for illustration? [31]It is like a grain of mustard seed that a farmer planted in his field. Although it is the tiniest of all seeds, [32]it became the largest plant in the field, so large that birds can perch in its branches and enjoy its shade."

[33]With many such illustrations, Jesus taught the people as much as they could understand. [34]No one heard him speak without some kind of story. In private, he explained everything to his followers.

[35]That evening, Jesus said to his disciples, "Let's cross over to the other side of the lake." [36]They dismissed the crowd and took him in their boat. Other boats followed.

[37]A violent wind struck the lake, so the boat was nearly swamped by large waves crashing over the side. [38]Jesus was asleep in the back of the boat, his head resting on a cushion. His disciples woke him, crying, "Teacher, don't you care that we are about to die?"

[39]Standing, Jesus rebuked the wind and said to the waves, "Peace, be still."

Suddenly, the wind died and the waters became calm.

[40]"Why are you so afraid? You have such weak faith."

[41]The disciples looked at one another with amazement. "What sort of man is this? Even the wind and the waves obey him!"

Chapter 5

¹After crossing the lake, Jesus and the disciples came to the region of the Gadarenes. ²As Jesus climbed out of the boat, a man with an evil spirit ran from the tombs to meet him. ³The man lived among the tombs and was so fierce and violent no one could restrain him, not even with chains. ⁴Frequently, people bound him with shackles and chains, but he always broke free. No one could control him. ⁵Night and day, he cut himself with stones and cried out from the tombs in the hills.

⁶From a distance, he saw Jesus, ran to him, and kneeled down. ⁷"What do you want with me," he screamed, "Jesus, son of the Most High God? I implore you by God, do not torment me!"

⁸Jesus had already commanded the spirit to come out of the man.

⁹"What is your name?" Jesus asked.

The man answered, "My name is Legion, because there are so many of us."

¹⁰The evil spirits kept begging Jesus not to send them out of the region. ¹¹A large herd of pigs was feeding on the hillside. ¹²The spirits begged, "Send us to the pigs so we may enter them."

¹³After Jesus gave them permission, they came out of the man and entered the pigs. Suddenly, the whole herd of about two thousand stampeded down the steep bank, plunged into the water, and drowned.

¹⁴The herdsmen ran into the town and told what had happened, how the man had been delivered and the pigs were lost. The townspeople rushed out to see for themselves. ¹⁵When they saw the man who had been possessed, sitting there, clothed and in his right mind, they were frightened. ¹⁶All the eyewitnesses repeated what they had seen happen to the man and the pigs. ¹⁷The townspeople begged Jesus to leave their country.

¹⁸As Jesus returned to the boat, the man begged to go along.

¹⁹"No," Jesus said. "Go home to your people and tell them what great things the Lord has done for you, how you received mercy."

²⁰So the man left and spread the word in the ten cities of the region, telling what Jesus had done. Everyone was amazed.

²¹After again crossing the sea by boat, Jesus met a large crowd at the shore.

²²A synagogue official named Jairus came, knelt before him, ²³and earnestly pleaded, "My little daughter is dying, but if you will come lay your hand on her, she will live."

²⁴So Jesus went with him, and a large crowd followed, pressing him from all sides.

²⁵A woman who had suffered twelve years from constant bleeding, ²⁶had endured the painful treatments of many physicians, and had spent all her money, had become worse instead of better. ²⁷After hearing about Jesus, she pushed through the crowd from behind and touched his robe ²⁸because she had thought, *If I can just touch his clothes, I will be healed.* ²⁹Immediately, her bleeding stopped, and she could feel the difference in her body. She knew she was healed.

³⁰At the same time, Jesus realized that power had gone out from him. He turned and asked, "Who touched me?"

³¹His disciples could see no reason for the question. "What are you talking about? All along the way, people have been pushing against you and touching you. Why are you asking, 'Who touched me?'"

³²Still, Jesus kept looking around as if only one person had touched him.

³³The woman, knowing she was the one, trembled with fear as she fell at Jesus' feet and told him what had happened.

³⁴"Daughter," Jesus said, "your faith has made you well. Go in peace, and be healed of your disease."

³⁵While Jesus was still speaking, men came from Jairus's house and said to him, "Your daughter has died. There is no need to trouble the teacher anymore."

³⁶Overhearing, Jesus said to Jairus, "Do not worry; she will be all right. Trust me."

³⁷Jesus held everyone back, allowing no one to follow except for brothers James and John, and Simon Peter.

³⁸At the house, Jesus saw family and friends weeping and heard the mourners crying their funeral dirge. ³⁹As he went in, he said to the people in the house, "Why are you crying? The child is not dead. She's asleep."

⁴⁰They laughed and said he was crazy, because they knew she was dead.

After making everyone else leave, he went with the parents and three disciples into the room where the child was. ⁴¹He took the girl by the hand. "*Talitha koumi!*" he said, which means "Little girl, rise up!"

⁴²At that moment, the twelve-year-old got up and walked. The parents and disciples were overwhelmed and amazed.

⁴³Jesus ordered them not to tell anyone what had happened. "Give her something to eat," he said.

Chapter 6

¹Jesus left the Capernaum area and went with his followers to his hometown, Nazareth. ²On the Sabbath, he taught in the synagogue, and many were amazed at his teaching, saying, "Where did he get such wisdom and the power to do miracles? ³Isn't he just a carpenter, the son of Mary, the brother of James, Joseph, Judas, and Simon? Do not his sisters live here in town?" They did not trust his actions or what he said.

⁴Jesus said to them, "A prophet has honor everywhere except in his own country, among his relatives, and in his own household."

⁵He could not do many miracles there. He only healed a few sick people. ⁶He was amazed at their unbelief. Then he went to teach in the towns nearby.

⁷He called the twelve disciples, gave them authority over evil spirits, and began to send them out in pairs. ⁸"Other than a walking stick, take nothing for your journey. Do not take a bag, bread, or money. ⁹Take one pair of sandals and no change of clothes. ¹⁰In whatever house you are welcomed, stay until you leave for another town. ¹¹When people do not welcome you or listen to your words, shake off the offense like dust from your feet as a testimony against them. I assure you, on Judgment Day, the people of Sodom and Gomorrah will be better off than that place."

¹²So the disciples went out and preached that men should turn from their sins. ¹³They cast out many evil spirits and anointed with oil many who were sick, healing them.

¹⁴King Herod heard about Jesus because news was spreading everywhere. "The spirit of John the Baptizer has returned from the dead," some said. "That is why he has the power to do such miracles." ¹⁵Others said, "He is Elijah," or, "He is like one of the great prophets who lived long ago." ¹⁶But when Herod heard all of this, he said, "It is John. The one I beheaded has come back from the dead."

¹⁷Earlier, Herod had taken Herodias, his brother Philip's wife, to be his wife. He had John arrested, bound in chains, and put in prison ¹⁸for saying to him, "Under God's law, you have no right to be married to her." ¹⁹Herodias was furious with John and wished she had the power to have him killed. She could not, ²⁰because Herod respected John as a righteous and holy man. He found John's words to be disturbing, yet he liked listening to him.

²¹An opportunity came for Herodias during Herod's birthday feast. Important government officials, military commanders, and prominent citizens of Galilee attended. ²²Her daughter danced before Herod and his guests in a way that immensely pleased him. "Ask me for anything you want," he said, "and I will give it to you. ²³I swear, whatever you ask I will give, up to half my kingdom."

²⁴The dancer left and asked her mother, "What should I ask for?"

Her mother said, "The head of John the Baptizer."

²⁵Immediately, she went before the king and said, "Bring me John the Baptizer's head on a platter."

²⁶This grieved the king, but because he had sworn an oath before his guests, he gave the order ²⁷to the executioner to bring John's head. So the executioner went to the prison and beheaded John. ²⁸He brought the head on a platter and gave it to the girl, who took it to her mother.

²⁹When John's disciples heard what had happened, they claimed the body and buried him.

³⁰After their tour of ministry, the disciples gathered around Jesus and told him all they had said and done. ³¹People constantly came and went, so much so that they did not even have an opportunity to eat.

Jesus said, "Let's go to a desolate place where we can rest for a while."

³²So they left by boat to an isolated place.

³³Many people saw them leave and the direction they were heading. Out of all the nearby towns, they hurried on foot and were already at the shore when the boat arrived.

³⁴Jesus saw the huge crowd waiting for him. He was moved with compassion because he saw them as helpless and confused, like sheep without a shepherd. He taught them many things.

[35]Late in the afternoon, the disciples said to Jesus, "We are far from town, and it is getting late. [36]Send the people away so they can go to the farms and towns nearby and buy food."

[37]Jesus said, "Why don't you feed them?"

"With what?" they said. "It would take over six months' wages to buy enough food for this crowd!"

[38]"How many loaves do you have? Go and see."

After checking, they said, "All we have are five loaves and two fish."

[39]"Have the people sit down in groups on the green grass."

[40]So they sat in groups of fifty to a hundred.

[41]Jesus took the five loaves and two fish, looked toward heaven, and gave thanks. He broke the loaves and fish and handed them to his disciples, who distributed the pieces to the people.

[42]They all ate as much as they wanted [43]and the disciples gathered twelve baskets full of leftover bread and fish. [44]Besides the women and children, about five thousand men were fed.

[45]After the five thousand had been fed, Jesus told his disciples to get into their boat and go from Bethsaida to the other side while he dismissed the crowd. [46]When the people had gone, he went up the mountain to pray. [47]In the evening, he was there alone and the boat was well out to sea.

[48]He watched them strain at the oars as they tried to push into a strong headwind. In the fourth watch of the night, between three and six o'clock in the morning, Jesus walked toward them on the water and was about to pass by.

[49]When the disciples saw him, they screamed because they thought he was a ghost. [50]There were terrified at what they saw, but Jesus said, "It's all right. I am Jesus. You do not need to be afraid."

[51]When Jesus climbed into the boat, the wind calmed.

The disciples were completely amazed. ⁵²Even after the miracle of the loaves, they had not learned what God could do.

⁵³After crossing the lake, Jesus and the disciples came to shore near Gennesaret. ⁵⁴As soon as they stepped out of the boat, people recognized him. ⁵⁵News of his arrival spread throughout the region. People carried the sick on pallets to wherever he stayed. ⁵⁶Whenever Jesus entered a town or small community, he would pass the sick in the roadway. Some of them begged to touch the fringe of his robe. Those who touched his robe were healed.

Chapter 7

¹Pharisees and teachers of the Law who had come from Jerusalem ²saw some of Jesus' disciples eat bread without washing their hands. ³Devout Jews, especially the Pharisees, always washed their hands before eating, a long-standing rule since ancient times. ⁴After buying food at the market, they would not put the food to their mouths until they had properly washed. They also followed other traditions, such as washing cups, pots, and pitchers brought to the table.

⁵The Pharisees and teachers of the Law asked Jesus, "Why do your disciples violate the rules of behavior that were established by our ancestors? When they eat bread, they do not wash their hands."

⁶"Hypocrites! You fulfill what Isaiah said about you: *These people offer praise with their lips, but their hearts are somewhere else. ⁷Their reverence for me is nothing but a ritual.*

⁸"You ignore God's commandments by following your own tradition. ⁹How beautifully you nullify God's commandments so you can have your own way. ¹⁰Moses wrote, *Honor your father and mother*, and, *Anyone who curses father or mother must be put to death.* ¹¹By your rules, it is all right for a man to say to his parents, 'I have dedicated all my possessions to God. What I might have given to you is no longer mine to give.' ¹²In this manner, you excuse the man

from helping his father or mother. [13]With your tradition, you nullify God's commandment. And you do many other, similar things."

[14]Jesus called the people closer. "Listen, and understand what I am saying. [15]You are not defiled by what goes into your mouth. It is what comes out that makes you unclean. [16]If you have ears, pay attention to what I am saying."

[17]Later, when Jesus had left the people and entered the house, his disciples asked him to explain his analogy.

[18]"You still do not understand? You should know that anything going into a man from the outside cannot make him unclean. [19]What you eat does not enter the heart but simply passes through the stomach and out. [20]But what comes out of a person is from the heart, revealing the filth that exists inside. [21]From the heart come evil thoughts, murder, adultery, erotic sexual acts, [22]theft, greed, cruelty, lies, lewdness, lust, cursing, pride, and foolishness. [23]All such things come from within and make a person unclean."

[24]Leaving Gennesaret, Jesus went to a region near Tyre and Sidon. He did not want anyone to know the house where he was staying, but the news could not be kept secret. [25]A woman who lived in the area had a young daughter who was possessed by an evil spirit. When she heard about Jesus, she knelt at his feet [26]and begged him to cast out the evil spirit.

Since she was Greek, born in Syrian Phoenicia, [27]he said to her, "The children of Israel should be fed first. It is not right to take the children's bread and throw it to the dogs."

[28]"That is true, sir. But the little dogs under the table eat the children's crumbs."

[29]"You have answered well. You may go now. The evil spirit has left your daughter."

[30]When the woman arrived home, she found her daughter lying on her bed, and the evil spirit had gone.

[31]After Jesus left the vicinity of Tyre and Sidon, he walked back toward the Sea of Galilee, to an area of the Decapolis.

[32]A deaf man had difficulty speaking and begged Jesus to lay his hand on him.

[33]After leaving the crowd for a place more private, Jesus put his fingers into the man's ears, then spat and touched the man's tongue. [34]Looking up to heaven, he said in a deep groan, "*Ephphatha!*" which means "Be opened!" [35]Immediately, the man's ears were opened, his tongue was set free, and he spoke clearly. [36]Jesus told the people not to tell anyone, but the more he told them to keep quiet, the more they spread the news.

[37]The crowd was thoroughly amazed, saying, "All his works are spectacular! He even causes the deaf to hear and gives speech to those who cannot talk."

Chapter 8

[1]During these days, another huge crowd gathered. Because they had nothing to eat, Jesus called his disciples. [2]"I feel sorry for all these people who have been with me for three days and have nothing left to eat. [3]If I send them away hungry, they might faint on their way home because many have come from far away."

[4]The disciples said, "In a desolate place like this, where can we get enough food to feed so many?"

[5]"How many loaves do you have?"

"Seven," they said.

[6]Jesus told the people to sit on the ground. He took the loaves, gave thanks, and broke them. He gave the pieces to the disciples, who distributed them to the crowd. [7]They also had a few small fish that he blessed and gave to the disciples to serve. [8]After all had eaten as much as they wanted, the disciples gathered seven full baskets of

leftover pieces. [9]Jesus sent the people home—four thousand men, plus women and children.

[10]Immediately after feeding the four thousand, Jesus got into a boat with his disciples and went to the area of Dalmanutha.

[11]Some Pharisees came to test his claim that he had been sent by God. So they asked him to show them a miraculous sign from heaven.

[12]He gave a deep groan. "Why do people keep asking for a sign? Without a doubt, no such proof will be given to this generation."

[13]So he left them standing there.

He got back into the boat and headed for the other side of the lake.

[14]The disciples had forgotten to take bread and had only a single loaf in the boat.

[15]"Watch out!" Jesus said. "Be careful to avoid the yeast of the Pharisees and those partial to Herod."

[16]They reasoned among themselves what Jesus meant. "He must have said this because we failed to bring enough bread."

[17]Jesus knew what they were saying. "Why do you think it's a problem that we have no bread? Do you not yet understand? Do you still have hardened hearts? [18]Are you like those who have eyes that cannot see or ears that cannot hear? Don't you remember? [19]When I broke the five loaves to feed the five thousand, how many baskets of leftovers did you have?"

"Twelve," they said.

[20]"When I broke the seven loaves to feed the four thousand, how many did you have?"

"Seven," they said.

[21]"How is it, then, that you still do not understand?"

[22]At Bethsaida, people brought a blind man and begged Jesus to touch him. [23]He took the man by the hand and led him out of town.

There, he spat on his eyes and laid his hands on him. "Can you see now?"

²⁴The man looked around. "Yes, I can see people, but they look like trees walking."

²⁵Again Jesus laid his hands on the man's eyes. This time when the man looked, his eyes were fully opened, and he could see everything clearly.

²⁶Jesus sent the man straight home, saying, "Do not go into town, and do not tell anyone how you were healed."

²⁷Leaving Galilee, Jesus and his disciples headed toward one of the towns near Caesarea Philippi. As they walked, he asked, "Who do people say that I am?"

²⁸They said, "Some say you are John the Baptizer. Others say you are Elijah or one of the other prophets."

²⁹"Who do you say that I am?"

Simon Peter answered, "You are the Anointed One, the Messiah!"

³⁰He gave a stern warning: "Do not tell anyone that I am the Messiah."

³¹Jesus began to explain to his disciples his need to go to Jerusalem and endure great suffering at the hand of government officials, chief priests, and teachers of the Law. "I will be killed," he said, "but three days later I will rise to life." ³²He talked to them plainly, clearly explaining what he meant.

Simon Peter took Jesus aside and privately reprimanded him for saying such things.

³³Jesus turned and saw the other disciples, then looked at Peter. "Do not stand in my way, adversary. You do not understand the plan of God. You see only from a human point of view."

³⁴When a crowd had gathered with his disciples, he began to teach. "If anyone wants to follow me, he must sacrifice his selfish

desires. Take up your cross, and then you can follow me. [35]If you try to save your life for yourself, you will lose it. But if you lose your life for my sake and for spreading the good news, you will find it. [36]What have you gained if you own the whole world but lose your life? [37]Nothing has sufficient value that you should want to exchange it for your life. [38]Those who are ashamed of me in this wicked and unfaithful generation will cause the Son of Man to be ashamed of them when he comes in his Father's glory with the holy angels."

Chapter 9

[1]"I guarantee, some of you standing here will not die before they see the Kingdom of God come with power."

[2]Six days after Jesus told his disciples about his need to die, he took Simon Peter, James, and John, to be alone, high up on the mountain. The three saw his whole appearance change. [3]His clothes became dazzling white, whiter than anyone could bleach them. [4]Moses and Elijah appeared and talked with him.

[5]Peter said, "Teacher, it is wonderful to be here. Let's build three shrines here—for you, Moses, and Elijah." [6]He really did not know what to say, because they were all afraid.

[7]A cloud overshadowed them, and a voice came from the cloud. "This is my dearly loved son. Listen to him!"

[8]When they looked around, no one was there except Jesus.

[9]As they came down the mountain, Jesus told them, "Do not tell anyone what you saw, not until after the Son of Man has risen from the dead."

[10]They kept the event to themselves. But they questioned one another about what rising from the dead might mean. [11]They asked Jesus, "Why do the teachers of the Law say Elijah must come before the Messiah comes?"

¹²"They are right," Jesus said. "Elijah comes first, to prepare for the Messiah's coming. What does the scripture mean where it says the Son of Man must suffer greatly and be despised? ¹³The truth is, Elijah has already come, and they chose to abuse him, exactly as the prophet said."

¹⁴When they returned to the other disciples, they saw a large crowd around them and some teachers of the Law arguing with them. ¹⁵As soon as the people saw Jesus, they were awestruck and ran to greet him.

¹⁶Jesus asked the teachers of the Law, "What are you arguing about?"

¹⁷A man from the crowd said, "I brought my son, who has an evil spirit that prevents him from speaking. ¹⁸Whenever it controls him, he is thrown into convulsions. He foams at the mouth, grinds his teeth, and becomes physically exhausted. I asked your disciples to cast out the evil spirit, but they could not do it."

¹⁹Jesus said, "How long must I be with this faithless generation? How long must I put up with you? Bring your son to me."

²⁰So they brought the boy, and he went into convulsions as soon as he saw Jesus. The boy fell to the ground, writhing and foaming at the mouth.

²¹"How long has he been this way?" Jesus asked.

"Ever since he was little. ²²The evil spirit often throws him into the fire or into the water, trying to kill him. Please have mercy and help us if you can."

²³"For those who believe, anything is possible."

²⁴"I do believe," the father said, crying. "Help my unbelief."

²⁵When Jesus saw that more people were gathering around, he spoke against the evil spirit, commanding it to come out of him and never return. ²⁶The spirit shrieked and threw the boy into another violent convulsion. Then it left, leaving the body motionless.

"He is dead," people said.

²⁷Jesus took him by the hand and helped him stand.

²⁸Later, when they were alone in the house, the disciples asked Jesus, "Why couldn't we cast out the evil spirit?"

²⁹"This kind," he said, "requires prayer and fasting."

³⁰They left the area and passed through Galilee. Jesus did not want people to know where he was, ³¹because he wanted to privately teach his disciples. "The Son of Man will soon be betrayed into the hands of men who will kill him," he said. "On the third day, he will rise to life again."

³²They did not understand everything Jesus said but were afraid to ask what he meant.

³³When the disciples entered the house, Jesus asked, "Back there on the road, what were you deliberating so strongly about?"

³⁴They did not want to answer, because they had been arguing about which of them was the greatest.

³⁵Jesus called the twelve to gather around him. "Anyone who wants to be the greatest must take the lowest seat and become servant to all."

³⁶He reached out to a little boy, brought him into their midst, and wrapped his arms around him. ³⁷"Anyone who welcomes such a child in my name is welcoming me. And anyone who welcomes me is welcoming the one who sent me."

³⁸John said, "Teacher, we saw someone casting out evil spirits in your name. We told him to stop because he was not part of our group."

³⁹"Don't stop him!" Jesus said. "No one with power in my name will say anything bad about me. ⁴⁰Anyone who is not against us is for us.

⁴¹"Believe me, people who give something as insignificant as a cup of cold water under my direction and authority, because you are

my disciples, are sure to be rewarded. [42]But if you cause one who believes in me to stumble, it would be better to have a millstone tied around your neck and be thrown into the sea.

[43]"If your hand causes you to sin, cut it off. You are better off entering eternal life maimed than to keep both hands and go to hell, with its unquenchable fire, [44]where the flesh-eating worms never die and the fire never goes out.

[45]"If your foot causes you to sin, cut it off. You are better off entering eternal life lame than to keep both feet and go to hell, with its unquenchable fire, [46]where the flesh-eating worms never die and the fire never goes out.

[47]"If your eye causes you to sin, gouge it out. You are better off entering the Kingdom of God blind in one eye than to keep both eyes and be thrown into hell, with its unquenchable fire, [48]where the flesh-eating worms never die and the fire never goes out. [49]Everyone there will be preserved in torment with fire.

[50]"Salt is a good preservative, but if it loses its saltiness, how will you make it any good? Have good salt in yourselves by living in peace with one another."

Chapter 10

[1]Jesus left Galilee and went to the area of Judea on the east side of the Jordan River. Crowds gathered and, as usual, he taught them.

[2]The Pharisees came to trap Jesus into saying something they could use against him, so they said, "Is it lawful for a man to divorce his wife?"

[3]"What did Moses command you?"

[4]"Moses allows a man to write a bill of divorce and send her away."

[5]"Because of your hard hearts, Moses allowed you to divorce your wives, [6]but in the creation's beginning, God made them male

and female. [7]That is why a man leaves his father and mother and is united with his wife, [8]and the two become one. Since they are no longer two but one, [9]and God has joined them, no one should separate them."

[10]Later, when Jesus was alone in the house, his disciples brought up the issue again.

[11]Jesus said, "Any man who divorces his wife and marries someone else commits adultery. [12]And any woman who divorces her husband and marries someone else commits adultery."

[13]Parents brought their children so Jesus could lay his hands on them and pray, but the disciples rebuked them.

[14]Jesus was upset when he saw what they were doing. "Don't stop them," he said. "Allow the little ones to come to me. Of such is the Kingdom of God. [15]Without exception, I tell you, those who do not accept the Kingdom of God like a young child cannot enter." [16]Then he took the children into his arms, laid his hands on them, and blessed them.

[17]While Jesus walked along the road, a man ran up and knelt before him. "Most excellent Teacher, what good deed must I do to have eternal life?"

[18]"Why do you call me most excellent?" Jesus said. "No one is most excellent except God. [19]You know the commandments. Do not murder, commit adultery, steal, or give false testimony. Never cheat. Honor your parents."

[20]"I've done all that since I was young."

[21]Jesus looked at him with love in his eyes. "You lack one thing. Go and sell everything you own, and give the money to the poor. You will have treasure in heaven and can follow me."

[22]After hearing this, he walked away sad, because he was very wealthy.

²³Looking around, Jesus said to his disciples, "It is nearly impossible for a rich man to enter the Kingdom of God."

²⁴The disciples were amazed.

Jesus said, "Those who trust in riches will have a very difficult time entering the Kingdom. ²⁵It is harder for a man of great wealth to enter the Kingdom than for a camel to get through a needle's eye."

²⁶The disciples could not believe what Jesus was saying. They said among themselves, "If that is true, who can be saved?"

²⁷Jesus looked intently at them. "With men, it is impossible. But with God, all things are possible."

²⁸Simon Peter said to him, "We have left everything to follow you."

²⁹Jesus said, "Those who have sacrificed their homes, relatives, or possessions for my sake and for the good news ³⁰will receive a hundred times more and will have eternal life. ³¹Those who were thought to be least important are first, and the first are last."

³²While going up to Jerusalem, Jesus walked ahead of the disciples. Amazed that he was going there, they trailed behind, afraid. He took them aside and again told them what must happen to him. ³³"Listen, we are going to Jerusalem. The Son of Man will be handed over to the chief priests and teachers of the Law, who will sentence him to die. They will deliver him to the Romans, ³⁴who will mock him and spit at him. He will be whipped and crucified, but he will rise again on the third day."

³⁵Zebedee's sons, James and John, went to see Jesus. "Master, we have a favor to ask of you."

³⁶"What do you want?"

³⁷"In your glorious Kingdom, let us have the seats of honor on your right and left."

[38]"You have no idea what you are asking. Are you able to drink the cup that I am about to drink and suffer the same baptism I must receive?"

[39]They answered, "Yes, we are."

"Indeed you will drink from my cup and suffer the same baptism, [40]but the places on my right and left are not mine to give. They are reserved for the ones for whom they have been prepared."

[41]When the other ten disciples heard what had happened, they were angry with James and John.

[42]So Jesus called them together. "You know that the most honored among the Gentiles exercise dominion over others. Great rulers command unquestioned service. [43]But you will not be like the kings. Your greatness depends on how well you serve others. [44]If you want the highest place of honor, you must be everyone's servant, [45]just like the Son of Man, who has come to serve and sacrifice his life for many."

[46]As Jesus and the disciples left Jericho, a large crowd followed. A blind man named Bartimaeus (son of Timaeus) sat by the side of the road, begging. [47]When he heard that Jesus of Nazareth was coming, he cried out, "Jesus, Son of David, have mercy on me."
[48]Many rebuked him, telling him to be quiet, but he shouted even louder, "Jesus, Son of David, have mercy on me!"

[49]So Jesus stopped and called for him.

"You can quit yelling now," people said to the blind man. "He has asked to see you."

[50]He threw his coat aside, stood up, and was led to Jesus.

[51]"What do you want me to do for you?" Jesus asked.

"Teacher, heal my eyes so I can see."

[52]"Look around. Because you believed, you now can see."

Immediately, his eyes were healed and he joined those who followed him.

Chapter 11

¹As Jesus and the disciples approached Jerusalem, past Bethany and near Bethphage, they stopped at the Mount of Olives. Jesus sent two disciples, ²saying, "Go into the next village. As soon as you enter, you will see a young donkey. Untie it, and bring it to me. ³If someone asks what you are doing, say, 'The Master needs it!' and he will allow you to take it without hesitation."

⁴The disciples did as they were told and found the colt on the street, tethered outside the front door. While untying it, ⁵some bystanders asked, "What are you doing, taking that colt?" ⁶After answering exactly as Jesus had instructed, they were allowed to leave.

⁷So they brought the colt and laid their coats on its back for Jesus to sit upon.

⁸People spread their garments on the road before him. Others cut palm branches to lay a carpet in his path. ⁹A crowd walked ahead of Jesus while others followed, all shouting, "Hail to the King! Blessed is the one who comes in God's name. ¹⁰Blessed is the kingdom of our father David. Praise God in the highest heaven."

¹¹After entering Jerusalem, Jesus went to the Temple and spent time there, observing and interacting with people until evening. Then he and the disciples went to Bethany.

¹²On his way from Bethany to Jerusalem the next morning, Jesus was hungry. ¹³After seeing a fig tree in the distance, covered with leaves, he went to pick its fruit. On arrival, he found nothing but leaves, because it was too early in the season. ¹⁴"Never will a man eat of your fruit."

The disciples heard what he said.

¹⁵When they arrived in Jerusalem, Jesus entered the Temple and began to drive out the merchants doing business there. He turned

over the tables of the moneychangers and the cages of those who sold doves. [16]He would not allow anyone to carry merchandise through the Temple.

[17]In teaching the people, he said, "The scriptures say the Temple will be called a house of prayer for all nations, but you have turned it into a hangout for robbers."

[18]When the chief priests and teachers of the Law heard about what Jesus had done, they looked for some way to get rid of him. They feared him because the crowds were so captivated by his teaching.

[19]That evening, Jesus and the disciples left the city, [20]and they returned the following morning. As they walked along the road, the disciples noticed the fig tree, dried up from the roots.

[21]Peter remembered what Jesus had said. "Teacher, look! The fig tree that you cursed has withered away."

[22]"If you have unwavering faith in God for what he wants to do, [23]you can be sure that whoever says to this mountain, 'Rise and be thrown into the sea,' will see it happen. [24]Under those conditions, whatever you ask in prayer, believing, is as good as done. [25]Whenever you are praying, forgive others for their offenses so your heavenly Father will forgive you. [26]If you do not forgive, your heavenly Father will not forgive your sins."

[27]Jesus and the disciples again went to Jerusalem. As Jesus was moving about in the Temple, the chief priests, Jewish leaders, and teachers of the Law [28]asked, "What right do you have to do these things? Who gave you the authority?"

[29]"Let me ask you a question. If you can give me the answer, I will tell you by what authority I do these things. [30]From where did John receive his authority to baptize? Was it from God or men?"

[31]They discussed the question among themselves. "If we say, 'From God,' he will ask why we did not believe him. [32]But if we say, 'From

men,' we will turn the people against us because they all regard John as a prophet." ³³So they said to Jesus, "We don't know."

"Then I won't tell you by what authority I do these things."

Chapter 12

¹Jesus used this illustration as he spoke to the people. "A landowner planted a vineyard, put a fence around it, dug a winepress, and built a watchtower. He left the vineyard under the care of sharecroppers and went to another country. ²At harvest season, he sent a servant to collect his share from the vineyard, ³but the sharecroppers grabbed and beat him, sending him away with nothing. ⁴So the landowner sent another servant. They threw stones at him, wounding him in the head, and ran him off with their insults. ⁵When yet another servant was sent, they killed him. And so it was with all who were sent. Some were beaten, others were killed, ⁶until the only one left to send was the landowner's only son. Finally, he sent him, saying, 'They will respect my son.' ⁷When the sharecroppers saw him coming, they said to themselves, 'He is the heir. If we kill him, we can have his inheritance.' ⁸So they grabbed him, dragged him out of the vineyard, and killed him.

⁹"What do you think the landowner will do to those sharecroppers?"

"He will destroy those men and find others who will give him his share of the harvest."

¹⁰"Haven't you read the scripture? *The stone that the builders rejected has become the cornerstone.* ¹¹*God has done this, and it is a wonderful sight to behold.*"

¹²The Jewish leaders realized that he was talking about them. They wanted to arrest him but went on their way because they feared the people.

¹³Jewish leaders sent Pharisees and people loyal to Herod to trap Jesus into saying something that could be used against him. ¹⁴"Teacher, we know you are sincere and completely honest. You teach the truth about God's ways without concern for what people think. Is it right to pay taxes to Caesar? ¹⁵Should we pay or not?"

Jesus recognized their scheming. "Why are you testing me? Show me a coin used to pay the tax so I can look at it."

¹⁶They handed him a Roman coin.

"Whose image and inscription is this?"

"Caesar's," they said.

¹⁷"Then pay to Caesar what belongs to him, and give God all that is God's."

They were amazed at his answer.

¹⁸Some Sadducees, who believed there was no resurrection, came to question Jesus. ¹⁹"Teacher, Moses said, *If a brother dies with no children, the widow must not marry someone outside the family. The surviving brother should marry her and have children for him.*

²⁰"Once, there were seven brothers, and the oldest brother married and died without children. ²¹After marrying the widow, the second brother had no children when he died, and the third brother did the same. ²²This continued until the barren wife had married all seven brothers. Finally, the woman died, still childless. ²³On the day when the dead rise to life, whose wife will this woman be? All seven were married to her."

²⁴"Your logic is wrong," Jesus said, "because you do not know the scriptures, and you do not understand how God works. ²⁵In the resurrection, people will not marry, but will be like the angels of heaven. ²⁶Now, on the issue of rising from the dead, haven't you read in the book of Moses where God speaks from the burning bush, *I am the God of Abraham, the God of Isaac, and the God of Jacob?*

[27]He is a God of the living, not of the dead. You have made a serious error in judgment."

[28]After hearing Jesus reason with the others and seeing how well he answered them, one of the teachers of the Law asked, "What is the most important of all commandments?"

[29]Jesus said, "The most important is, *Listen, Israel, and never forget. The Lord our God is the one and only true God. *[30]*You must love God with your whole heart, with all your being and all your strength.* This is the most important commandment. [31]But the second commandment is equally important. *Love your neighbor as yourself.* Of all the commandments, none is greater than these."

[32]"Teacher, you are right in saying there is only one God and no other. [33]To love him with our whole heart, with all our being and all our strength, and to love others as much as ourselves is more important than all the burnt offerings and sacrifices."

[34]When Jesus saw that he had spoken with such insight, he said, "You are not far from the Kingdom of God."

After that, no one dared ask him any questions.

[35]While teaching in the Temple, Jesus asked, "How can the teachers of the Law say the Messiah is the son of David? [36]David himself said, *God said unto my Lord, 'Sit here at my right hand until I have put all your enemies beneath your feet.'* [37]If David called him Lord, how can he be his son?" This kind of questioning greatly pleased the crowd.

[38]While teaching, Jesus said, "Watch out for the teachers of the Law who wear luxurious robes and love to be recognized in the marketplace. [39]At feasts and in the synagogues, they love the seats of honor. [40]Because they take advantage of widows while making long prayers to appear righteous, they will be punished most severely."

[41]Sitting across from the offering box, Jesus watched people giving their money. Many rich people put in large amounts. [42]A poor widow put in two copper coins that were worth next to nothing.

[43]Jesus called his disciples and said, "The truth is, this poor widow has given more than all those rich people together. [44]The rich gave a portion of their abundance that they will never miss, but she has given all she had to live on."

Chapter 13

[1]As Jesus left the Temple, one of his disciples said, "Teacher, look at the impressive stone work and the beauty of these buildings."

[2]"Do you see all these buildings as something great?" Jesus asked. "Their destruction will be so great, one stone will not be left standing on the other."

[3]Across the valley from the Temple, Peter, James, John, and Andrew came privately to Jesus while he sat on the slopes of the Mount of Olives. [4]"Tell us," they said, "when will all these things happen? How will we know when the time is at hand?"

[5]"Be careful," Jesus said. "Do not let anyone deceive you. [6]Many will claim to be the Messiah and will fool a multitude. [7]Do not panic when you hear about wars or battle threats. Such things must happen, but the end is not yet. [8]Nation will war against nation and kingdom against kingdom. There will be famines and earthquakes in various places. This is only the beginning of tragedies.

[9]"Watch out for yourselves, because people will take you to court and have you flogged in the synagogues. You will stand before kings and magistrates and testify about me. [10]The good news must be preached to people around the world. [11]When you are arrested and taken to trial, do not worry about how you will answer the charges brought against you. When the time comes, you will speak the words that come from the Holy Spirit. [12]Brothers will turn against one another, fathers against their children, and children against their parents to have them executed. [13]Because of me, all men will hate you, but those who stand firm until the end will be saved."

¹⁴(Readers, understand and pay attention.)

"When you see the abominations as predicted by the prophet Daniel, and desecration standing where it ought not to be, those in Judea should flee to the mountains. ¹⁵People on their housetops should not take time to gather belongings from their houses. ¹⁶A man in the field should not go back for his coat. ¹⁷How terrible it will be for pregnant women and nursing mothers. ¹⁸Pray that you will not have to flee in winter, ¹⁹because this will be the worst time of suffering that has ever been or ever will be. ²⁰Except those days be few, no one would survive, but the time will be shortened for the sake of God's people.

²¹"If anyone says, 'Look! Here is the Messiah," or, "There he is," do not believe it. ²²False messiahs and ministers will perform such great signs and wonders that even God's people would be deceived, if that were possible. ²³Pay attention, because I've warned you ahead of time.

²⁴"After those days of suffering, darkness will blanket the sky. The sun will hide and the moon will give no light. ²⁵All the stars will disappear, and the powers of the universe will be shaken.

²⁶"The people will see the Son of Man arrive in the clouds, with power and great glory. ²⁷He will send his angels to gather his people from everywhere on earth.

²⁸"From the fig tree, you can understand how it will be. When the branches bud and start to put on leaves, you know that summer is near. ²⁹In the same way, when you see these things come to pass, you will know the time is near, right at the door.

³⁰"You can be sure, when all these things have been fulfilled, this age will come to its close. ³¹Heaven and earth will pass away, but my words will stand forever.

³²"No one knows the exact date and time, not even the Son or the angels in heaven. Only the Father knows. ³³Always be watching,

because you do not know when your Lord will come. [34]My coming will be like a man who took a long journey. When he left home, he instructed his servants about the work they were to do and told the doorman to keep watch.

[35]"Always be watching, because you do not know when the master of the house will come, whether at midnight, before dawn, or after the sun comes up. [36]Do not let him catch you sleeping when he arrives unexpectedly. [37]I am warning everyone to always be alert."

Chapter 14

[1]Two days before Passover, the Feast of Unleavened Bread, the chief priests and teachers of the Law sought a means to covertly capture Jesus and put him to death.

[2]"We must not do it during the feast," they agreed, "or we will cause a riot."

[3]At Bethany, Jesus was in the home of Simon the leper when a woman came with a jar made of fine gypsum filled with expensive perfume, broke the seal, and poured it on Jesus' head as he sat at the table.

[4]Some of the people there were upset when they saw what she had done. "Why this waste?" they said among themselves. [5]"That perfume could have been sold for more than a year's wages and given to the poor." They rebuked her.

[6]"Leave her alone," Jesus said. "Why are you criticizing the woman for doing good for me? [7]You will always have the poor with you, so you can help them whenever you want, but you will not always have me. [8]She has done what she could, anointing my body ahead of time for burial. [9]I assure you, everywhere the good news is proclaimed throughout the world, this woman's deed will be remembered and told."

[10]Judas Iscariot, one of the twelve disciples, went to the chief priests with an offer to betray Jesus to them. [11]They were delighted and promised to pay, so he looked for a good place and time when he could hand him over.

[12]On the first day of the Feast of Unleavened Bread, when the Passover lambs were killed, the disciples asked Jesus, "Where shall we prepare for you to eat the Passover meal?"

[13]He gave two of his disciples specific instructions: "Go into the city. When you see a man carrying a pitcher of water, follow him. [14]Say to the owner of the house that he enters, 'The Teacher says, "Where is the room where I shall eat the Passover meal with my disciples?"' [15]He will show you a large upstairs room that is furnished and ready for our use. Make preparations there."

[16]The disciples went into the city, found everything exactly as Jesus had said, and prepared the meal.

[17]In the evening, Jesus arrived with the twelve disciples.

[18]While they were at the table, Jesus said, "I tell you the truth. One of you eating with me will turn against me."

[19]Everyone was deeply grieved and said, "Sir, you are not talking about me, are you?"

[20]"It is one of you who eats with me now. [21]I, the Son of Man, must suffer according to the scriptures, but how terrible it will be for the man who betrays me. It would be better for him if he had not been born."

[22]While they ate, Jesus took the bread, blessed it, broke it, and passed it to the disciples. "Take this bread and eat. This is my body." [23]He held the cup, offered thanks, and passed it to the disciples. They all drank from it. [24]"This is my blood of the new agreement between God and his people, to be poured out for many. [25]I tell you, I will not drink wine again until I drink with you in the Kingdom of God."

²⁶After they had sung a hymn, they left for the Mount of Olives.

²⁷"Tonight," Jesus said, "all of you will leave me, for the scripture says, *Strike the shepherd, and the sheep will be scattered.* ²⁸But after I have risen, I will reach Galilee before you do."

²⁹Peter said, "Everyone else may abandon you, but I never will."

³⁰"I guarantee," Jesus said, "before the rooster crows twice tonight, you will deny me three times."

³¹"Even if I have to die," Peter insisted, "I will not deny you."

The rest of the disciples said the same thing.

³²When they arrived at Gethsemane, Jesus said to his disciples, "Sit here while I pray."

³³Jesus took with him Peter, James, and John. He became grieved and was filled with distress. ³⁴"Stay here and watch with me," he said. "My heart is overcome with sorrow to the point of death."

³⁵He went a little farther, fell on his face, and prayed that if possible, he would escape this time of suffering. ³⁶"Dearest Father, everything is possible for you. Let me escape this suffering. Nevertheless, I want your will, not mine."

³⁷He returned to his disciples and found them asleep. "Simon," he said to Peter, "can't you watch with me for an hour? ³⁸Stay alert and pray so you do not fall into temptation. The spirit is willing, but the body is weak."

³⁹Again, Jesus left to pray the same words as before.

⁴⁰Once more, he returned to find his disciples asleep. They could not keep their eyes open and did not know what to say.

⁴¹When he returned for the third time, he said, "How can you be at ease, sleeping? You have slept long enough. Look! It is time for the Son of Man to be handed over to wicked men. ⁴²Get up. Let's go! My betrayer is coming."

⁴³While Jesus was still speaking, Judas, one of the twelve, arrived with a mob carrying swords and clubs, men sent by the chief priests

and Jewish leaders. ⁴⁴To identify Jesus, the traitor had arranged a signal, saying, "The man I kiss is the one you want. Seize him and take him away." ⁴⁵Without hesitation, Judas approached Jesus. "Hello, Teacher." After he gave Jesus the customary kiss of greeting, ⁴⁶men grabbed Jesus and held him captive.

⁴⁷One of the bystanders drew a sword and cut off the high priest's servant's ear.

⁴⁸Jesus looked at the mob surrounding him. "Am I a hardened criminal that you must capture me with swords and clubs? ⁴⁹Every day, I taught in the Temple. Why didn't you arrest me there? It has happened this way to fulfill the scriptures."

⁵⁰All the disciples abandoned him and escaped.

⁵¹A young man who had followed Jesus stood there, wearing only a linen sleeping garment. When the mob tried to grab him, ⁵²they tore off his garment, and he ran away naked.

⁵³The arresting guards took Jesus to the high priest and a gathering of chief priests, Jewish leaders, and teachers of the Law.

⁵⁴Peter followed at a distance and entered the high priest's palace courtyard, where he sat with the guards and warmed himself by the fire.

⁵⁵The chief priests and Jewish council brought in witnesses who were to give false testimony about Jesus so they could sentence him to die. Their efforts failed. ⁵⁶Although many false witnesses came, they could not get any two testimonies to agree. ⁵⁷Finally, some more men appeared before the council to give false testimony. ⁵⁸"This man claimed he could destroy the Temple of God and rebuild it in three days without any help." ⁵⁹Even in this testimony, their statements failed to agree.

⁶⁰The high priest stood and looked at Jesus. "Aren't you going to answer? What do you have to say about the charges brought against you?"

[61]Jesus said nothing.

"Are you the Messiah, the Son of God?"

[62]"Yes," Jesus said, "I am. In the future you will see the Son of Man sitting on God's right hand and arriving on the clouds of the sky."

[63]The high priest ripped his clothes. "Why do we need more witnesses? [64]With your own ears you have heard his blasphemy. What is your verdict?"

"Guilty," they answered. "He should be put to death."

[65]Some of them spat at him. Others blindfolded him and struck him with their fists. "Prophesy to us, Messiah," they scoffed. Tell us who hit you." The guards slapped him on the face.

[66]In the courtyard outside, one of the high priest's servant girls came to where Peter was. [67]She looked closely at him as he warmed himself. "You are one of those with Jesus of Nazareth."

[68]He denied having been with Jesus. "It was not me," he said. "I do not know what you are talking about."

As he left the courtyard and came near the entrance, a rooster crowed.

[69]Another servant girl noticed him and said to those standing nearby, "This man is one of them."

[70]Again, he denied any knowledge of Jesus.

Later, some of those who stood near Peter said, "You must be one of them. Your accent is clearly Galilean."

[71]With cursing and swearing, Peter denied any connection with Jesus. "I tell you, I do not know this man you are talking about."

[72]For the second time, a rooster crowed, and Peter remembered what Jesus had said: "Before the rooster crows twice, you will deny me three times."

And he broke down crying.

Chapter 15

¹At dawn, the chief priests, Jewish leaders, and teachers of the Law convened in the full council. They had Jesus bound and delivered to Pilate.

²Pilate asked Jesus, "Are you the king of the Jews?"

Jesus said, "Yes, you could say that."

³The chief priests accused Jesus of many things, but he said nothing.

⁴"Aren't you going to say something?" Pilate asked. "Haven't you heard all their accusations?"

⁵Jesus gave no response, not the slightest word, so Pilate was greatly impressed.

⁶At every Passover feast, Pilate would release one prisoner to the people, anyone they wanted. ⁷A criminal named Barabbas was in prison at the time, a man who had committed murder when he led a rebellion. ⁸After a large crowd gathered, the people shouted for Pilate to do as he had done before.

⁹Pilate asked, "Shall I release to you the king of the Jews?" ¹⁰He knew the chief priests had condemned Jesus because they envied his popularity with the people.

¹¹The chief priests had persuaded the people to ask for the release of Barabbas instead.

¹²"What shall I do with Jesus the Messiah?" Pilate asked.

¹³They all shouted, "Crucify him!"

¹⁴"Why? What crime has he committed?"

But the crowd roared, "Crucify him!"

¹⁵Pilate wanted to satisfy the people, so he released Barabbas and ordered the flogging and crucifixion of Jesus.

¹⁶The soldiers took Jesus into their headquarters, where they assembled the entire regiment. ¹⁷They dressed him in a purple robe and placed a woven crown of thorns on his head. ¹⁸In mockery, they

saluted him, saying, "Hail, king of the Jews." [19]They spat on him and struck him on the head with a staff. They knelt before him, pretending to give him honor. [20]When they tired of mocking him, they removed the purple robe, dressed him in his own clothes, and took him to be crucified.

[21]On the way, the soldiers met Simon, a native of Cyrene, father of Alexander and Rufus, who had come from the country. They forced him to carry Jesus' cross. [22]They took Jesus to Golgotha, which means "skull," [23]where they offered him wine mixed with a bitter drug, but he refused the drink. [24]After the soldiers nailed Jesus to the cross, they threw dice for the fair dividing of his clothes.

[25]It was nine o'clock when he was crucified.

[26]The sign to show the charge against him said, "The king of the Jews."

[27]Two criminals were crucified with him, one on the right, the other on the left.

[29]People who walked by insulted him and shook their heads. "You said you could tear down the Temple and rebuild it in three days. [30]If you have such power, save yourself. Come down from the cross."

[31]In a similar manner, the chief priests and teachers of the Law mocked him. "He saved others," they said. "Let's see if he can save himself. [32]If he is the king of Israel, let him come down from the cross. Then we will believe he is who he says he is." The criminals who were crucified with him joined in the mockery.

[33]From noon until three o'clock, darkness covered the land.

[34]At three o'clock, Jesus screamed, "*Eloi, Eloi, lema sabachthani*," which means "My God, my God, for this I was born."

[35]Some of those standing there said, "Listen! He calls for Elijah."

[36]One of them ran to fill a sponge with sour wine and lifted the sponge on the end of a branch so Jesus could drink.

"Wait. Let's see if Elijah will come to save him."

³⁷After Jesus screamed again, he quit breathing.

³⁸The Temple veil ripped in two, from top to bottom.

³⁹When the centurion who stood guard in front of Jesus heard him scream and saw how he died, he said, "This man really was the Son of God."

⁴⁰From a safe distance away, women were watching. Among them were Mary Magdalene, Mary the mother of Joses and the younger James, and Salome. ⁴¹They had followed Jesus and served him in Galilee. Many other women who had come with Jesus to Jerusalem were also there.

⁴²In the late afternoon of the day of preparation, before the beginning of the Sabbath, ⁴³Joseph of Arimathea, a respected member of the council who looked for the coming of God's Kingdom, went boldly before Pilate and asked for the body of Jesus.

⁴⁴Pilate doubted whether Jesus could already have died, so he asked the centurion whether his death was certain. ⁴⁵After the centurion assured him that Jesus was, in fact, dead, he granted the request.

⁴⁶Joseph took Jesus down from the cross and wrapped his body in the fine linen that he had purchased. He laid him in a tomb that was cut into the rock and rolled a stone to close the entrance.

⁴⁷Mary Magdalene and Mary the mother of Joses saw where Jesus was buried.

Chapter 16

¹After sundown, as soon as the Sabbath had ended, Mary Magdalene, Mary the mother of James, and Salome bought the sweet-smelling spices they needed to anoint Jesus' body.

²At the break of dawn on Sunday, the first day of the week, they headed to the tomb ³but asked one another, "Who will roll away the stone so we can enter?"

[4]When they arrived, they saw that the huge stone had already been rolled back. [5]Inside the tomb, they were frightened by the sight of a young man dressed in white, sitting on the right.

[6]"Do not be afraid," he said. "You are looking for Jesus of Nazareth, who was crucified. He is not here, because he has risen. Come and see where his body was. [7]Go tell his disciples, including Peter, that he will go before you, and you will see him in Galilee as he said you would."

[8]With fear and amazement, they ran from the tomb and spoke to no one along the way, because they were afraid.

[9]Mary Magdalene, the woman from whom Jesus had cast out seven evil spirits, was the first to see Jesus after he rose from the dead on the first day of the week. [10]She went to tell his disciples, who grieved and wept. [11]She told them he was alive, that she had seen him. They did not believe her.

[12]Later, Jesus appeared in a different form to two of his disciples as they walked from Jerusalem into the country. [13]They went back and told the others. But no one believed them.

[14]Later, Jesus appeared to the eleven disciples while they were eating. He rebuked them for their lack of faith and their rejection of those who had seen him after he had risen.

[15]Jesus told them, "Go into all the world and proclaim the good news to everyone. [16]Those who believe and are baptized will be saved, but those who do not believe will be condemned. [17]These miraculous signs will follow those who believe: Under my direction and authority, they will cast out evil spirits, and they will speak in new languages. [18]If they pick up serpents or drink something poisonous, they will not be harmed. They will place their hands on the sick, and they will recover."

[19]After Jesus had finished speaking, he was taken up into heaven, where he sat at the right hand of God.

²⁰The disciples preached the good news everywhere. God was with them and confirmed their message with miraculous signs.

Luke

Chapter 1

[1]Many people have written about what God has done in fulfillment of his promises. [2]All these accounts owe their source to the early disciples and other eyewitnesses who saw him with their own eyes and touched him with their own hands. [3]They have been carefully investigated, [4]so you may be certain that this record is accurate.

[5]During the reign of Herod the Great over Judea, Zechariah of the priestly order of Abijah and his wife, Elizabeth, a descendant of Aaron, [6]were upright in God's sight, blameless in following the commandments and regulations of the Law. [7]Despite their righteousness, they had lived beyond the age of childbearing and were still childless.

[8]Zechariah was chosen by lot to fulfill his priestly duties. [9]He entered the Holy Place to burn incense to God. [10]While the people gathered outside to pray, he stood before the altar. [11]Suddenly, an angel appeared, [12]and Zechariah became paralyzed with fear.

[13]"Do not be afraid, Zechariah," the angel said. "God has heard your prayer. Your wife, Elizabeth, will give birth to a son. You must name him John. [14]He will bring you great joy, and many will rejoice at his birth. [15]God will recognize him as a great man. He must never drink wine or other fermented beverages. Even before birth, he will be filled with the Holy Spirit.

[16]"He will turn many Israelites back to the Lord their God. [17]In the spirit and power of Elijah, he will soften the hearts of fathers toward their children and cause the rebellious to accept godly wisdom. He will prepare the people for the Lord's coming."

¹⁸"How can this be?" Zechariah asked. "This is impossible. I am an old man, and my wife is also too old."

¹⁹"I am Gabriel, sent from God to bring you this good news. ²⁰Because you have not believed me, you will be unable to speak a word until the day of your son's birth. All I have said will be fulfilled in due time."

²¹Outside, the people waited and wondered why the priest had stayed so long in the Holy Place. ²²When he came out and could not speak, but kept making signs with his hands, they were sure he had seen a vision.

²³After completing his time of service in the Temple, he returned home.

²⁴His wife, Elizabeth, became pregnant and went off by herself for five months. ²⁵"This is the Lord's doing," she said. "In these last days, he has shown his favor and has taken away my disgrace."

²⁶In the Galilean town of Nazareth, the angel Gabriel ²⁷appeared to a virgin named Mary, who was engaged to marry Joseph, a descendent of Israel's King David. ²⁸"Greetings, favored woman!" the angel said. "God is with you."

²⁹Mary was deeply shaken. She trembled at what the angel's greeting might mean.

³⁰"Do not be frightened, Mary. God is pleased with you. ³¹You will become pregnant and give birth to a son. You must name him Jesus. ³²He will be great and will be called the Son of the Most High. The Lord God will make him king like his ancestor David, ³³and he will rule over Israel forever."

³⁴"How is this possible?" Mary asked. "I have never slept with a man."

³⁵"The Holy Spirit will come upon you, and the power of the Most High will overshadow you. Therefore, your child will be holy and will be called the Son of God. ³⁶No one thought your relative

Elizabeth could have a child, either, but she is now in her sixth month. ³⁷Nothing is impossible with God."

³⁸"I am God's servant," Mary said. "Let all you have said happen to me according to his will."

Then the angel left.

³⁹Sometime after seeing the angel, Mary hurried to the Judean hill country, to the town ⁴⁰where Zechariah lived. As she entered the house, she greeted Elizabeth.

⁴¹The instant Elizabeth heard Mary's voice, the Holy Spirit filled her, and she felt the baby leap in her womb. ⁴²Overwhelmingly thrilled, she exclaimed, "Of all women, you are most blessed because of the child in your womb. ⁴³Why am I so honored that the mother of my Lord should come to see me? ⁴⁴When I heard your greeting, the baby in my womb leaped for joy. ⁴⁵You are blessed because you believed that every word God has spoken will come to pass."

⁴⁶"Oh, how my soul sings praise to the Lord," Mary said. ⁴⁷"I rejoice in God my Savior, ⁴⁸who took notice of me, a lowly servant. From now on, every generation will call me blessed ⁴⁹because the Mighty One has done a miraculous work in me.

⁵⁰"His mercy reaches to all who fear him. ⁵¹With his might, he does tremendous things, scattering the proud and arrogant. ⁵²He has brought rulers down from their thrones while lifting up the humble. ⁵³With good food, he has filled the stomachs of the poor, but he has sent the rich away with empty bowls. ⁵⁴He has remembered his promise to Abraham and his children, ⁵⁵showing mercy and helping his servant Israel."

⁵⁶For about three months, Mary stayed with Elizabeth. Then she returned home.

⁵⁷After Elizabeth gave birth to a son, ⁵⁸relatives and neighbors who knew how God had been merciful and healed her barrenness

came to celebrate with her. [59]The baby was eight days old when they gathered for the circumcision ceremony. They called him Little Zechariah, [60]but when Elizabeth heard them, she said, "No, his name is John."

[61]"What?" they said in disbelief. "You have no relatives with that name." [62]Making gestures with their hands, they asked the baby's father what he would name him.

[63]Zechariah motioned for a writing slate. To everyone's amazement, he wrote the name *John*. [64]Immediately, his tongue was loosed, and he began to speak, praising God.

[65]The neighbors were filled with awe, and throughout the Judean hill country, [66]people talked and wondered about these things and kept asking one another, "What will this child become? The hand God is surely upon him."

[67]Filled with the Holy Spirit, Zechariah prophesied, [68]"Praise the Lord God of Israel, who has come to set his people free. [69]From the house of his servant David, he has sent a mighty Savior, [70]as the prophets promised long ago, [71]to deliver us from our enemies and all those who hate us. [72]He has been merciful to our ancestors by remembering his sacred covenant [73]sworn with an oath to Abraham. [74]We are freed from our enemies so we can serve God without fear, [75]in holiness and righteousness, for the rest of our lives.

[76]"And you, my infant son, will be called the prophet of the Most High because you will prepare the way for the Messiah, [77]who will offer salvation to his people and forgive their sins. [78]In God's tender mercy, heaven's early light is about to shine [79]on those living in darkness, in the shadow of death. He will show us the way of peace."

[80]As John grew, he became strong in spirit. He lived in the wilderness until he preached to Israel.

Chapter 2

[1]When Caesar Augustus ordered a census throughout the Roman Empire [2](this was the first census taken while Quirinius was governor of Syria), [3]everyone went to his own town to register.

[4]Joseph went to Bethlehem in Judea, the home of his ancestors, because he was a descendent of King David. [5]He took Mary, his fiancée, who was pregnant and near the time of delivery, and left their village, Nazareth in Galilee.

[6]While they were in Bethlehem, [7]Mary gave birth to a son, wrapped him snugly, and placed him in a manger because no lodging was available.

[8]That night, in a nearby field, shepherds watching their flocks [9]were terrified when an angel of God appeared in brilliant light.

[10]"Do not be afraid," the angel said. "My good news will bring great joy to everyone. [11]Today in the city of David, a savior has been born, the anointed Messiah. [12]You will know who he is when you see a baby wrapped in cloth and lying in a manger."

[13]Suddenly, a host of angels appeared, praising God and singing, [14]"Glory to God in the highest, and on earth peace, good will toward men."

[15]After the angels returned to heaven, the shepherds said, "Let's go to Bethlehem and see this miracle that God has revealed to us." [16]They left their flocks, hurried to the city, and found Joseph, Mary, and the baby, who was lying in a manger. [17]After seeing the baby, the shepherds told everyone what had happened.

[18]All who heard their story were amazed.

[19]Mary treasured the experience and pondered what it all might mean.

[20]As the shepherds returned to their fields, they praised and glorified God for all they had seen and heard, how everything had been exactly as the angel had said.

²¹Eight days later, it was time for the circumcision ceremony and to name the baby Jesus, the name given by the angel before he was conceived.

²²After the thirty-three days required for purification were completed, Joseph and Mary took the baby to the Temple in Jerusalem. ²³The Law required every firstborn male to be consecrated to God. ²⁴Unable to afford the cost of a lamb for the consecration offering, they brought the alternative sacrifice of a pair of doves, one for the burnt offering, the other for the purification offering.

²⁵At the same time, the Holy Spirit led a righteous man named Simeon to enter the Temple. Simeon had eagerly anticipated the arrival of the Messiah, who would restore Israel. ²⁶The Holy Spirit had shown him that he would not die until he had seen God's anointed. ²⁷So he was there when the parents came to present their baby to God as the Law required. ²⁸After taking the infant into his arms, he praised God, saying, ²⁹"God, now that your promise is fulfilled, your servant can die in peace. ³⁰With my own eyes, I have seen your salvation ³¹prepared for all people, ³²a guiding light to the Gentiles and the glory of your people Israel."

³³As Joseph and Mary marveled at his words, ³⁴he turned to Mary. "This child will cause the rise and fall of many in Israel. He will be a sign from God that many people will oppose ³⁵as he reveals the thoughts of many hearts and pierces your own soul like a sword."

³⁶Anna, a prophet, daughter of Phanuel of the tribe of Asher, was also in the Temple. Her husband had died after seven years of marriage. ³⁷From then until now, at the age of eighty-four, she had been a widow, who never left the Temple but stayed there from dawn to dusk, worshiping God in fasting and prayer. ³⁸While Simeon was still speaking, she came to them and likewise praised God, saying Jesus was the child for whom all were looking because he would redeem Jerusalem.

[39]After Joseph and Mary had done all that was required in the Law, they returned to Galilee, to their hometown of Nazareth. [40]The child grew and became strong. He was filled with wisdom, and God's grace was upon him.

[41]The family went to Jerusalem to celebrate the Passover festival, according to Jewish custom, [42]when Jesus was twelve. [43]Afterward, when leaving for home, his parents did not realize that he had stayed behind. [44]They traveled for a whole day, assuming he was elsewhere in the caravan. When he did not show up that evening, they looked for him among relatives and friends. [45]Unable to find him, they went back to Jerusalem and searched.

[46]Finally, after three days, they found him in the Temple, sitting among the teachers, listening and asking questions. [47]His understanding and his answers had amazed everyone.

[48]Joseph and Mary were shocked. "Son," Mary said, "why have you treated us this way? Your father and I have been frantically searching everywhere."

[49]"Why?" Jesus asked. "Didn't you know I would have to be here, doing the work of my Father?"

[50]They did not understand what he meant, [51]but Mary held this event dear to her heart.

Jesus returned to Nazareth with them, submitting to their authority.

[52]As the years passed, he grew physically and spiritually, enjoying the favor of God and the people.

Chapter 3

[1]In the fifteenth year of the reign of Tiberius, the Roman emperor, when Pontius Pilate was governor over Judea, Herod Antipas ruled over Galilee, and his brother Philip ruled over Iturea and Traconitis. Lysanias ruled over Abilene. [2]This was during the high priesthood

of Annas and Caiaphas, when the word of God came to John, son of Zechariah, in the wilderness.

[3]In those days, John traveled the areas near the Jordan River and preached that people should repent, be forgiven by God for their sins, and be baptized.

[4]Long ago, the prophet Isaiah referred to John when he wrote: *Listen! Someone is shouting, "Clear a path in the wilderness, for the Lord our God is coming. [5]Fill the valleys and flatten the mountains. Straighten the curves and smooth the rough places. [6]The glory of the Lord will appear for all to see."*

[7]Then he said to the multitude coming to be baptized, "You bunch of snakes. Who warned you to flee God's judgment? [8]The way you live proves whether you have left your sins and turned to God. Do not say to one another, 'We are all right because we are Abraham's descendents.' That does not mean anything. God can make these stones into children of Abraham. [9]His ax is raised, ready to sever the roots of every tree that does not produce good fruit. You will be chopped down and thrown into the fire."

[10]"What should we do?" the people asked.

[11]"If you have two garments, give one to the poor. Share your food with people who are starving."

[12]Even the cheating tax collectors asked what to do.

[13]To them, he said, "Do not collect any more taxes than the government requires."

[14]To the soldiers, he said, "Be content with your pay. Never extort money or make false accusations."

[15]People who anticipated the coming of the Messiah asked if John might be the Messiah.

[16]"No, I am not the Messiah," he answered. "He will come after me and will be much greater than I am. I am not worthy to stoop down and untie the straps of his sandals. I baptize with water, but he will

baptize you with the Holy Spirit and fire. [17]He is ready to separate the wheat from the chaff and clean up the threshing area. He will gather the wheat into his barn but burn the chaff with eternal fire."

[18]With many other words, he encouraged the people and preached about how they could gain hope for salvation.

[19]John had openly rebuked Herod Antipas, ruler of Galilee, for marrying his brother's wife, Herodias, and for all the evils he had done. [20]So Herod put him in prison, adding this to his many sins.

[21]As the people were being baptized, Jesus was also baptized. While he prayed, the sky opened [22]and the Spirit of God descended like a dove, lighting upon him. A voice spoke from heaven: "You are my son, whom I love. I am well pleased with you."

[23]Jesus began his public ministry when he was about thirty years old. He was known as the son of Joseph, who was preceded by Heli, [24]Matthat, Levi, Melki, Jannai, Joseph, [25]Mattathias, Amos, Nahum, Esli, Naggai, [26]Maath, Mattathias, Semein, Joda, [27]Joanan, Rhesa, Zerubbabel, Shealtiel, Neri, [28]Melki, Addi, Cosam, Elmadam, Er, [29]Joshua, Eliezer, Jorim, Matthat, Levi, [30]Simeon, Judah, Joseph, Jonam, Eliakim, [31]Melea, Menna, Mattatha, Nathan, David, [32]Jesse, Obed, Boaz, Salmon, Nahshon, [33]Amminadab, Admin, Arni, Hezron, Perez, Judah, [34]Jacob, Isaac, Abraham, Terah, Nahor, [35]Serug, Reu, Peleg, Eber, Shelah, [36]Cainan, Arphaxad, Shem, Noah, Lamech, [37]Methuselah, Enoch, Jared, Mahalalel, Kenan, [38]Enosh, and Seth, who was the son of Adam, the son of God.

Chapter 4

[1]Full of the Holy Spirit, Jesus left the Jordan River and was led by the Spirit into the wilderness. [2]For forty days, he fasted, eating nothing at all. Afterward, it was time to eat.

[3]Satan said to him, "Since you are the Son of God, command these stones to become bread."

⁴Jesus refused, quoting from Deuteronomy: *"People do not live by bread only but by everything God says."*

⁵Satan took him to a high mountain and showed him the kingdoms of this world. ⁶"I will give you all this power and glory," he said. "I can give it to anyone I please. ⁷Simply worship me, and you can have it all."

⁸Again, Jesus refused. "Get out of here, Satan. The scriptures say: *Love the Lord your God and serve only him."*

⁹Satan took him to the Temple in Jerusalem and stood him on a high place. "Since you are the Son of God, jump. ¹⁰For it is written, *God will command his angels to protect you.* ¹¹*They will hold you in their hands lest you strike your foot against a stone."*

¹²"It is also written," Jesus said, *"You must not test the Lord your God."*

¹³After Satan had finished these temptations, he left for a while.

¹⁴Jesus entered Galilee in the power of the Spirit. Reports about him quickly spread throughout the countryside. ¹⁵Everyone praised him as he taught in their synagogues.

¹⁶Jesus came to Nazareth, his boyhood home. As usual, he went to the synagogue on the Sabbath. When he stood to read, ¹⁷someone handed him the scroll of the prophet Isaiah. He unrolled it and read from the place where Isaiah had written: ¹⁸*"The Spirit of the Lord is upon me because he has anointed me to preach good news to the poor. He has sent me to comfort the brokenhearted and to proclaim liberty to the captives, freedom for the oppressed, and recovery of sight for the blind—*¹⁹*to tell those who mourn that the time of the Lord's favor has come."*

²⁰He rolled up the scroll, handed it to the attendant, and sat down. Everyone looked intently at Jesus ²¹as he spoke. "This very day, that scripture has been fulfilled."

²²The people marveled at his eloquent words. "How can this be?" they asked. "Isn't he the son of Joseph?"

²³"No doubt," Jesus said, "you will say this proverb to me: 'Physician, heal yourself.' You will ask me to do the same things here that you heard I did in Capernaum. ²⁴Well, I can tell you for sure, no prophet is accepted in his hometown. ²⁵In Elijah's day, many widows suffered from the severe famine that devastated the land during those three and a half years of drought. ²⁶Yet God did not send Elijah to any of them. God sent him only to a foreigner—a widow in Zarephath in the land of Sidon. ²⁷And in the time of the prophet Elisha, there were many lepers in Israel, but the only one healed was Naaman from Syria."

²⁸When the people heard this, they became a furious mob.

²⁹They dragged him out of the synagogue, through the town, and to the brow of the hill on which the town was built. They intended to push him over the cliff, ³⁰but he walked right through the crowd and went on his way.

³¹Jesus went to Capernaum, a city in Galilee, where he taught on the Sabbath.

³²People were amazed at the authority with which he spoke.

³³In the synagogue, a man possessed by an evil spirit screamed in torment. ³⁴"What do you want with us, Jesus of Nazareth?" he asked. "I know who you are, the Holy One sent from God. Have you come to destroy us?"

³⁵"Silence!" Jesus commanded. "Come out of him."

The evil spirit threw him to the floor among the people but did him no harm before leaving.

³⁶People were astonished and asked one another, "What is going on? What powerful new teaching is this? Even the evil spirits obey him."

³⁷The news quickly spread throughout the region of Galilee.

³⁸After leaving the synagogue, Jesus entered Simon's home. There, Simon's mother-in-law was sick with a burning fever.

"Please," everyone begged, "heal her."

³⁹He went to her bedside and ordered the fever to go, and it left. At once, she got up and began to prepare a meal for them.

⁴⁰After sunset, people brought to Jesus those who suffered from various diseases. With a touch of his hand, he healed each one. ⁴¹As evil spirits came out of many people, they screamed, "You are the Son of God!" Because they knew he was the Anointed One, he did not allow them to say more.

⁴²The next day, he left for a solitary place, but the people came looking for him and begged him not to leave.

⁴³"I must preach the Kingdom of God in the other towns also," Jesus said. "That is why I came."

⁴⁴So he continued to preach in the synagogues of Galilee.

Chapter 5

¹One day, Jesus stood on the shore of the Sea of Galilee, and the people crowded around him to hear the word of God. ²Two boats had been pulled onto the beach, left by fishermen who were washing their nets. ³He climbed into the boat that belonged to Simon and asked him to put out a short distance from the shore. He sat down and taught the multitude.

⁴When he finished speaking, he turned to Simon. "Go to deep water and let down your net for a catch."

⁵"Master, we have worked hard all night and caught nothing. But because you say so, I will go out and let down the net."

⁶This time, they caught so many fish their net started to break. ⁷They motioned for help from their partners and filled both boats so full they were on the verge of sinking. ⁸When Simon Peter realized what had happened, he turned to Jesus and fell to his knees. "Leave me, Master, for I am a sinful man." ⁹He and those working

with him were amazed at the huge number of fish they had caught, [10]including James and John, the sons of Zebedee.

"You do not need to worry," Jesus said. "From now on, you will fish for people."

[11]So they brought their boats to the shore, left everything, and followed him.

[12]Near one town, a leper kneeled before Jesus, begging, "Sir, you could make me well if you wanted to."

[13]"I want to." Moved with compassion, Jesus touched him. "Be cleansed."

Immediately, all signs of the leprosy disappeared.

[14]"Do not tell anyone about this. Show yourself to the priest and offer the sacrifices, taking two birds as commanded by Moses. Your healing will become public record so you will no longer be regarded as a leper."

[15]As the report of Jesus' power rapidly spread, large crowds gathered to hear his teaching and ask for healing of their diseases.

[16]He often retreated to a secluded place where he could be alone and pray.

[17]One day, a crowd packed the room where Jesus was teaching, including Pharisees and teachers of the Law, seemingly from every Galilean and Judean town, so there was no space left, not even outside the door. The power to heal was present.

[18]Some men carried a paralyzed man on a mat. They tried to enter the house, to lay him before Jesus. [19]They could not find a way into the house, so they went up onto the roof and lowered him through an opening in the tiles, into the midst of the crowd and right in front of Jesus.

[20]Impressed by their faith, Jesus said, "My friend, your sins are forgiven."

²¹Some of the Pharisees and teachers murmured among themselves, "What is he saying? That is blasphemy. Only God can forgive sins."

²²Immediately, Jesus recognized their reaction. "Why are you thinking I've done something wrong? ²³Which is easier to say, 'Your sins are forgiven,' or, 'Stand and walk'? ²⁴So you may know the Son of Man has authority on earth to forgive sins . . ." He turned to the paralyzed man. "Get up. Take your mat and go home."

²⁵Without hesitation, the man stood, grabbed his mat, and walked to his own house, praising God.

²⁶Everyone marveled and glorified God, saying, "We've never seen anything like this before."

²⁷As Jesus walked along, he saw the tax collector Matthew, also called Levi, sitting at the place where people paid taxes. "Follow me," he said.

²⁸Matthew got up, left everything, and followed.

²⁹Later, Matthew had a big feast for Jesus at his house. Many tax collectors and other outcasts were among the dinner guests who ate with Jesus and his disciples.

³⁰The Pharisees and the teachers of the Law asked his disciples, "Why does he eat with such people?"

³¹"Healthy people do not need a doctor. The sick do. ³²I have not come to invite to repentance those who think they are righteous. I have come for those who know they are sinners."

³³One day, some people asked Jesus, "Why do the Pharisees and John's disciples fast, but your disciples never do?"

³⁴Jesus answered, "At a wedding, the friends of the bridegroom do not go without eating while he is still with them. ³⁵But the day will come when he will be gone. Then they will fast."

³⁶He gave this illustration: "No one uses a piece of new cloth to patch old clothes. The patch would shrink, pull away from the old,

and make the tear worse. ³⁷Men do not pour new wine into old skins. If they did, the wineskin would burst, ruining both the wine and the wineskin. ³⁸New wine is always kept in fresh skins so both are preserved. ³⁹After tasting fine, aged wine, no one would want new, because the old is better."

Chapter 6

¹On a Sabbath day, Jesus went through the grain fields. His disciples picked some heads of grain. They rubbed off the husks with their hands and ate the kernels.

²The Pharisees said, "Why are you doing work that is not permitted on the Sabbath?"

³"Haven't you read," Jesus said, "what David and his men did when they were hungry? ⁴He entered the house of God and ate the sacred bread that only the priests were allowed to eat. He also gave loaves to his men. ⁵The Son of Man is Lord, even of the Sabbath."

⁶On another Sabbath, Jesus taught in the synagogue. A man with a crippled hand was there. ⁷The Pharisees and the teachers of the Law were looking for a reason to accuse Jesus, so they watched closely to see if he would heal the man. ⁸Knowing their intentions, he said to the man, "Come stand in front of everyone." The man came forward.

⁹Jesus asked them, "Is it lawful to do good or evil on the Sabbath, to save life or destroy it?"

¹⁰He said to the man, "Stretch out your hand." As the man reached out, his hand became completely restored, as healthy as the other.

¹¹The Pharisees and teachers were furious and began to plot what they might do to Jesus.

¹²One day, Jesus went up on a mountain and spent the whole night praying to God.

¹³The next morning, he invited his followers and chose twelve men, whom he named apostles, to stay with him. ¹⁴They were Simon, whom he named Peter, his brother Andrew, and James, John, Philip, Bartholomew, ¹⁵Matthew, Thomas, James the son of Alphaeus, Simon the Zealot, ¹⁶Judas the son of James, and Judas Iscariot, who became a traitor.

¹⁷When Jesus saw a crowd gathering, he and his disciples went down the mountain to level ground. A great multitude was there from Judea, Jerusalem, and the coastal cities of Tyre and Sidon—some of his followers and other people who had come to hear him and be healed of their diseases.

¹⁸People who were tormented by evil spirits also came and were cured. ¹⁹They tried to touch him because they saw he had power to heal them.

²⁰Jesus looked at his followers who had come to hear his teaching. "Blessed are the poor in spirit, those who recognize their need for God, for the Kingdom of Heaven belongs to them. ²¹Blessed are the righteous, those who hunger and thirst to please God, for they will find true satisfaction. Blessed are the mourners, those who are grieving, for God will bring comfort, joy, and laughter to their aching hearts. ²²Blessed are the hated, those who are rejected, insulted, and falsely accused because of me. ²³In their day of abuse, they will rejoice because their reward in heaven is great. The ancient prophets were treated the same way.

²⁴"Woe to the rich, those unwilling to help those who have less, for they already have their blessing. ²⁵Woe to the well fed, those who think they have no need, for they will be hungry. Woe to the joyful, those who depend on circumstances for happiness, for they will weep and cry. ²⁶Woe to the politically correct, those who say what people want to hear, for that is what their fathers liked about the false prophets.

²⁷"Love your enemies. Do good to those who hate you. ²⁸Show kindness to those who curse you. Pray for those who mistreat you. ²⁹If people slap you on the cheek, do not retaliate, but allow them to slap the other cheek. If someone wants your shirt, be willing to give up your coat as well. ³⁰Give to everyone who asks, and when things are taken from you, do not demand their return. ³¹Do what you would have others do to you. ³²What is commendable about loving only those who love you? Even sinners do that. ³³You get no credit for showing kindness to those who treat you well, because sinners do that much. ³⁴Will you receive compliments for lending money only to those you are sure will pay you back? Even sinners lend to sinners when they are confident of repayment. ³⁵Lend when you have no assurance of being paid back. Then you will be rewarded as children who are like their Father God, who is kind to the wicked and ungrateful. ³⁶Show mercy to others, just as your Father has shown mercy to you.

³⁷"Do not judge, and you will not be judged. Do not condemn, and you will not be condemned. Forgive, and you will be forgiven.

³⁸"Give, and you will not have to worry about receiving. You will receive a full measure, packed down, shaken together, and spilling into your lap. The measure you give determines the measure you will receive."

³⁹Jesus used these analogies: "Can one blind person lead another? Wouldn't both of them fall into a ditch?

⁴⁰"A student is not above the teacher, but the one who is fully taught will be like the teacher.

⁴¹"Why do you worry about the sawdust in your brother's eye but never notice the board in your own eye?

⁴²"How can you say, 'Brother, let me take the speck out of your eye,' and not admit the existence of something much larger in your own eye? Hypocrite! First take the large object from your eye. Then

you can see clearly to remove the small piece from your brother's eye.

⁴³"A good tree cannot produce bad fruit, and a bad tree cannot produce good fruit. ⁴⁴Each tree is identified by its own fruit. No one picks grapes from thorn bushes or figs from briers. ⁴⁵Out of the treasury of a good heart, people do good things. From an evil heart, people do evil things. What they say flows from what is in their hearts.

⁴⁶"Why do you call me your master and not do what I say? ⁴⁷Everyone who not only hears my words but also puts them into practice is like ⁴⁸a wise man who dug deep and laid the foundation of his house on solid rock. When a storm brought torrential rain, flooded streams, and hurricane-force winds, his house did not collapse, because it was well built on an unshakable foundation. ⁴⁹Anyone who hears my words but never acts on them is like a foolish man who built his house on sand, without a foundation. The rain fell, causing the streams to rise. As soon as the high winds came, the house fell with a great crash and was completely destroyed."

Chapter 7

¹When Jesus finished speaking to the people, he went to Capernaum.

²There, a Roman officer had a dear servant who was sick and near death. ³When he heard about Jesus, he sent respected Jewish leaders to ask him to come heal his servant. ⁴Immediately upon arriving, they pleaded, "This man is worthy of your help ⁵because he loves our people and has built a synagogue for us."

⁶So Jesus went with them, but as he came to a place not far from the house, friends brought a message from the officer. "Sir, do not put yourself to any trouble. I am not important enough to have you

enter my house, [7]nor did I consider myself worthy to see you. Just give the order, and my servant will be healed. [8]For I also am a man under authority. At my command under Caesar, my soldiers come and go and do exactly what I say."

[9]Jesus marveled at the message. To those following him, he said, "In all of Israel, I have never seen such faith."

[10]When the messengers arrived at the officer's home, they found that the servant had completely recovered.

[11]Soon after the healing of the Roman officer's servant, Jesus walked toward the town of Nain. His disciples and a huge crowd followed him. [12]As they approached the town gate, they met a large funeral procession for the only son of a widow.

[13]When Jesus saw the widow, he was filled with compassion and said to her, "Do not cry." [14]He walked over and touched the stretcher while the bearers stood still. "Young man! I say to you, arise!"

[15]The dead son sat up and began to speak.

Jesus presented him to his mother.

[16]A deep reverence came upon all who saw what had happened. They praised God, saying, "A great prophet has risen among us," and, "Today, God has visited us."

[17]The news about Jesus spread throughout Judea and beyond.

[18]John the Baptizer heard from his disciples about all that Jesus was doing. [19]He sent two of them to ask, "Are you the one to fulfill God's promise, or must we look for someone else?"

[20]So the men went to Jesus and said, "John the Baptizer has sent us to ask, 'Are you the one to fulfill God's promise, or must we look for someone else?'"

[21]At that time, Jesus was healing many who were sick or had physical handicaps. He cast out evil spirits and gave sight to the blind. [22]"Go tell John what you have seen and heard," Jesus replied. "The blind see, the lame walk, and the lepers are cleansed. The deaf

can hear, the dead are raised, and the needy receive words of hope. [23]Tell him a man is blessed when he puts his faith in me."

[24]As the two left, Jesus asked the people about John. "What did you go into the wilderness to see? A reed blown over by the wind? [25]Why did you go? Was it to see a man dressed in fine clothes? No, those people live in the royal palaces. [26]What did you expect to see? A prophet? Yes, and I tell you, he is more remarkable than a prophet. [27]He is the one the prophet Malachi talked about when he wrote: *See, I will send my messenger to prepare the way before me.* [28]Believe me, John the Baptizer is greater than any other person ever born. Yet the lowliest one in the Kingdom of Heaven is greater than John. [29]Everyone who heard John, including the tax collectors, yielded to God's way when they were baptized, [30]but the Pharisees and scholars of the Law rejected God when they refused to be baptized."

[31]Jesus asked, "What are the people of this generation like? [32]They are like children in the marketplace, whining to get what they want. They say, 'We played our flutes, but you would not dance for us. We wailed our funeral songs, but you never shed a tear with us.' [33]John the Baptizer did not party with the people. He chose not to eat or drink with others, and they said, 'He has an evil spirit.' [34]When the Son of Man came, he ate bread and drank wine. They condemned him as well, calling him a drunkard and a glutton, a friend of dishonest tax collectors and other sinners. [35]However, the results show the actions to be wise."

[36]A Pharisee invited Jesus to dinner, so Jesus went to his house and sat at his table.

[37]A sinful woman from the town heard Jesus was there and brought a jar made of fine gypsum filled with perfume. [38]Kneeling behind him, she wept. She wiped his feet with her hair, kissed them, and rubbed them with the perfume.

³⁹When the Pharisee saw this, he reasoned, *This man cannot be a prophet or he would know the woman who is touching him is a sinner.*

⁴⁰"Simon," Jesus said, "I need to tell you something."

"What is it?"

⁴¹"Two men owed a debt to a money lender. One owed five hundred days' wages, the other, fifty. ⁴²Neither of them had any money, so he cancelled their debts. Which man do you think loved the lender more?"

⁴³Simon answered, "I suppose it would be the one whose large debt was cancelled."

"You have judged correctly."

⁴⁴Jesus turned toward the woman and said to Simon, "Have you seen her gratitude? When I arrived, you did not give me water to wash my feet. But she has washed my feet with her tears and wiped them with her hair. ⁴⁵You did not greet me with a kiss, but she has covered my feet with kisses. ⁴⁶You put no oil on my head, but she has anointed my feet with expensive perfume. ⁴⁷Isn't it obvious? Her sins were very great, so she is exceptionally grateful to be forgiven. Those who receive only a little forgiveness have little love to give."

⁴⁸Jesus said to her, "Your sins have been forgiven."

⁴⁹Other guests at the table whispered among themselves, "Who does this man think he is, that he can forgive sins?"

⁵⁰Ignoring them, Jesus said to the woman, "Your faith has set you free. Go in peace."

Chapter 8

¹After this, Jesus traveled through cities and towns, preaching the good news about the Kingdom of God. The twelve disciples were with him, ²and also women whose diseases had been cured and people whom he had delivered from evil spirits, including Mary Magdalene, who once had seven evil spirits, ³Joanna, whose

husband, Chuza, was a manager for King Herod, and Susanna. There were many others who brought resources to support Jesus and his disciples.

[4]When a large crowd had gathered from many towns, Jesus gave this illustration: [5]"A farmer went to sow his seeds in the field. As he scattered the seeds, some fell on the road, where they were trampled and were eaten by the birds. [6]Some fell on rocky ground, where the plants sprang up but soon wilted for lack of moisture. [7]Some seeds fell among thorny weeds that grew more quickly and choked out the tender plants. [8]Other seeds fell on fertile soil and became healthy plants, producing a hundred times the amount of seed sown. If you have ears, pay attention to what I am saying."

[9]His disciples asked what the illustration meant.

[10]Jesus said, "I have given you insights into the mysteries of the Kingdom of God, but others have only the stories. With open eyes, they choose to see nothing. They listen with their ears but do not want to understand. [11]This is what the illustration means: The seed is the word of God. [12]The seeds that fell on the road are people who hear the Kingdom message but do not understand. The devil takes away the seed that was planted in their hearts and prevents them from believing and being saved. [13]The seeds that fell on rocky ground are those who hear the message and eagerly accept it, but their roots are shallow. In times of temptation, they forsake their faith. [14]The seeds that fell among thorny weeds are the people who allow the worries of this life and the enticement of wealth and the pleasures of this life to choke the message, so no fruit is produced. [15]The seeds that fell on fertile soil are the people who hear, understand, and act on God's word, in patience yielding a huge harvest.

[16]"Is a lighted candle ever put under a basket or couch? No. It is always placed where its light will shine. [17]Everything hidden will one day be revealed, and all secrets will be brought to light.

[18]Believe me, because more knowledge will be given to those who listen carefully. But those who are not listening will lose what little understanding they have."

[19]Jesus' mother and brothers arrived outside the house but could not reach Jesus because of the crowd.

[20]Someone said, "Your mother and your brothers are outside, asking for you."

[21]Jesus replied, "My mother and brothers are those who hear God's word and do it."

[22]One day, Jesus got into a boat with his disciples, saying, "Let's cross over to the other side of the lake."

So they left.

[23]Under smooth sailing, Jesus went to sleep.

Soon afterward, a violent wind struck the lake, so the boat was nearly swamped by large waves crashing over the side.

[24]His disciples woke him, crying, "Teacher! Teacher! Help us or we are going to drown!"

Standing, Jesus ordered the wind and waves to be still. Suddenly, the wind died and the waters became calm. [25]"Where is your faith?" he asked.

The disciples looked at one another with amazement. "What sort of man is this? Even the wind and the waves obey him!"

[26]After crossing the lake, Jesus and the disciples came to the region of the Gadarenes, near Galilee.

[27]As Jesus climbed out of the boat, he was met by a man from town who was possessed by evil spirits. For a long time, the man had been homeless and naked, living among the tombs. [28]When he saw Jesus, he screamed and kneeled before him. "What do you want with me," he screamed, "Jesus, Son of God? I beg you, do not torment me!"

²⁹Jesus had already commanded the evil spirit to come out of the man.

Many times, the spirit had grabbed hold of the man. He had been bound with shackles and chains, but he always broke free and ran into the wilderness, under the evil spirit's control.

³⁰"What is your name?" Jesus asked.

The man answered, "My name is Legion, because there are so many of us."

³¹The spirits kept begging Jesus not to send them to the bottomless pit. ³²A large herd of pigs was feeding on the hillside. The spirits begged, "Send us to the pigs that we may enter them."

And Jesus said, "Go!"

³³They came out of the man and entered the pigs. Suddenly, the whole herd stampeded down the steep bank, plunged into the water, and drowned.

³⁴The herdsmen ran into town and countryside and told what had happened, how the man had been delivered and the pigs were lost. ³⁵The people rushed out to see for themselves. When they saw the man who had been possessed, sitting at Jesus' feet, clothed and in his right mind, they were frightened.

³⁶All the eyewitnesses repeated what they had seen happen to the man and the pigs.

³⁷The whole crowd of Gadarenes begged Jesus to leave their country because they were overcome with fear.

So Jesus returned to his boat.

³⁸The man who had been possessed begged to go along, but Jesus said, "No. ³⁹Go home to your people and tell them what great things the Lord has done for you."

So the man left and spread the word throughout the region, telling what Jesus had done.

Everyone was amazed.

⁴⁰When Jesus returned to the other side of Galilee, a crowd welcomed him. People had been waiting for his arrival.

⁴¹A synagogue official named Jairus came, knelt before him, and begged him to come to his house. ⁴²His only daughter, about twelve years old, was at home, dying. On the way to Jairus's home, a crowd of followers pressed in on Jesus.

⁴³A woman who had suffered twelve years from constant bleeding, and had spent all her money on physicians, had been unable to find a cure. ⁴⁴She came through the crowd from behind and touched the fringe of his robe. Immediately, her bleeding stopped.

⁴⁵"Who touched me?" Jesus said.

When no one admitted it, Simon Peter said, "Master, what are you talking about? All along the way, people have been pushing against you and touching you. Why are you asking, 'Who touched me?'"

⁴⁶"Someone touched me," Jesus said. "I felt power go out from me."

⁴⁷When the woman realized she could not hide, she trembled with fear as she fell at Jesus' feet and told him what had happened.

⁴⁸"Daughter," Jesus said, "your faith has made you well. Go in peace."

⁴⁹While Jesus was still speaking, men came from the house to tell Jairus, "Your daughter has died. There is no need to trouble the teacher anymore."

⁵⁰Overhearing, Jesus said to Jairus, "Do not worry; she will be all right. Trust me."

⁵¹At the house, Jesus allowed no one to go in except Simon Peter, James, John, and the child's parents. ⁵²To those who were crying and mourning the child's death, Jesus said, "Do not cry. The child is not dead. She's asleep."

⁵³They laughed and said he was crazy, because they knew she was dead.

⁵⁴Taking the girl by the hand, he said, "Little girl, rise up!"

⁵⁵At that moment, life returned to her body. She got up, and Jesus said, "Give her something to eat."

⁵⁶The parents were amazed, but Jesus ordered them not to tell anyone what had happened.

Chapter 9

¹Jesus called the twelve and gave them authority to cast out evil spirits and heal all kinds of sicknesses. ²And he sent them out to preach the Kingdom of God and to heal the sick. ³"Take nothing with you—no money, walking stick, or bag with extra clothes. ⁴In whatever house you are welcomed, stay until you leave for another town. ⁵When people do not welcome you or listen to your words, shake off the offense like dust from your feet, as a testimony against them."

⁶The disciples went through the towns, preaching the good news of the Kingdom of God and healing the sick.

⁷When Herod the tetrarch received reports about Jesus, he was troubled because some had said the spirit of John had returned from the dead. ⁸Others said, "He is Elijah," or, "He is like one of the great prophets who lived long ago."

⁹"I had John beheaded," Herod said, "so who is the man who is doing such amazing things?" Herod wanted to see him.

¹⁰After their tour of ministry, the disciples gathered around Jesus and told him all they had said and done. Then he directed the disciples toward a desolate place in the region of Bethsaida. ¹¹Many people saw them leave, and they followed him. Jesus welcomed them, preached the Kingdom of God, and healed their sick.

¹²Late in the afternoon, the twelve said to Jesus, "We are far from town. Send the people away so they can go to the farms and towns nearby and buy food."

¹³Jesus said, "Why don't you feed them?"

"With what?" they said. "All we have are five loaves and two fish. Or do you expect us to buy enough food for this gigantic crowd?"

¹⁴Besides the women and children, about five thousand men were there.

Jesus said, "Have the people sit down in groups of about fifty."

¹⁵So everyone sat down.

¹⁶Jesus took the five loaves and two fish, looked toward heaven, and gave thanks. He broke the loaves and fish and handed them to his disciples, who distributed the pieces to the people. ¹⁷They all ate as much as they wanted, and the disciples gathered twelve baskets full of leftover bread and fish.

¹⁸One day, after Jesus had been alone, he asked his disciples, "Who do people say that I am?"

¹⁹They said, "Some say you are John the Baptizer. Others say you are Elijah or one of the other prophets, who has come back to life."

²⁰"Who do you say that I am?"

Simon Peter answered, "You are the Anointed One, the Messiah sent from God!"

²¹He gave a stern warning: "Do not tell anyone that I am the Messiah."

²²Jesus explained that the Son of Man must endure great suffering at the hand of government officials, chief priests, and teachers of the Law. "I will be killed," he said, "but three days later I will rise to life."

²³Then he taught his disciples. "If you want to follow me, you must sacrifice your selfish desires. Take up your cross, and then you can follow me. ²⁴If you try to save your life for yourself, you will lose it. But if you lose your life for my sake and for spreading the

good news, you will find it. ²⁵What have you gained if you own the whole world but lose your life?

²⁶"Those who are ashamed of me and my words will cause the Son of Man to be ashamed of them when he comes in glory and in his Father's glory, with the holy angels. ²⁷I guarantee, some of you standing here will not die before they see the Kingdom of God."

²⁸About eight days after Jesus told his disciples about his need to die, he took Simon Peter, James, and John to pray alone, high up on the mountain. ²⁹As Jesus prayed, the three saw his whole appearance change. His clothes became dazzling white. ³⁰Moses and Elijah appeared and talked with him. ³¹They also stood in brilliant glory while they talked about his death that was to take place in Jerusalem.

³²Simon Peter and the others had been overcome with sleep, but when they awakened, they saw Jesus in his glory and the two men with him.

³³Peter said to Jesus, "Master, it is wonderful to be here. Let's build three shrines here—for you, Moses, and Elijah." He spoke without considering what he was saying.

³⁴While Peter was still speaking, a cloud overshadowed them. They were terrified as the cloud enveloped them. ³⁵A voice came from the cloud. "This is my dearly loved son. Listen to him!"

³⁶After they heard the voice, they saw that Jesus was alone. They kept the event to themselves, telling no one what they had seen.

³⁷The day after Jesus and the three disciples came down from the mountain, they met a large crowd.

³⁸A man from the crowd shouted, "Teacher, I beg you, help my son. He is my only child. ³⁹An evil spirit takes control of him, so he screams, foams at the mouth, and goes into convulsions. It will not leave him alone until after he is physically exhausted. ⁴⁰I begged your disciples to cast out the evil spirit, but they could not do it."

⁴¹Jesus said, "How long must I be with this faithless and corrupt generation? How long must I put up with you? Bring your son to me."

⁴²When the boy came near, he went into convulsions and fell to the ground. Jesus spoke against the evil spirit, healed the boy, and gave him back to his father.

⁴³Everyone was amazed at God's mighty power.

While people were still marveling at the miracles, Jesus taught his disciples. ⁴⁴"Listen carefully. The Son of Man will soon be betrayed into the hands of men."

⁴⁵They did not understand everything Jesus said but were afraid to ask what he meant.

⁴⁶An argument arose about which of them was the greatest.

⁴⁷Knowing their thoughts, Jesus brought a little boy to his side.

⁴⁸"Anyone who welcomes this child in my name is welcoming me. And anyone who welcomes me is welcoming the one who sent me. The least of those among you is the greatest."

⁴⁹John said, "Master, we saw someone casting out evil spirits in your name. We told him to stop because he was not part of our group."

⁵⁰"Don't stop him!" Jesus said. "Anyone who is not against us is for us."

⁵¹As the time drew closer to when he would ascend to heaven, Jesus decided he would go to Jerusalem. ⁵²He sent messengers ahead to arrange a place for him to stay in a Samaritan town. ⁵³After hearing that Jesus was determined to go to Jerusalem, the Samaritans refused to welcome him.

⁵⁴When James and John heard about their rejection, they said, "Sir, should we call down fire from heaven to consume them, just as Elijah did?"

[55]Jesus turned and rebuked them. "You do not know what kind of spirit you have. [56]The Son of Man has not come to destroy lives, but to save them."

They went on to another town.

[57]As they walked down the road, a man said to Jesus, "Wherever you are going, I will follow."

[58]"Foxes have dens, and birds have nests," Jesus said, "but the Son of Man has no home where he can lay his head."

[59]To another man, he said, "Follow me." But the man said, "Sir, let me first go and care for my father until he dies."

[60]Jesus replied, "The dead can bury their dead. You need to preach the Kingdom of God."

[61]Someone else said, "Sir, I would like to follow you, but I need to go back home and say good-bye to my family."

[62]"After a man puts his hand to the plow," Jesus said, "he is not fit for the Kingdom of God if he keeps looking back."

Chapter 10

[1]Jesus chose another seventy-two disciples, sending them in pairs to every town and community where he planned to visit. [2]"The harvest is great," Jesus said, "but there are not many workers. So pray to the Lord of the harvest, and ask him to send more people into the fields. [3]Take care as you go, for I am sending you like lambs into a pack of wolves.

[4]"Do not carry a money bag, traveling sack, or extra pair of sandals. Do not stop to greet anyone on the way. [5]Whenever you enter a house, first greet the family and say, 'May God's peace be upon this house.' [6]If a peace-lover lives there, your blessing will be received, but if not, it will be rejected. [7]Do not move from house to house, but remain in the same place, accepting their hospitality as workers deserving their pay.

⁸"In every town where you are welcomed, eat whatever is set before you. ⁹Heal those who are sick, and tell the people, 'The Kingdom of God is near.' ¹⁰But wherever you are not welcome, take the street out of town and say, ¹¹'As a testimony against you, we wipe your town's dust from our feet. Nevertheless, you have had the opportunity to know, the Kingdom of God is near.' ¹²I tell you, on Judgment Day, the wicked of Sodom will be better off than that town.

¹³"How terrible it will be for you, Korazin! And for you, Bethsaida! If the miracles I did before you had been seen in Tyre and Sidon, they would have turned to God long ago in sackcloth and ashes. ¹⁴On Judgment Day, Tyre and Sidon will be better off than you. ¹⁵And you in Capernaum who think you are so high and mighty will be brought to the lowest depths.

¹⁶"Those who listen to you are listening to me, and those who reject you are rejecting me and the one who sent me."

¹⁷When the seventy-two returned, they said with delight, "Sir, we even commanded the evil spirits in your name!"

¹⁸"So what?" Jesus said. "I have seen Satan fall like lightning from heaven. ¹⁹Sure, I have given you authority to trample snakes and scorpions and have power over the enemy, so nothing can harm you in any way. ²⁰However, you should not rejoice that evil spirits obey your commands. Instead, rejoice because your citizenship in heaven has been recorded."

²¹Jesus rejoiced in his spirit. "Thank you, Father, ruler of heaven and earth, for hiding these things from those who think they are so smart and revealing them to infants of faith. I know, Father, that it pleases you to have it happen this way."

²²He reminded them of what he had said before. "My Father has entrusted everything to me. Only the Father knows the Son. And the Father is known only by the Son and those to whom the Son chooses to reveal him."

²³He turned to his disciples as if privately addressing a special group. "How blessed are the eyes that see what you see! ²⁴I tell you, many prophets and kings have desired to see what you now see, but they never saw it. They longed to hear what you hear, but they did not get to hear it."

²⁵One day, a teacher of the Law stood up from the crowd to test Jesus. "Teacher, what should I do to receive eternal life?"

²⁶"What is written in the Law?" Jesus said. "How do you read it?"

²⁷"You must love God with your whole heart, with all your being and all your strength. And you must love your neighbor as yourself."

²⁸"That's right. If you do that, you will have eternal life."

²⁹Wanting to justify himself, the man asked Jesus, "And how do I know who my neighbors are?"

³⁰"A man once went down from Jerusalem to Jericho and was attacked by robbers who took his clothes, beat him, and left him half dead beside the road. ³¹A priest happened to be going that way. When he saw the bleeding man, he walked by on the other side. ³²After that, a Levite came, saw the man's injuries, and also walked by on the other side. ³³A Samaritan traveler saw the man suffering and was moved with compassion. ³⁴He went to him, used wine and oil to cleanse and soothe his wounds, and stopped the bleeding with bandages. He lifted him onto his own donkey and took him to the inn, where he cared for him. ³⁵The next morning, he left two days' wages with the innkeeper, telling him, 'Take care of this man. If you spend more, I will reimburse your expenses when I return.' ³⁶Which of the three travelers do you think was a neighbor to the man who was robbed and beaten?"

³⁷The teacher of the Law answered, "The one who helped the man."

Jesus said, "Go and do the same thing."

³⁸As they journeyed, Jesus and his disciples came to a village where a woman named Martha welcomed them into her house. ³⁹Mary, Martha's sister, sat at Jesus' feet, listening to him teach. ⁴⁰Martha was frantic, trying to get everything ready for the evening meal. "Sir, don't you care that my sister has left all the work for me to do alone? Tell her she should come help me."

⁴¹Jesus said to her, "Martha, Martha. You are worried and frustrated over so many trivialities, ⁴²but only one thing is most important. Mary has chosen what is best—that which will never be taken from her."

Chapter 11

¹One day, Jesus was praying at a certain place. When he finished, one of his disciples said, "Sir, teach us how to pray, just as John the Baptizer taught his followers."

²"When you pray," Jesus said, "say something like this: Our Father in heaven, may your name be honored. May your Kingdom come and your will be done, on earth as it is in heaven. ³Give us the bread we need for today. ⁴Forgive our wrongs as we forgive the wrongs of others. Keep us from temptation and protect us from evil."

⁵He used this illustration: "Suppose you knock on a friend's door at midnight and say, 'Please let me borrow three loaves of bread ⁶because a friend of mine has arrived from his journey to see me and I have no food for him.' ⁷From inside he will answer, 'Do not bother me. The door is locked, and my family and I are in bed. I am not getting up to give you anything.' ⁸I tell you, he will not get up because of friendship. But because of the persistent knocking, he will rise and answer your needs.

⁹"Ask and you will receive, seek and you will find, knock and the door will be opened for you. ¹⁰Those who keep asking will receive.

Those who keep seeking will find what they are looking for. And the door will be opened to those who keep knocking."

[11]He repeated this illustration: "If a son asks his father for bread, will he receive a stone? If he asks for a fish, will he be handed a serpent? [12]Or if he asks for an egg, will he give him a scorpion? No, of course not. [13]If you who are evil know how to give good gifts to your children, you can be sure your heavenly Father will give the Holy Spirit to those who ask him."

[14]One day, Jesus met a man who was unable to speak because of an evil spirit. At Jesus' command, the evil spirit left, and the man began to speak.

The crowd was amazed.

[15]Some of them said, "He gets his authority from Beelzebub, the ruler of evil spirits."

[16]Others wanted to test him by asking for a miraculous sign from heaven.

[17]Aware of what they were thinking, he said, "A kingdom working against itself will soon be destroyed. Any city or family who fights internally cannot last very long. [18]If Satan wars against himself, his kingdom cannot survive. You say Beelzebub gives me power over evil spirits. [19]If Beelzebub is my power over evil spirits, by whom do your followers cast them out? They prove you have a double standard of judgment. [20]But if I cast out evil spirits by the Spirit of God, the Kingdom of God has come unto you. [21]When a fully armed strong man guards his house, his property is safe. [22]But when someone stronger attacks and overpowers him, the owner will lose his weapons and personal belongings.

[23]"Anyone who is not with me is against me. If you are not gathering with me, you are scattering.

[24]"When an evil spirit leaves a person, it wanders through barren places, seeks rest, but finds none. It then says, 'I know. I will return

to the person I left.' ²⁵It finds its former home empty, swept clean, and ready to be occupied. ²⁶So it finds seven spirits more evil than itself, and they go in to live there. That person is worse off than before."

²⁷While Jesus was teaching, a woman shouted from the crowd, "Blessed is the womb that bore you and the breasts that nursed you."

²⁸"No," he said, "the most blessed are those who hear God's word and obey him."

²⁹As the crowd grew larger and pressed in, Jesus said, "This is a wicked and adulterous people who demand miraculous signs. No sign will come except the sign of the prophet Jonah. ³⁰Just as Jonah was a sign to the people of Nineveh, so shall the Son of Man be to this generation. ³¹The Queen of Sheba will testify and condemn this generation, because she came from far away to hear the wisdom of Solomon. Now someone wiser than Solomon is here, but you refuse to listen. ³²The people of Nineveh give evidence to condemn this generation, because they repented at the preaching of Jonah. Behold, someone greater than Jonah is here, but you do not repent.

³³"People do not light a lamp and hide it under a bowl. It is placed on a stand to give light to everyone in the house. ³⁴Your eyes are like a lamp for the body. If your eyes are good, your whole body will be full of light. But if your eyes are bad, darkness fills your body. ³⁵So make certain that the light you think you have is not actually darkness. ³⁶If your whole body is filled with light, with no darkness in the corners, your life will radiate the light like a lamp on a stand that brightens your whole house."

³⁷While Jesus was speaking, a Pharisee asked him to dinner. He entered the man's house and sat to eat. ³⁸His host was amazed to see that Jesus did not wash his hands first.

³⁹Jesus said, "You Pharisees wash the outside of cups and platters, but you leave the inside dirty, full of greed and wickedness. ⁴⁰How foolish! The same one who made the outside also made the inside. ⁴¹If you would become givers of what you have, you could be fully clean.

⁴²"How terrible for you Pharisees, because you give a tenth of your mint, rue, and the tiniest amounts of other herbs, but you neglect what is right in giving to others and in loving God. You should not do one while neglecting the other.

⁴³"How terrible for you Pharisees, because you love the seats of honor in the synagogues. You love to be admired as you walk through the markets.

⁴⁴"How terrible for you Pharisees and teachers of the Law. Hypocrites! You are like unmarked graves that people walk over and never know it."

⁴⁵A teacher of the Law said, "Teacher, when you say these things about our people, you insult us too."

⁴⁶"How terrible for you teachers of the Law," Jesus said. "You place unbearably heavy burdens on others but will carry none of the weight yourselves. ⁴⁷How terrible for you, because you build memorials for the prophets your ancestors killed. ⁴⁸With your monuments, you give testimony that you approve of their deeds. ⁴⁹God in his foresight has said, 'I will send prophets and messengers, and they will kill some and persecute others.' ⁵⁰So this generation will be held responsible for the blood of all the prophets since the beginning of the world, ⁵¹from the murder of Abel in the beginning to Zechariah, who died between the altar and the Temple sanctuary. I tell you, their deaths will be charged against this generation.

⁵²"How terrible for you teachers of the Law, because you have stolen from the people the key to knowing God. You will not enter the Kingdom, and you hinder others who would like to get in."

[53]As Jesus left the house, the Pharisees and teachers of the Law were in bitter opposition to him and looked for ways to turn his words against him. [54]They stalked him, waiting for him to say something incriminating so they could have him arrested.

Chapter 12

[1]The crowd grew into the thousands, more than anyone could count, until they were pressing against one another and stepping on one another's feet. Mainly to his followers, Jesus taught what he had said many times before. "Watch out for the yeast of the Pharisees, and recognize their hypocrisy. [2]Everything hidden will one day be revealed, and all secrets will be brought to light. [3]What you have whispered in the darkness will be shouted in broad daylight. What your ears have heard in a secluded room will be preached from the housetops.

[4]"My friends, never fear those who can kill the body and nothing more. [5]Let me tell you whom you should fear: God, who can destroy both body and soul in hell. He is the one you need to fear.

[6]"The price of five sparrows is not much, but one sparrow cannot die without God's knowledge. [7]He even knows the number of hairs on your head. Don't worry. You are worth more than many sparrows.

[8]"I assure you, anyone who publicly acknowledges me before men, the Son of Man will publicly acknowledge before the angels of God. [9]But anyone who denies me before men will be denied before God's angels. [10]Those who speak against the Son of Man will be forgiven, but speaking evil of the Holy Spirit cannot be forgiven. Never ever.

[11]"When you are arrested and stand before synagogue authorities, governors, and kings, do not worry about what to say. [12]At the time you must speak, you will be given the right words to say."

¹³Someone from the crowd asked Jesus, "Teacher, would you instruct my brother to share our father's inheritance with me?"

¹⁴"Sir," Jesus answered, "who made me your arbitrator?" ¹⁵He said to the crowd, "Look, do not be greedy. Satisfaction in life does not come from having an abundance of possessions."

¹⁶He gave this illustration: "A rich man had an unusually productive farm that produced huge harvests. ¹⁷'What shall I do?' he asked himself. 'I have no place to store all my crops. ¹⁸I know. I will tear down my granaries and build bigger ones in their place. Then I will have enough room for all my goods, ¹⁹and I can tell myself, *Now you can relax and enjoy life because you have saved enough to last for many years. Eat, drink, and be merry.*' ²⁰But God said, 'You fool! Tonight, you will die, so what good is all the wealth you have accumulated?' ²¹This is what happens to all who store treasure for themselves and are not rich toward God in their giving."

²²Jesus said to his followers, "That is why I keep telling you not to worry about your life, whether you have enough food and drink or clothes to wear. ²³Life is more important than food, and the body is more important than clothes. ²⁴Look at the birds. They do not plant seeds, gather a harvest, or store grain in barns. Yet God feeds them. Aren't you far more valuable to him than they are? ²⁵Can all of your worrying increase your lifespan by just one minute? ²⁶If you cannot do that, why fret about the rest?

²⁷"Look how the wildflowers grow in the fields. They do not spin yarn or weave fabric. Yet Solomon in his greatest splendor was never dressed like one of them. ²⁸If God clothes the wildflowers that are here now and gone tomorrow, don't you suppose he will care for you? Why do you have such weak faith? ²⁹Do not trouble yourselves with questions like 'What shall we eat?' or 'What shall we drink?' Do not worry about such things. ³⁰People who do not know God seek such things, but your heavenly Father already knows what you need.

[31]"Seek first his Kingdom, and he will give you everything you need. [32]Little flock, do not be afraid you will not have enough. Your Father is delighted to give you the Kingdom. [33]If you sell what you have and give to those in need, you will store up treasure for yourselves in heaven, where it is safe from moths and rust and thieves. [34]For wherever your treasure is, your heart will be there also.

[35]"Be dressed and ready for action," Jesus said. "Have your lamps burning. [36]Be like servants waiting for their master's return from a wedding feast, so whenever he comes and knocks, they immediately open the door. [37]Blessed are those servants whom the master finds watching for his arrival. I am telling you, the master will dress to serve, ask them to dinner, and be their server. [38]Whenever the master comes, perhaps in the middle of the night or at dawn, blessed are those servants who are ready. [39]Certainly, if a homeowner knew when a thief was coming, he would be ready and would not allow him to break in. [40]Likewise, you must always be ready, or the Son of Man will come at an unexpected time."

[41]Peter asked, "Sir, are you giving this illustration only for us or for everyone?"

[42]"I am talking to all the faithful and wise servants whom the master puts in charge of caring for his possessions and serving food at mealtime. [43]Blessed are those servants whom the master finds at work when he comes. [44]I guarantee, he will put them in charge of everything he owns. [45]But if a servant thinks, *My master will not be back for a while*, so he abuses other servants, spends his time partying, and pursues personal pleasures, [46]his master will return unexpectedly and cut him off. He will put the servant with those who cannot be trusted. [47]The servant who knows what his master wants but fails to prepare and do the work will be severely punished, [48]but the one who does wrong out of ignorance will receive a lighter sentence.

Much is required of those who are given much responsibility, and more is required of those who are given more.

⁴⁹"I have come to set the world on fire, and I wish it were already burning. ⁵⁰But first I have a baptism of suffering to endure, and I am pressed to see it completed. ⁵¹Do you think I've come to bring peace to the world? No, I bring division. ⁵²From now on, five in a household will be divided concerning me, three against two and two against three. ⁵³A father will oppose his son, and the son, his father. A mother will oppose her daughter, and the daughter, her mother. A mother-in-law will oppose her daughter-in-law, and the daughter-in-law, her mother-in-law."

⁵⁴Jesus said to the crowd, "When you see a cloud rise in the west, you say, 'It is going to rain,' and it does. ⁵⁵When the wind blows from the south, you say, 'It is going to be a hot day,' and it is. ⁵⁶Hypocrites! You can read the signs of the earth and sky to determine what the weather will be. How can you not see what is happening now? ⁵⁷Why can't you decide for yourselves what is right?

⁵⁸"Suppose someone brings an accusation against you. You should seek to settle the dispute before going to court. Otherwise, you may find yourself before a judge, who will have an officer put you in prison. ⁵⁹If that happens, you will not be free until you have paid all that is due."

Chapter 13

¹At this time, some people came to tell Jesus about the Galileans who had been murdered as they were offering sacrifices in the Temple.

²Jesus said, "Do you think, because they suffered in this way, that these Galileans were greater sinners than others? ³I assure you, they were not. But unless you turn to God, you will suffer a similar fate.

[4]What about those eighteen people who died when the tower of Siloam fell? Do you think they were greater sinners than everyone else in Jerusalem? [5]I assure you, they were not. But unless you turn to God, you will suffer a similar fate."

[6]He gave this illustration: "A man planted a fig tree in his vineyard but was disappointed when he came looking for fruit and found none. [7]So he said to his gardener, 'Look, for three years I've expected to pick fruit from this fig tree, and it is still barren. Cut it down. Why should it be allowed any space in the ground?'

[8]"'Sir,' the gardener said, 'give it one more year to bear fruit. I will cultivate it and fertilize it. [9]Maybe it will yield figs next season. If not, I will cut it down.'"

[10]Jesus was teaching in the synagogue on the Sabbath.

[11]A woman there, crippled by an evil spirit for eighteen years, was bent over and could not straighten up.

[12]When Jesus saw her, he said, "Woman, you are now set free from your infirmity." [13]After he placed his hands on her, she immediately stood up straight and praised God.

[14]The leader of the synagogue was indignant because Jesus had done work on the Sabbath, so he said to the people, "If you want to be healed, come on one of the six days when men should work, not on the Sabbath."

[15]"You hypocrites!" Jesus said. "Don't you do work when you untie your donkey or ox from the stall and lead it to water? [16]Shouldn't this daughter of Abraham, who has been tied up by Satan for eighteen years, be released on the Sabbath?"

[17]Those words humbled his critics, and the people rejoiced at the wonderful things Jesus was doing.

[18]Jesus said, "What is the Kingdom of God like? What analogy will help you understand? [19]It is like someone planting a tiny mustard

seed in his garden, and the plant grows until it becomes so big that birds can perch in its branches."

[20]Again he said, "What is the Kingdom of God like? [21]It is like a little yeast that a woman kneaded into three measures of flour and made the whole batch of dough rise."

[22]On the way to Jerusalem, Jesus passed through towns and villages, teaching as he went.

[23]Someone asked, "Sir, will only a few people be saved?"

Jesus said, [24]"You must give a wholehearted effort to enter the Kingdom, because the entrance is narrow. With a halfhearted effort, many will try to enter but will fail.

[25]"After the homeowner rises to lock the door, it will be too late. You will stand outside, knocking, and saying, 'Sir, open the door!' but he will say, 'I do not know you or where you are from.' [26]You will beg, saying, 'We ate and drank with you. We heard you teaching in our streets.' [27]But he will answer, 'No. I am telling you, I do not know where you are from. Get out of here, you workers of unrighteousness.'

[28]"When you see Abraham, Isaac, Jacob, and all the prophets in the Kingdom of God, you will cry and grit your teeth in pain because you have been shut out. [29]People will come from everywhere, from the east, west, north, and south, to sit at God's table in the Kingdom. [30]You see, some who have the seat of lowest honor here will have the highest there. And some who have the seat of highest honor here will have the lowest there."

[31]At that time, some Pharisees said to Jesus, "You must get away from here to a safer place. Herod wants to kill you."

[32]Jesus said, "Go tell that fox I am too busy to leave. Today and tomorrow, I will deliver people from evil spirits and heal the sick. On the third day, I will finish what I could not get done on the first two days. [33]I must carry on my work here today, tomorrow, and the

next day, because it would never do for a prophet to die outside of Jerusalem.

³⁴"O Jerusalem, Jerusalem! You kill the prophets and those who have been sent to you. Many times, I have wanted to gather you to myself like a hen brings her chicks under her wings, but you were not willing.

³⁵"So now you have your desolate Temple to yourselves. You will not see me again until the day when you say, 'Blessed is he who comes in the name of the Lord!'"

Chapter 14

¹On a Sabbath, Jesus went to eat at the home of a prominent Pharisee. The people watched Jesus closely. ²Sure enough, right in front of him was a man suffering from badly swollen arms and legs.

³Jesus turned to the Pharisees and teachers of the Law. "Is it permitted to heal on the Sabbath?"

⁴No one said a word.

Jesus touched the man, healed him, and sent him away.

⁵He turned to the guests and repeated why it was necessary to work on the Sabbath. "If one of you had an ox or donkey that fell into a pit, wouldn't you immediately pull it out, even on the Sabbath?"

⁶Again, no one dared answer.

⁷After noticing how some of the guests had sought the seats of highest honor, he said, ⁸"When you arrive at a wedding feast, do not take a seat of honor. A more distinguished person might have been invited. ⁹Your host would say to you, 'Give this person your seat.' In shame, you would have to take the lowest seat. ¹⁰Instead, go to the lowest seat first. Then when your host says, 'Friend, move to this higher place,' you will be honored before the other dinner

guests. [11]Those who try to make themselves great will be humbled, and those who humble themselves will be exalted."

[12]Jesus turned to his host. "When you serve the morning or evening meal, do not just invite friends, relatives, and rich neighbors who will return the favor. [13]When you spread a feast, invite the poor, handicapped, lame, and blind. [14]You will be blessed because they have nothing from which they can repay you. When the righteous are raised from the dead, you will be rewarded."

[15]Hearing this, a man sitting at the table said, "Blessed is the man who eats at the feast in the Kingdom of God!"

[16]"A man once planned a huge banquet," Jesus said, "and invited many guests. [17]The hour arrived when everyone should come. He sent his servant to tell them, 'Come, for everything is now ready.' [18]One after another, they made excuses.

"One person said, 'I've just bought a piece of land and must go to see it. Please excuse me.'

[19]"Another said, 'I have purchased five teams of oxen and need to see how they plow. Please accept my apologies.'

[20]"Someone else said, 'I just got married. I am sorry, I cannot come.'

[21]"When the servant returned with the messages, the host was furious. 'Quick!' he told the servant. 'Go into the city streets and alleys and bring in the poor, handicapped, lame, and blind.'

[22]"Soon afterward, the servant said, 'Master, I did what you commanded, and there is still room.'

[23]"'Then go into the country lanes and shaded hedge rows,' the host said. 'Urge people to come. I want my house to be full. [24]I assure you, none of those I first invited will get even a taste of my banquet.'"

[25]Jesus turned to the large crowd that followed him. [26]"Any man who follows me must be willing to forsake father and mother, wife,

brothers and sisters, and children. You must even be willing to give up your own life or you cannot be my disciple. ²⁷Those who will not take up their cross and follow in my footsteps cannot be my disciples.

²⁸"If you were going to build a tower, wouldn't you first sit down and calculate the cost, to be sure you had the resources to complete it? ²⁹Otherwise, you might finish the foundation but not have enough to continue. Others would see your failure and laugh at you, ³⁰saying, 'See that fool? He started to build the tower but was not able to finish.' ³¹What king would ever plan war without first sitting down with his captains to determine whether his ten thousand soldiers could defeat the twenty thousand coming against him? ³²If not, while the opposing forces were still far away, he would send an ambassador to negotiate conditions for peace. ³³Likewise, if you are not ready to give up everything you have, you cannot be my disciple.

³⁴"Salt is a good preservative, but if it loses its saltiness, how will you make it any good? ³⁵Because it has no use, either for food or fertilizer, you would throw it away.

"If you have ears, pay attention to what I am saying."

Chapter 15

¹At this time, many tax collectors and sinners came to hear Jesus.

²The Pharisees and teachers of the Law complained, saying, "This man eats and has fellowship with outcasts."

³So Jesus repeated this illustration: ⁴"What do you think? If a man has a hundred sheep and one wanders away, won't he leave the ninety-nine on the hillside to find the one that is lost? ⁵When he finds the stray, he will carry it on his shoulders, rejoicing. ⁶At home, he will call his friends and neighbors and say, 'Let's celebrate

because I have found my sheep that was lost.' ⁷I assure you, it is the same way in heaven. There will be more rejoicing in heaven over one sinner who repents than for ninety-nine who have not strayed.

⁸"If a woman loses one of her ten silver coins, won't she light a lamp and sweep the house, searching until she finds it? ⁹And when she finds the coin, she will call her friends and neighbors, saying, 'Come rejoice with me! I have found the coin that was lost.' ¹⁰In the same way, there is joy in the presence of God's angels when one sinner repents."

¹¹Jesus said, "There once was a man with two sons, ¹²and the younger son said, 'Father, give me my portion of your estate now.' So his father divided his wealth between the two sons.

¹³"Before long, the young son collected all he had and went to a faraway country, where he wasted all his inheritance on the pursuit of pleasure. ¹⁴About the time his money was gone, a severe famine spread across the land. Penniless and hungry, ¹⁵he went to work for a country farmer, who sent him to feed the pigs. ¹⁶He would have gladly eaten the bean pods he fed to the pigs, but no one gave him anything.

¹⁷"When he came to his senses, he said to himself, *My father's hired men have enough food to throw away, and here I am, starving.* ¹⁸*I will go home and say, 'Father, I have sinned against heaven and before you.* ¹⁹*I am no longer worthy to be called your son, so let me be one of your hired men.'* ²⁰So he headed home.

"He was still a long way off when his father saw him coming. Full of compassion, the father ran to embrace and kiss his son.

²¹"'Father,' the son said, 'I have sinned against heaven and before you. I am no longer worthy to be called your son.'

²²"But the father said to his servants, 'Bring the finest robe and get him cleaned up and dressed. Put a ring on his hand and sandals on his feet. ²³Butcher the best calf so we can have a feast and celebrate,

²⁴because my son was dead and has returned alive. He was lost but now is found.' So they began to celebrate.

²⁵"The older son had been in the field. As he came closer to the house, he heard the sound of music and dancing, ²⁶so he called one of the servants to learn what was going on.

²⁷"'Your brother has returned,' the servant answered. 'Your father has killed the best calf and called for a celebration because your brother is alive and well.'

²⁸"The brother was angry and refused to go in, so his father came out and pleaded with him. ²⁹The brother said, 'For all these years, I have served you and never disobeyed your instructions. You never gave me as much as a scrawny goat so I could have a feast with my friends. ³⁰But the moment this rebel son of yours comes home, the one who wasted your wealth on prostitutes, you kill our best calf for him.'

³¹"'Son, you are always with me,' the father said. 'Everything I have is yours. ³²We had to celebrate, because your brother was dead and has returned alive. He was lost but now is found.'"

Chapter 16

¹Jesus said to his disciples, "Once, a rich man had a manager who was accused of wasting his employer's money. ²He called the manager in. 'What is this I hear about you? I want a complete report of what you have done with my money, because you cannot be my employee any longer.'

³"The manager said to himself, *What am I to do? I am about to be fired. I cannot do hard labor, and I am too proud to beg.* ⁴*I know what I must do so people will receive me into their homes when I no longer have a job.* ⁵One by one, he contacted each of his employer's debtors.

"To the first, he asked, 'How much do you owe?'

⁶"He replied, 'One hundred barrels of olive oil.'

"'Take your bill,' the manager said. 'Sit down right now and write fifty.'

⁷"To the next debtor, he said, 'How much do you owe?'

"'A hundred sacks of wheat,' he replied.

"'Here,' the manager said. 'Take your bill and change it to eighty.'

⁸"The rich man praised the dishonest manager for his creative solution, because the people of the world are more clever in their dishonesty than the godly who do right.

⁹"Here is the point: Use the world's resources to build relationships and help others. When you have nothing left on earth, you will be welcomed at your eternal home in heaven.

¹⁰"Those who are faithful in small concerns will be faithful when much is at stake. And he who is dishonest in petty matters will be dishonest in what is most important. ¹¹If you have not been faithful in handling worldly wealth, how can you be trusted with heaven's riches? ¹²If you cannot be trusted with what belongs to others, who can trust you to do right with what you own?"

¹³As on earlier occasions, he explained, "No one can serve two masters, because you will hate one and love the other, or you will be devoted to one and cheat the other. You cannot serve God and riches at the same time."

¹⁴When the Pharisees heard this, they made fun of Jesus because they loved riches.

¹⁵"You make yourselves look good in public," Jesus told them, "but God sees your heart. That which is most highly admired by people is detested by God. ¹⁶The Law and the prophets spoke until the time of John the Baptizer. Since then, we have preached the Kingdom of God, but people still try to make their own way into the Kingdom. ¹⁷It would be easier for heaven and earth to disappear than for the smallest point of the Law to fail.

¹⁸"Any man who divorces his wife and marries someone else commits adultery. And anyone who marries a divorced woman commits adultery.

¹⁹"There was a rich man," Jesus said, "who dressed in expensive clothes and lived in luxury. ²⁰At the gate to his house lay a poor beggar named Lazarus, covered with sores. ²¹While Lazarus longed for a few leftover scraps from the rich man's table, the dogs licked his sores. ²²One day, the beggar died and was carried by the angels to be with Abraham. The rich man also died and was buried, ²³but his soul was in torment.

"In the place of the dead, the rich man saw Abraham far away, with Lazarus by his side. ²⁴He shouted, 'Father Abraham, have mercy on me! Send Lazarus over here to dip the tip of his finger in water and cool my tongue, because I am suffering in these flames.'

²⁵"Abraham said, 'Son, remember all the good things you received during your life. Lazarus lived in misery, but now he is comfortable while you are in agony. ²⁶Besides, a great abyss separates you and me. No one can cross over.'

²⁷"The rich man said, 'I beg you, Father, if Lazarus cannot come to me, send him to my father's house. ²⁸At least he can warn my five brothers there so they will avoid this place of torment.'

²⁹"'They already have Moses and the prophets,' Abraham said. 'Your brothers can listen to them.'

³⁰"'Oh, no, Father Abraham. If a messenger is sent from the dead, they will surely turn from their sins.'

³¹"But Abraham said, 'If they will not listen to Moses and the prophets, they will not be convinced, even if someone rises from the dead.'"

Chapter 17

¹Jesus said to his followers, "Occasions for stumbling are sure to lead some people to sin, but how terrible it will be for those who bring the temptations. ²It would be better to have a millstone tied around your neck and be thrown into the sea than to cause the innocent to stumble.

³"Watch what you are doing. If a brother does wrong, rebuke him, and if he repents, forgive him. ⁴If he offends you seven times in a day, and seven times in a day he turns to you and says, 'I repent,' you must forgive him."

⁵"Sir," the apostles said, "we need more faith for that."

⁶"More faith? If you had faith as tiny as a mustard seed, you could say to this mulberry tree, 'Be pulled out by the roots and planted in the sea,' and it would obey.

⁷"When a servant comes in from plowing the field or feeding the livestock, does the master say, 'Go get something to eat'? ⁸Of course not. He will say, 'Go prepare dinner and serve me while I eat and drink.' The servant will eat later. ⁹Does the servant receive special thanks for doing what he was told? Probably not. ¹⁰In the same way, when you have done all you were told, say, 'We are unworthy servants who have only done our duty.'"

¹¹On his way back to Jerusalem, Jesus went through the area between Samaria and Galilee. ¹²As he came near to a town, ten leprous men approached. They kept their distance ¹³but cried out to him, "Lord Jesus, have mercy on us!"

¹⁴He looked upon them, fully aware of their condition. "Go show yourselves to the priests."

While they went, they were healed.

¹⁵One of the ten, when he realized he had been healed, turned back. With a loud voice, he kept saying, "Praise God!" ¹⁶He fell at Jesus' feet and thanked him. The man was a Samaritan.

¹⁷"Didn't I heal ten men?" Jesus asked. "Where are the other nine? ¹⁸Except for this foreigner, no one has returned to give glory to God. ¹⁹Stand up, now, and go. Your faith has made you well."

²⁰Some Pharisees asked Jesus when the Kingdom of God would come. "It will come," Jesus said, "but you will not see it. ²¹No one will say, 'Here it is,' or, 'It's right over there.' That is because the Kingdom of God is within you."

²²To his followers, he said, "The time will come when you will long to see the Son of Man, but you cannot. ²³People will say, 'Look, here he is,' or, 'There he is, over there,' but do not listen to them. ²⁴Just as the lightning stretches from one end of the sky to the other, the coming of the Son of Man will be unmistakable. ²⁵First he must suffer many things and be rejected by this generation.

²⁶"When the Son of Man returns, it will be like it was in the days of Noah. ²⁷People were partying and pursuing pleasures until the day Noah entered the ark and the flood came to destroy them. ²⁸It will be like it was in the days of Lot, when people were partying, having fun, working, and conducting business ²⁹until the day Lot left Sodom, and fire and brimstone destroyed the whole city. ³⁰That is how it will be when the Son of Man is revealed.

³¹"On that day, a man on the upper deck should not go back inside his house to get his belongings. He who is in the field should not return home.

³²"Remember what happened to Lot's wife. ³³If you try to save your life, you are going to lose it. But if you lose your life in surrender to God, you will save it.

³⁴"That night, two people will sleep in the same bed, and one will be taken, the other left. ³⁵Two women will be grinding together at the mill, and one will be taken, the other left. ³⁶Two men will be working in the field, and one will be taken, the other left."

³⁷One man asked, "Sir, where will this happen?"

Jesus said, "As the gathering of vultures shows where the carcass is, these signs indicate that the end is near."

Chapter 18

¹To illustrate their need to always pray and never give up, Jesus told a story, ²saying, "There was a judge in town who did not fear God and had no respect for people. ³A woman in his town kept coming to him and begging, 'Give me justice against the one who has done me harm.'

⁴"At first, he refused to hear her case, but he eventually changed his mind. He said to himself, 'I do not fear God or care about people, ⁵but this woman keeps pestering me. If I do not do something, she will wear me out with her endless pleas. Therefore, I will hear her case and give her the justice she wants.'

⁶"Consider how the unrighteous judge responded. ⁷Don't you know that God, who cares for his people, will hear the case and bring justice to those who cry to him day and night? He will not put them off forever. ⁸I am telling you, he will bring justice, and soon. But when the Son of Man comes, will he find such persistent faith on the earth?"

⁹He gave an illustration for those who trusted in themselves, were confident in their own goodness, and despised others. ¹⁰"Two men went to pray at the Temple. One was a Pharisee, the other a tax collector.

¹¹"The Pharisee stood and prayed, 'God, I thank you that I am not like others who are greedy, dishonest, and unfaithful. I thank you that I am nothing like that tax collector over there. ¹²Twice a week, I fast, and I never fail to give you a tenth of my income.'

¹³"The tax collector stood in the distance, away from other people, and would not so much as look up toward heaven. In despair, he

pounded his chest and prayed, 'God, have mercy on me, for I have sinned.'

[14]"I guarantee, the tax collector had peace with God when he went home, not the Pharisee. For those who try to make themselves great will be humbled, and those who humble themselves will be exalted."

[15]Parents brought their infants so Jesus could touch them, but the disciples rebuked them.

[16]"Don't stop them," Jesus said. "Allow the little ones to come to me. Of such is the Kingdom of God. [17]Without exception, I tell you, those who do not accept the Kingdom of God like a young child cannot enter."

[18]A religious leader asked Jesus, "Most excellent Teacher, what good deed must I do to have eternal life?"

[19]"Why do you call me most excellent?" Jesus said. "No one is most excellent except God. [20]You know the commandments. Do not murder, commit adultery, steal, or give false testimony. Honor your parents."

[21]"I've done all that since I was young."

[22]"You lack one thing. Go and sell everything you own, and give the money to the poor. You will have treasure in heaven and can follow me."

[23]Upon hearing this, he became very sad, because he had great wealth.

[24]When Jesus saw his sorrow, he said, "It is nearly impossible for a rich man to enter the Kingdom of God. [25]It is harder for a man of great wealth to enter the Kingdom than for a camel to get through a needle's eye."

[26]Those listening said, "If that is true, then who in the world can be saved?"

²⁷"With men," Jesus said, "it is impossible. But with God, all things are possible."

²⁸Simon Peter said to him, "We have left everything to follow you."

²⁹Jesus said, "I guarantee, those who have sacrificed their homes, relatives, or possessions for sake of the Kingdom ³⁰will receive much more in this life and will have eternal life."

³¹Jesus took the twelve disciples aside and said to them privately, "Listen, we are going to Jerusalem. Everything the prophets have written about the Son of Man must be fulfilled. ³²He will be delivered to the Romans, mocked, insulted, and spat upon. ³³He will be whipped and killed. But on the third day, he will rise again."

³⁴The disciples did not understand. What Jesus said was a mystery they could not figure out.

³⁵As Jesus was passing near Jericho, a blind man sat by the side of the road, begging.

³⁶Hearing the crowd going by, the blind man asked what was happening. ³⁷When he heard that Jesus of Nazareth was near, ³⁸he cried out, "Jesus, Son of David, have mercy on me."

³⁹Those in the crowd who were closest to him rebuked him, telling him to be quiet, but he shouted even louder, "Son of David, have mercy on me!"

⁴⁰So Jesus stopped and called for him.

⁴¹"What do you want me to do for you?" Jesus asked.

"Heal my eyes, sir, so I can see."

⁴²"Look around. Because you believed, you now can see."

⁴³Immediately, his eyes were healed, and he joined those who followed him, glorifying God.

All who saw the miracle praised God as well.

Chapter 19

¹Zacchaeus, a very rich tax collector, was in Jericho ²when Jesus passed through. ³He wanted to see Jesus but could not, because he was much too short to see over the crowd. ⁴So he ran ahead of the procession, climbed a fig tree, and waited for him to come his way.

⁵When Jesus came to the tree, he looked up and saw him. "Zacchaeus, hurry down from there, for I must be a guest at your house today."

⁶Zacchaeus scrambled down the tree and gladly welcomed Jesus.

⁷The people who saw what had happened complained, "He has gone to be the guest of a sinner."

⁸Later, Zacchaeus stood before Jesus. "Sir, I will give half my wealth to the poor. If I have defrauded anyone, I will pay back four times the amount."

⁹"Today," Jesus said, "salvation has come to this house, because this man has shown himself to be a true son of Abraham. ¹⁰For the Son of Man has come to find and save those who are lost."

¹¹While the people surrounded him, listening, he gave this illustration, because they were near Jerusalem and some people thought the Kingdom of God was about to appear. ¹²"A prince went to a faraway country to be made king and then return. ¹³Before leaving, he called ten servants and gave each of them three months' wages. 'Take care of business until I get back,' he said.

¹⁴"Citizens who hated the prince sent delegates to say to the one who would appoint him, 'We do not want this man ruling over us.'

¹⁵"Nevertheless, he was made king and came home. He called his servants to find out how they had done with his money.

¹⁶"The first said, 'Sir, I have gained ten times as much with your money.'

¹⁷"'Well done,' the king said. 'Because you have been faithful with a small amount, I am appointing you to govern ten of my cities.'

¹⁸"The second servant said, 'Sir, I have gained five times as much with your money.'

¹⁹"'Well done,' the king said. 'You will govern five of my cities.'

²⁰"Another servant said, 'Sir, here is your money back. I kept it wrapped up and safe while you were gone. ²¹I was afraid to do more, because I knew how demanding you are. You get a return with no investment. You reap a harvest where you have not planted.'

²²"The king said, 'You worthless servant! Your own words condemn you. If you knew I was demanding, reaping where I did not plant, ²³why didn't you at least invest the money with a lender? Then when I returned, I could have had my investment with added interest.'

²⁴"He said to those standing nearby, 'Take his money and give it to the one who earned ten times as much.'

²⁵"But they objected, saying, 'But sir, he already has so much.'

²⁶"The king said, 'More will be given to those who use what they have. But those who do not will lose what little they have. ²⁷Now, bring those citizens who did not want me to be king and let them be executed in my presence.'"

²⁸After saying this, Jesus left for Jerusalem.

²⁹As Jesus approached Bethphage past Bethany, he stopped at the Mount of Olives and sent two disciples ahead, ³⁰saying, "Go to the next village. There, you will find a colt that has never been ridden. Untie it, and bring it to me. ³¹If someone asks, 'Why are you taking that donkey?' say, 'The Master needs it.'"

³²The disciples did as they were told and found the colt, just as Jesus had said they would. ³³As they were untying it, the owners asked, "Why are you taking that donkey?" ³⁴and they said, "The

Master needs it." ³⁵They brought the colt and laid their coats on its back for Jesus to sit on.

³⁶As he went, people spread their garments on the road before him. ³⁷At the valley beyond the Mount of Olives, as Jesus came near to Jerusalem, a joyful crowd of followers cheered and shouted praises for all the miracles they had seen, ³⁸saying, "Blessed is the king sent by God, who brings peace. Let the heavens rejoice and God be glorified!"

³⁹Some Pharisees in the crowd complained to Jesus, "Teacher, you should rebuke your followers for saying such things."

⁴⁰"You can be certain," Jesus said, "that if they kept quiet, the stones would have to shout praises."

⁴¹As he came closer to the city, he wept. ⁴²"Oh, if you only knew the peace that is available to you today, but you cannot see it. ⁴³The day will come when your enemies will surround and lay siege upon you from all sides. ⁴⁴They will cut you down, level with the ground, with you and your children within the walls. Because you failed to recognize your time of visitation, they will not leave one stone standing on another."

⁴⁵When Jesus entered the Temple, he drove out the merchants doing business there, ⁴⁶saying to them, "The scriptures say the Temple will be called a house of prayer, but you have turned it into a hangout for robbers."

⁴⁷He continued to teach in the Temple, but the chief priests and teachers of the Law looked for some way to get rid of him. ⁴⁸But they were unable to do anything because the people were so captivated by his teaching.

Chapter 20

¹One day in the Temple, as Jesus was teaching and proclaiming the good news to the people, the chief priests, Jewish leaders, and

teachers of the Law ²asked, "What right do you have to do these things? Who gave you the authority?"

³"First, let me ask you a question. Tell me, ⁴from where did John receive his authority to baptize? Was it from God or men?"

⁵They discussed the question among themselves. "If we say, 'From God,' he will ask why we did not believe him. ⁶But if we say, 'From men,' the people will stone us because they all regard John as a prophet."

⁷So they said to Jesus, "We don't know."

⁸"Then I won't tell you by what authority I do these things."

⁹Jesus used this illustration as he spoke to the people. "A landowner planted a vineyard, left it under the care of sharecroppers, and went to another country for a long time.

¹⁰"At harvest season, he sent a servant to collect his share from the vineyard, but the sharecroppers grabbed and beat him, sending him away with nothing. ¹¹So the landowner sent another servant. They also beat him and ran him off with nothing but their insults. ¹²When a third servant was sent, they wounded him and threw him out.

¹³"The owner of the vineyard said, 'What can I do? I know. I will send my only son. Surely they will respect him.'

¹⁴"When the sharecroppers saw him coming, they said to themselves, 'He is the heir. If we kill him, we can have his inheritance.' ¹⁵So they dragged him out of the vineyard and killed him.

"What do you think the landowner will do to those sharecroppers? ¹⁶He will destroy those men and find others who will give him his share of the harvest."

After hearing this, the people listening to Jesus said, "This must never happen!"

¹⁷Looking straight at them, Jesus said, "Haven't you read the scripture? *The stone that the builders rejected has become the cornerstone.*

¹⁸Those who fall on this stone will be broken, but those on whom this stone falls will be crushed."

¹⁹The chief priests and teachers of the Law realized that he was talking about them, so they wanted to arrest him.

²⁰The Jewish leaders kept watching Jesus and sent spies who pretended to be interested in his teaching. They wanted to trap Jesus into saying something they could use against him, so they could arrest and deliver him to the Roman authorities. ²¹"Teacher," the spies said, "we know you are sincere and completely honest. You teach the truth about God's ways without concern for what people think. ²²Is it right to pay taxes to Caesar?"

²³Jesus recognized their scheming. "Why are you testing me? ²⁴Show me a coin used to pay the tax. Whose image and inscription does it have?"

"Caesar's," they said.

²⁵"Then pay to Caesar what belongs to him, and give God all that is God's."

²⁶His reply gave them nothing to use in accusation before the people. Amazed at his answer, they said no more.

²⁷Some Sadducees, who believed there was no resurrection, came to question Jesus. ²⁸"Teacher, Moses said, *If a brother dies with no children, the widow must not marry someone outside the family. The surviving brother should marry her and have children for him.*

²⁹"Once, there were seven brothers and the oldest brother married and died without children. ³⁰After marrying the widow, the second brother had no children when he died. ³¹The third brother did the same. This continued until the barren wife had married all seven brothers. ³²Finally, the woman died, still childless.

³³"On the day when the dead rise to life, whose wife will this woman be? All seven were married to her."

³⁴Jesus said, "People in this world get married, ³⁵but those worthy of resurrection enter another world, where marriage does not exist. ³⁶They cannot die, but are like the angels. They will be God's children because they have been raised to life.

³⁷"Now, on the issue of rising from the dead, consider what God said to Moses from the burning bush: *I am the God of Abraham, the God of Isaac, and the God of Jacob.* ³⁸He is a God of the living, not of the dead. To him, we are all alive."

³⁹Some teachers of the Law said, "Teacher, that is a very good answer!"

⁴⁰After that, no one wanted to question him further.

⁴¹Then Jesus asked the religious scholars a question. "How can the teachers of the Law say the Messiah is David's son? ⁴²David himself said in the Psalms, *God said unto my Lord, 'Sit here at my right hand* ⁴³*until I have put all your enemies beneath your feet.'* ⁴⁴If David called him Lord, how can he be his son?"

⁴⁵With everyone listening, Jesus said to his followers, ⁴⁶"Watch out for the teachers of the Law who wear luxurious robes and love to be recognized in the marketplace. At feasts and in the synagogues, they love the seats of honor. ⁴⁷Because they take advantage of widows while making long prayers to appear righteous, they will be punished most severely."

Chapter 21

¹In the Temple, Jesus watched the rich people putting their money into the offering box. ²He also saw a poor widow put in two copper coins that were worth next to nothing. ³Jesus said, "The truth is, the poor widow has given more than all the others. ⁴Everyone else gave a portion of their abundance that they will never miss, but she has given all she had to live on."

⁵Some were talking about the temple, how magnificent the stone-work was and the beauty of the furnishings that had been given.

⁶"Do you see these things as something great?" Jesus asked. "Their destruction will be so great, one stone will not be left standing on the other."

⁷His disciples asked, "Teacher, when will all these things happen? How will we know when the time is at hand?"

⁸"Be careful," Jesus said. "Do not let anyone deceive you. Many will claim to be the Messiah and say the time has come. Do not follow them. ⁹Do not panic when you hear about wars or battle threats. Such things must happen, but that does not mean the end has come.

¹⁰"Nation will war against nation and kingdom against kingdom. ¹¹There will be earthquakes, famines, and plagues in various places. There will be terrifying events and great signs from heaven.

¹²"Before the end, people will arrest you and have you flogged because you follow me. They will deliver you to their synagogues and prisons. You will stand before kings and magistrates, ¹³but this will be an opportunity for you to testify about me. ¹⁴Do not worry about how you will answer the charges brought against you. ¹⁵I will give you words of wisdom that your adversaries cannot refute.

¹⁶"Even relatives and friends will betray you, and some of you will be executed. ¹⁷Because of my name, you will be hated by people everywhere. ¹⁸Don't worry. Not even a hair of your head will actually be lost. ¹⁹By standing firm until the end, you will be saved.

²⁰"When you see Jerusalem surrounded by soldiers, you will know its destruction is at hand. ²¹Those in Judea should flee to the mountains. Those in the city must escape, and those in the country must not return to the city. ²²These will be days of vengeance when all that has been written will be fulfilled.

²³"How terrible it will be for pregnant women and nursing mothers. There will be disaster in the land, and people will suffer horribly. ²⁴They will die by the sword or be taken captive. Jerusalem will be trampled by the Gentiles until their time has been fulfilled.

²⁵"There will be signs in the sun, moon, and stars. The earth will be in turmoil, with violent tides and furious seas. ²⁶People will be terrified when they see what is happening in the earth, how the powers of the universe will be shaken. ²⁷They will see the Son of Man arrive in the clouds, with power and great glory.

²⁸"When these things begin to happen, look up and be glad, for your redemption is near."

²⁹Jesus gave this illustration about the fig and other trees: ³⁰"When the branches bud and start to put on leaves, you know that summer is near. ³¹In the same way, when you see these things come to pass, you will know the Kingdom of God is near. ³²You can be sure, when all these things have been fulfilled, this age will come to its close. ³³Heaven and earth will pass away, but my words will stand forever.

³⁴"Be careful. Do not let partying and the pursuit of pleasures overcome your heart, or that day will come unexpectedly, ³⁵like a trap. For that day will come upon everyone on earth. ³⁶Always be watching. Constantly pray so you can escape the terrors and stand before the Son of Man."

³⁷During the day, Jesus taught in the Temple. He spent each night on the Mount of Olives.

³⁸People came early to hear him in the Temple.

Chapter 22

¹It was almost time for Passover, the Feast of Unleavened Bread. ²The chief priests and teachers of the Law sought a means to covertly

capture Jesus and put him to death, because they feared how the people might react.

³Judas Iscariot, one of the twelve, thought of a devilish plan, ⁴left the other disciples, and talked to the chief priests and teachers of the Law about how he could betray Jesus to them. ⁵They were delighted and promised to pay, ⁶so he agreed and looked for a good place and time when he could hand him over without any people around.

⁷On the day of Unleavened Bread, when the Passover lambs must be killed, ⁸Jesus said to Simon Peter and John, "Go prepare the Passover meal so we may eat together."

⁹They asked, "Where do you want us to go?"

¹⁰"Go into the city. When you see a man carrying a pitcher of water, follow him. ¹¹Say to the owner of the house that he enters, 'The Teacher says, "Where is the room where I shall eat the Passover meal with my disciples?"' ¹²He will show you a large upstairs room that is furnished and ready for our use. Make preparations there."

¹³The disciples went into the city, found everything exactly as Jesus had said, and prepared the meal.

¹⁴When the time came, Jesus sat with the disciples at the table. ¹⁵Jesus said, "I have looked forward to eating this Passover meal with you before I suffer. ¹⁶I will not eat of it again until all has been fulfilled in the Kingdom of God."

¹⁷He held the cup, offered thanks, and passed it to the disciples. "Take this wine and drink, all of you. ¹⁸I will not drink wine again until the Kingdom of God has come."

¹⁹He took the bread, blessed it, broke it, and passed it to the disciples. "This is my body that is given for you. Do this to remember me."

²⁰In the same way, he held the cup after they had eaten and said, "This cup is the new agreement sealed with my blood.

²¹"Listen. The one who will turn against me is with me at this table. ²²I, the Son of Man, must suffer as it has been planned, but how terrible it will be for the man who turns against me."

²³The disciples talked among themselves as they questioned who would do such a thing.

²⁴They got into an argument over which one of them would be considered greatest in the Kingdom.

²⁵Jesus said to them, "Pagan kings exercise power over their subjects and are honored as if they cared for the people. ²⁶You shall not be like them. The greatest among you must behave as the least. The leader is the one who serves. ²⁷Who is greater, the man who sits at the table or the one who serves him? You think it is the one at the table, but I am with you as a servant.

²⁸"You have stuck with me throughout my trials. ²⁹I confer power upon you as my Father conferred power upon me ³⁰so you may eat and drink at my table in my Kingdom and sit on thrones, judging the twelve tribes of Israel.

³¹"Simon, listen. Satan has asked to test you as a farmer sifts the good grain from the chaff. ³²I have prayed that your faith will not fail. After you have repented, strengthen your brothers."

³³"Sir," Peter said, "I am ready to go anywhere with you, even to prison and death."

³⁴"I guarantee," Jesus said, "before the rooster crows tonight, you will deny me three times."

³⁵Jesus asked his disciples, "When I sent you without money, a change of clothes, or extra sandals, did you lack anything?"

They replied, "Nothing."

³⁶"But now, take money and provisions. If you have no sword, sell your clothes and buy one. ³⁷What the scripture says about me must be fulfilled. *He was treated as one of the criminals.* These things are coming to a close."

³⁸"Look, sir," the disciples said. "Here are two swords."

"That is enough."

³⁹Jesus left the city for the Mount of Olives, as he often did. His disciples followed him. ⁴⁰When they arrived at Gethsemane, Jesus said to his disciples, "Pray that you do not fall into temptation."

⁴¹He went about a stone's throw away, knelt, and prayed, ⁴²"My Father, if you are willing, let me escape this suffering. Nevertheless, I want your will, not mine."

⁴³An angel from heaven appeared and strengthened him.

⁴⁴In extreme agony, Jesus prayed more earnestly. His sweat was like drops of blood falling to the ground. ⁴⁵Afterward, he found his disciples asleep, exhausted from grief. ⁴⁶"Why are you sleeping? Stay alert and pray so you do not fall into temptation."

⁴⁷While Jesus was still speaking, Judas, one of the twelve, arrived to give Jesus the customary kiss of greeting. He was followed by a mob.

⁴⁸"Judas," Jesus said, "would you betray the Son of Man with a kiss?"

⁴⁹When the disciples saw what was about to happen, they asked, "Sir, shall we use our swords to fight?" ⁵⁰One of them drew a sword and cut off the high priest's servant's right ear.

⁵¹"Stop! That is enough." Jesus touched the servant's ear and healed him.

⁵²He turned to the mob and spoke to the chief priests, Temple guards, and Jewish leaders. "Am I a hardened criminal that you must capture me with swords and clubs? ⁵³Every day, I taught in the Temple. Why didn't you arrest me there? This is your time, when the power of darkness prevails."

⁵⁴The arresting guards took Jesus to the house of the high priest. Peter followed at a distance. ⁵⁵After the guards built a fire in the

middle of the courtyard and were seated together, Peter joined them.

⁵⁶A servant girl looked closely at him as he sat in the firelight. "This man was with Jesus."

⁵⁷He denied having been with Jesus. "Woman, I do not know the man."

⁵⁸Another servant girl noticed him and said, "You are one of them."

Again, he denied any knowledge of Jesus, and said, "No, I am not!"

⁵⁹An hour later, someone else insisted, "It's true. This man was with him, for he is also Galilean."

⁶⁰Peter denied any connection with Jesus. "I do not know this man you are talking about." While he was still speaking, a rooster crowed.

⁶¹Jesus turned and looked at him.

Then Peter remembered what Jesus had said: "Before the rooster crows, you will deny me three times."

⁶²He went outside and broke down crying.

⁶³The guards who held Jesus mocked him and beat him. ⁶⁴After blindfolding him, they slapped him on the face. "Prophesy to us. Tell us who hit you." ⁶⁵They insulted him with many other cruel words.

⁶⁶At dawn, the chief priests, Jewish leaders, and teachers of the Law convened in the full council. ⁶⁷"Tell us," they said, "are you the Messiah?"

"If I tell you," Jesus said, "you will not believe me. ⁶⁸If I asked you a question, you would not answer. ⁶⁹From now on, the Son of Man will sit at the right hand of almighty God."

⁷⁰"Then you claim to be the Son of God?"

"Yes, you could say that."

[71]"We do not need any more testimony," they said. "From his own lips, we have heard his blasphemy."

Chapter 23

[1]The entire council took Jesus to Pilate [2]and began to accuse him. "We judged this man for misleading the people. He forbids paying taxes to Caesar and says he is the anointed king."

[3]Pilate asked him, "Are you the king of the Jews?"

"Yes, you could say that."

[4]Pilate said, "I do not find this man guilty of any crime."

[5]They became more insistent. "He stirs up trouble among people from Galilee to Jerusalem with his teaching."

[6]When Pilate heard about Galilee, he questioned whether Jesus was Galilean. [7]As soon as he ascertained that Jesus was under the jurisdiction of Herod Antipas, he sent him to Herod, who was in Jerusalem at the time.

[8]Herod was delighted to see Jesus, because he had heard many stories and had wanted to meet him for a long time. He hoped to see him perform a miracle. [9]He asked many questions, but Jesus said nothing.

[10]The chief priests and teachers of the Law shouted accusations against him.

[11]Herod and his soldiers made fun of Jesus, taunting and mocking him. They dressed him in a kingly robe and sent him back to Pilate.

[12]On that day, Herod and Pilate, who had been enemies, became friends.

[13]Pilate called the people, including the chief priests and Jewish leaders, [14]and said to them, "You brought this man to me, saying he was a troublemaker who misled the people. While you were here, I questioned him thoroughly concerning your accusations, and I found him not guilty. [15]Herod arrived at the same conclusion

and sent him back to me. He has done nothing to deserve death. [16]Therefore, I will order him flogged and released."

[17]At every Passover feast, Pilate would release one prisoner to the people.

[18]All the people shouted in protest, "Take this man away, and release Barabbas to us."

[19]Barabbas had been imprisoned for murder and leading a rebellion in Jerusalem.

[20]Again, Pilate appealed to the crowd, because he wanted to release Jesus.

[21]"Crucify him," the crowd screamed. "Crucify him!"

[22]For the third time, he defended Jesus. "Why? What crime has he committed? I find no reason to sentence him to death. Therefore, I will order him flogged and released."

[23]The crowd went into an uproar, shouting for Jesus to be crucified. The violent cries of the people and chief priests prevailed. [24]So Pilate granted the sentence that the people demanded. [25]To satisfy the people's desire, he released Barabbas, who had been imprisoned for murder and rebellion, and ordered Jesus to be crucified.

[26]On the way, the soldiers met Simon, a native of Cyrene, who had come from the country. They forced him to walk behind Jesus and carry his cross.

[27]A large crowd followed, including many women who mourned and cried.

[28]Jesus turned to them. "Daughters of Jerusalem, do not cry for me. Cry for yourselves and your children. [29]The day will come when people will say, 'Blessed are the childless who have never nursed a baby.' [30]They will say to the mountains, 'Fall on us,' and beg the hills to hide them. [31]If they do these things to a living tree, what will they do to you who are dry wood?"

[32]Two others, both criminals, were taken with Jesus to be crucified.

³³When the soldiers reached the place called the "skull," they nailed Jesus to the cross. The criminals were crucified with him, one on the right, the other on the left.

³⁴"Father, forgive them," Jesus prayed, "because they do not know what they are doing."

The soldiers threw dice for the fair dividing of his clothes.

³⁵The people stood there, watching.

The Jewish leaders mocked him. "He saved others," they said. "Let's see if he can save himself. Then we'll know if he's really the Messiah, the chosen of God."

³⁶The soldiers also mocked him. They offered him sour wine ³⁷and said, "If you are the king of the Jews, save yourself."

³⁸A sign above his head said, "This is the king of the Jews."

³⁹One of the criminals joined in the mockery. "If you are the Messiah, save yourself, and save us too."

⁴⁰The second criminal said to the first, "Don't you fear God since you have been sentenced to the same death? ⁴¹We deserve our punishment, but this man has done nothing wrong." ⁴²He said to Jesus, "Sir, remember me when you enter your Kingdom."

⁴³"I guarantee," Jesus said, "you will be with me in paradise today."

⁴⁴From about noon until three o'clock, darkness covered the land. ⁴⁵The sun gave no light, and the Temple veil ripped in two.

⁴⁶Jesus screamed, "Father, I place my life in your hands," and he quit breathing.

⁴⁷When the centurion saw what had happened, he honored God by saying, "Truly, this man was innocent."

⁴⁸The crowd that had come to witness the crucifixion left in deep sorrow after they saw Jesus die. ⁴⁹But those who knew Jesus, including the women who had followed from Galilee, continued to watch from a distance.

⁵⁰A good and righteous man named Joseph, a member of the council, ⁵¹disagreed with the decisions and actions of the other council members. He was from the Jewish city of Arimathea and waited for the Kingdom of God. ⁵²He went before Pilate and asked for the body of Jesus. ⁵³Then he took the body down from the cross, wrapped it in linen, and laid it in an unused tomb that was cut into the rock.

⁵⁴It was the day of preparation, almost at sundown that would begin the Sabbath. ⁵⁵The women from Galilee followed him and saw the tomb where Jesus' body was placed. ⁵⁶They went home to prepare spices and ointments but did not go back to the tomb, because it was the Sabbath day of rest required by the Law.

Chapter 24

¹At the break of dawn on the first day of the week, the women went to the tomb with spices they had prepared. ²The stone had already been rolled back from the entrance. ³They walked in, but Jesus' body was not there.

⁴While they stood there, wondering what had happened, two men appeared in dazzling clothes. ⁵Terrified, the women bowed their faces to the ground.

The men said to them, "Why do you look for the living among the dead? ⁶He is not here, because he has risen. Do you remember what he told you while he was in Galilee? ⁷The Son of Man must be delivered into the hands of sinful men to be crucified, and he will rise on the third day."

⁸Then the women remembered what Jesus had said. ⁹They left the tomb to tell the eleven apostles and all the other disciples. ¹⁰Mary Magdalene, Joanna, Mary the mother of James, and the women who were with them also told these things to the apostles. ¹¹But their words seemed like a fairy tale, so the men did not believe them.

¹²Peter ran to the tomb, stooped down, and saw the pieces of linen lying by themselves. Then he left, wondering what had happened.

¹³On the same day, two of Jesus' followers left for Emmaus, about seven miles from Jerusalem. ¹⁴As they walked, they talked about everything that had happened. ¹⁵While they discussed the events and reasoned together, Jesus came near and walked with them, ¹⁶but they were kept from recognizing him.

¹⁷"What are you talking about?" Jesus asked. "Why are you so sad?"

¹⁸One of the two, Cleopas, said, "Are you the only visitor to Jerusalem who does not know what has happened in the last few days?"

¹⁹"What are you talking about?"

"Jesus of Nazareth. He was a prophet who did incredible miracles and was a powerful teacher in the eyes of God and all the people. ²⁰Our chief priests and religious leaders delivered him to be sentenced to death and crucified. ²¹We had hoped he was the one who would liberate Israel. It has been three days since these things happened. ²²Some women of our group were at the tomb early this morning and brought an unbelievable report. ²³They could not find his body, they said, but they saw a vision of angels who said he was alive. ²⁴Some of our men went to the tomb and saw that the body was gone, just as the women had said, but they did not see him."

²⁵"Why don't you understand?" Jesus asked. "You are so slow to believe what the prophets have said. ²⁶Wasn't it necessary for the Messiah to suffer these things before entering his glory?" ²⁷Beginning with Moses and all the prophets, Jesus took them through the scriptures and explained everything concerning himself.

²⁸As they came to Emmaus, Jesus acted as if he would go farther.

²⁹"Stay with us," the two begged. "It's getting late, and there is little daylight left." So he went with them.

³⁰As they sat down to eat, Jesus took the bread and gave thanks. He broke off a piece and gave the loaf to them.

³¹Their eyes were opened, and they recognized him.

Then he disappeared.

³²They said to each other, "Didn't our hearts burn within us while we were on the road and he explained the scriptures?"

³³At once, they returned to Jerusalem and found the eleven disciples gathered with the others. ³⁴"It's true," Cleopas said. "The Lord Jesus has risen. It's not my word alone. Simon was with me, and he saw him too." ³⁵They told what had happened on the way to Emmaus and how they recognized Jesus when he broke the bread.

³⁶While the disciples talked about what had happened, Jesus appeared and stood among them. "Peace be with you."

³⁷Startled by what they thought was a ghost, they were terrified.

³⁸"Why are you fearful?" Jesus asked. "Why do you question who I am? ³⁹Look at my hands and feet. Touch me, and see for yourself. Ghosts do not have flesh and bone as I have."

⁴⁰As he spoke, he showed them his scarred hands and feet.

⁴¹In their joy and amazement, this seemed too good to be true. Jesus asked them, "May I have something to eat?"

⁴²They gave him a piece of broiled fish ⁴³and watched him eat it.

⁴⁴Jesus said to them, "When I was with you, I told you that everything written in the Law of Moses, the prophets, and the psalms concerning me must be fulfilled." ⁴⁵He opened their minds to understand the scriptures ⁴⁶and said, "It is written that the Messiah must suffer and will rise from the dead on the third day. ⁴⁷Beginning in Jerusalem, repentance and forgiveness of sins must be preached among all nations. ⁴⁸You have been eyewitnesses of these things. ⁴⁹As my Father promised, I will send the Holy Spirit upon you. Wait in Jerusalem until you are equipped with power from heaven."

⁵⁰After leading them to a place near Bethany, Jesus lifted his hands and blessed them. ⁵¹While he blessed them, he was lifted up into heaven.

⁵²They worshiped him and returned to Jerusalem, rejoicing.

⁵³They were continually in the Temple, praying and praising God.

John

Chapter 1

[1]The Word was with God, and he was God, in the beginning. [2]He already existed. [3]Everything was created by him. Nothing exists that he did not make. [4]Life itself came from him, and this life gives light to everyone. [5]The light shone in the darkness, and the darkness could not overcome it.

[6]God sent John the Baptizer to spread the news about the light [7]so people might believe. [8]John was not the light, but he came to testify [9]that the true light would come into the world to shine on everyone.

[10]Although the Word made the world, people in the world did not recognize him when he came. [11]He lived among his own people. Despite his unfailing love and faithfulness, most people did not accept him. [12]But he gave those who believed and accepted him the right to become God's children. [13]They were born again, not physically out of human desire, but spiritually by the will of God.

[14]The Word became human and we have seen the majestic splendor of Jesus Christ, the Word of Life, and the glory of the only son of the Father.

[15]John the Baptizer pointed out Jesus, then shouted to the crowds, "This is the one I was talking about when I said, 'Someone is coming who is far greater than I am, because he existed long before I did.'"

[16]All believers can benefit from his rich grace by which he has blessed us repeatedly. [17]Moses gave us the Law, but Jesus Christ gave us grace and truth.

[18]No one has ever seen God. However, his son, who came from him, has revealed him to us.

[19]The Jews sent a group of priests and Temple officials to inquire about John's identity. "Who are you?" they asked.

[20]Without hesitation, John answered, "I am not the Messiah."

[21]"Who are you? Elijah?"

"No, absolutely not."

"Are you the Prophet, the one foretold by Moses?"

"No, I am not."

[22]"Then who are you? We must give an answer to those who sent us. What do you have to say about yourself?"

[23]Quoting from Isaiah the prophet, John said, "I am the one who is shouting, *'Clear a path in the wilderness, because the Lord our God is coming.'*"

[24]Some of the Pharisees [25]asked, "If you are not the Messiah, Elijah, or the Prophet, why do you baptize?"

[26]"I only baptize with water. One stands among you whom you do not recognize. [27]Although his ministry follows mine, I am not worthy to untie the straps of his sandals."

[28]This encounter happened at Bethany on the other side of the Jordan River, where John was baptizing.

[29]The next day, John saw Jesus coming and shouted, "Look! The Lamb of God, who takes away the sin of the world. [30]He is the one I was talking about when I said, 'A man is coming after me who is much greater than I am' because he existed long before me. [31]I did not know who he was. I only knew that I must baptize people so he might be revealed to Israel."

[32]John gave this proof: "I saw the Spirit of God descend from the sky like a dove and remain upon him. [33]I would not have known him, but the one who sent me to baptize said, 'The man on whom you see the Spirit descend and remain is he who will baptize with the

Holy Spirit.' ³⁴With my own eyes, I saw it and can testify without reservation. He is the Son of God."

³⁵The next day, John was again at the Jordan River, this time with two of his disciples. ³⁶When he looked up and saw Jesus passing by, he said, "Look! The Lamb of God."

³⁷So the two disciples decided to follow Jesus.

³⁸Jesus turned and saw them following. "What do you want?"

"Rabbi," they said, meaning Teacher, "where are you staying?"

³⁹"Come and see."

It was about ten o'clock in the morning, so they went to where he was staying and spent the day with him.

⁴⁰One of the two disciples who heard John and followed Jesus was Andrew, Simon Peter's brother. ⁴¹Before John reached his brother James, Andrew reached his own brother Simon and said, "We have found the Messiah, the Anointed One."

⁴²Andrew brought Simon to meet Jesus.

"You are Simon, son of Jonah," Jesus said, looking intently at him. "You will be called Cephas," which is translated Peter, meaning Rock.

⁴³The next day, Jesus left for Galilee. On the way, he met Philip and said, "Follow me."

⁴⁴Like Andrew and Peter, Philip was from the town of Bethsaida. ⁴⁵He ran ahead and found Nathanael sitting under a fig tree, meditating on who the Messiah would be: *Behold, a true Israelite in whom is no deceit*—

Philip interrupted his thoughts. "We've found the one Moses wrote about in the Law, the one described by the prophets—Jesus, the son of Joseph, from Nazareth."

⁴⁶"Nazareth? Can anything good come from there?"

Philip answered, "Come see for yourself."

[47]As Nathanael approached, Jesus said, "Behold, a true Israelite in whom is no deceit."

[48]"How can you know what I was thinking?" Nathanael asked.

"I saw you while you were still under the fig tree, before Philip called you."

[49]"Teacher!" Nathanael exclaimed. "You really are the Son of God, the King of Israel."

[50]"Do you believe just because I told you I saw you under the fig tree? You will see greater things than this. [51]Without a doubt, you will see the skies open and the angels of God going up and down on the Son of Man."

Chapter 2

[1]Three days later, there was a wedding at Cana in Galilee. Jesus' mother, Mary, was there. [2]Jesus and his disciples were guests.

[3]When the supply of wine ran low, Mary said to him, "They have no more wine."

[4]"Mother," Jesus said, "you must not tell me what to do. My time has not yet come."

[5]Mary said to the servants, "Do whatever he tells you."

[6]Six stone water jars stood nearby, the kind used for ritual washings. Each could hold twenty to thirty gallons.

[7]"Fill the jars with water," Jesus said.

So the servants filled them to the brim.

[8]"Now, dip some out and take it to the host."

[9]When the host tasted the water that had been turned into wine, he did not know where it had come from. Of course, the servants knew. The host called the bridegroom aside and said, [10]"Normally, everyone brings the choice wine first. After the guests have had too much to drink, they bring the cheaper wine. You have saved the best until now."

¹¹This miracle at Cana in Galilee was the first sign of Jesus' majesty, and his disciples believed in him.

¹²After this, Jesus went with his mother, brothers, and disciples to Capernaum, but he did not stay there very long. ¹³That spring, when it was almost time for the Jewish Passover celebration, Jesus went up to Jerusalem.

¹⁴In the Temple, he found merchants selling cattle, sheep, and doves for sacrifices. Dealers had set up tables to exchange foreign money for the half-shekel Temple tax. ¹⁵After making a whip from small cords, Jesus drove out the sheep and cattle, scattered the moneychangers' coins, and overturned their tables.

¹⁶To those who sold the doves, he said, "Get these things out of here. Do not make my Father's house a marketplace."

¹⁷Then his followers were reminded of the passage from the Psalms: *Passion for your house burns like fire within me.*

¹⁸The Jewish leaders demanded of him an answer. "What miraculous sign can you show us to prove you have the right to do this?"

¹⁹"All right," Jesus said. "Destroy this temple, and in three days I will raise it up."

²⁰"It took forty-six years to build this Temple," they said in disbelief. "Can you rebuild it in three days?"

²¹When Jesus said "this temple," he referred to his own body.

²²After he had risen from the dead, his disciples remembered what he had said. They believed the scriptures and his words.

²³Many people came to the Passover celebration in Jerusalem. When they saw the miracles Jesus did, they believed. ²⁴But Jesus did not trust them, because he understood human nature. ²⁵No one had to explain to him what people were really like.

Chapter 3

¹Nicodemus, a Pharisee and member of the Jewish ruling council, ²came to Jesus at night. "Rabbi, we know you are a teacher sent from God. Your miracles prove your authority."

³"I can guarantee," Jesus said, "you will never see the Kingdom of God unless you are born again."

⁴"What do you mean? A grown man cannot enter his mother's womb and be born a second time."

⁵"I assure you, no one will enter the Kingdom of God without being born of water and the Spirit. ⁶Flesh gives birth to flesh, but the Spirit gives birth to spirit. ⁷You should not be surprised at my saying, 'You must be born again.' ⁸You do not doubt the existence of the wind that blows wherever it wants, although you cannot tell where it comes from or where it is going. So it is with those born of the Spirit."

⁹"I still do not understand how this is possible."

¹⁰"You teach the people of Israel, and you do not understand? ¹¹Reality is, we speak from what we know and testify to what we have seen. Instead of accepting my testimony, you question it. ¹²If I give you an earthly example and you cannot grasp the truth, how will you believe what is heavenly? ¹³No one has seen God except the one who came from him—the Son of Man. ¹⁴Moses attached a bronze serpent to a pole in the wilderness. In the same way, the Son of Man must be lifted up ¹⁵so everyone who believes in him may live.

¹⁶"For God so loved the world that he gave his only son, so that everyone who believes in him will not die but will live forever. ¹⁷God sent the Son, not to judge, but to save the world. ¹⁸God will not condemn whoever believes in him, but he has already judged unbelievers for choosing not to accept God's one and only son.

¹⁹"This is why God condemns people: Light has come into the world, but people love the darkness, not the light, because their deeds are evil. ²⁰People who do evil hate the light and will not come near it for fear that the light will expose their sins. ²¹But those who love truth and desire to do right will come to the light so others can see they are doing what God wants."

²²After the meeting with Nicodemus, Jesus and his disciples left Jerusalem and went into the Judean countryside. They spent a significant amount of time there, baptizing people.

²³John the Baptizer was at Aenon near Salim because the water there was plentiful, and people were constantly coming to be baptized.

²⁴This was before John had been imprisoned.

²⁵John's disciples and a certain Jew argued over whose message about repentance was most effective. ²⁶They came to John and said, "Teacher, the man who was with you on the east side of the Jordan, the one you pointed out, is also baptizing, and everyone is going to him."

²⁷"A man can receive only what God gives him," John said. ²⁸"You heard me testify, 'I am not the Anointed One, only the one sent ahead of him.' ²⁹At a wedding, the groom gets married. The attendant only stands with him, glad to listen and do anything he asks. My joy is complete ³⁰as he becomes greater and I become less. ³¹He who comes from above is greater than those below.

³²"We speak of earthly things. He reveals the truth from heaven, yet not everyone believes him. ³³Anyone who believes his message confirms the truth of God. ³⁴The one sent from God speaks his words because he has the fullness of his Spirit. ³⁵The Father loves the Son and has given everything into his hands. ³⁶Everyone who believes in the Son will live forever. Those who reject him will never see life but will remain under God's wrath."

Chapter 4

¹Jesus was aware of the Pharisees who kept track and knew he baptized more people than John. ²Actually, it was not Jesus who baptized, but his disciples. ³He left Judea to go to Galilee. ⁴To get to Galilee, he insisted on taking the road through Samaria.

⁵Near the village of Sychar, not far from the field that Jacob gave to his son Joseph, ⁶he and his disciples came to Jacob's well. It was midday when Jesus, weary from the journey, sat down with John.

⁷When a Samaritan woman came to draw water, Jesus said, "Would you give me a drink?"

⁸The other disciples had gone to the village to buy food.

⁹The question surprised her because Jews normally have nothing to do with Samaritans. "You are a Jew," she said, "and I am a Samaritan woman. How can you ask me for a drink?"

¹⁰"If you understood God's generosity and who is asking for a drink, you would ask *me* for a drink. I would give you living water."

¹¹"Sir, where are you going to get this living water? You have no vessel to draw with, and the well is deep. ¹²How can you offer better water than our father Jacob, who gave us this well and drank from it, as did his children and his livestock?"

¹³Jesus said, "Everyone who drinks this water will thirst again. ¹⁴But those who drink the water I give will never become thirsty. My water is a fresh artesian spring, bubbling with everlasting life."

¹⁵"Sir, give me this water so I will not get thirsty and have to come to this well anymore."

¹⁶"Go and bring your husband here."

¹⁷"I have no husband."

Jesus said, "That's right. ¹⁸You have had five husbands, and the man you now live with is not your husband. You have certainly spoken truly."

¹⁹"Sir," the woman said, "you must be a prophet. ²⁰Tell me, why do you Jews say we must worship in Jerusalem while Samaritans say we should go to Mount Gerizim, the place where our ancestors worshiped?"

²¹"Believe me, woman, soon you will not worship the Father either here or in Jerusalem. ²²You Samaritans do not know what you worship. We know, because salvation comes through the Jews. ²³The time is coming—in fact, it is here now—when the Father looks for true worship that is an expression from your spirit. ²⁴God is spirit, so those people who truly worship must do so in spirit."

²⁵"I know the Messiah is coming—the one who is called Anointed. When he comes, he will explain everything."

²⁶Then Jesus told her, "I am the Messiah."

²⁷The disciples returned from town and were surprised to see Jesus talking with a woman. No one had the nerve to ask, "What do you want with her?" or, "Why are you talking with her?"

²⁸The woman left her water jar, went to the village, and told everyone she saw, ²⁹"Come see a man who told me everything I ever did. Could he be the Messiah?"

³⁰So they left the town to see Jesus.

³¹Meanwhile, the disciples urged him, "Rabbi, have something to eat."

³²"I have had food to eat that you know nothing about."

³³The disciples asked among themselves, "Did someone bring him food while we were gone?"

³⁴"My food," Jesus said, "is to do the will of him who sent me and to complete his work. ³⁵You should not say, 'It is another four months until harvest.' I say, open your eyes and look at the fields, already ripe and ready to harvest. ³⁶The reapers receive their reward by gathering a harvest for eternal life, so the sower and reaper may rejoice together. ³⁷The saying 'One sows and another reaps' is true.

[38]I am sending you where others have planted, and now you get to gather the harvest."

[39]Many Samaritans from the village believed in Jesus because the woman had said, "He told me everything I ever did." [40]After seeing him, they begged him to stay in their village.

He stayed for two days, [41]long enough for many more to hear and believe.

[42]The people said to the woman, "Not only do we believe because of what you said. We have seen and heard for ourselves and know for sure. He really is the Savior of the world."

[43]Jesus pointed out to the disciples as they left Samaria for Galilee [44]that a prophet has no honor in his own country.

[45]When Jesus entered Galilee, the people welcomed him because many had been in Jerusalem at the Passover celebration and had seen what he did there.

[46]A government official in Capernaum heard that Jesus had come from Judea to Galilee and was in Cana, the place where Jesus had turned the water into wine. [47]So the official went to Cana and begged Jesus to come to Capernaum and heal his son, who was about to die.

[48]"Some of you will never believe," Jesus said, "unless you see miracles and wonders."

[49]The official pleaded, "Sir, please come before my son dies."

[50]"You may go," Jesus said. "Your son will live."

The man took Jesus at his word and left. [51]While he was on the way home, his servants met him with the news that his son was alive and well.

[52]"When did he begin to get better?" he asked.

"Yesterday afternoon," they replied. "At seven o'clock, his fever suddenly disappeared."

⁵³The official knew this was the hour Jesus had said, "Your son will live," so he and his entire household believed in Jesus.

⁵⁴This was the second miracle Jesus did in Galilee, after he left Judea.

Chapter 5

¹Jesus went to Jerusalem for one of the Jewish feasts. ²In the city, not far from the Sheep Gate, was the pool called Bethesda, with five covered colonnades. ³Here, a great number of blind, crippled, and sickly people waited for a stirring of the water. ⁴They believed an angel sometimes came and caused a bubbling of the pool, and the first one to notice and step into the water would be healed.

⁵One man there had suffered from his affliction for thirty-eight years.

⁶Jesus saw him lying there and knew he had been in that condition for a long time. "Would you like to be healthy?"

⁷The feeble man answered, "Sir, when the water is stirring, I have no one to help me into the pool. While I am trying, someone else always gets there first."

⁸"Stand up!" Jesus said to him. "Pick up your mat and start walking."

⁹At the moment those words were spoken, the man was healed. He picked up his mat and walked, without regard for the Sabbath.

¹⁰Some Jewish leaders saw him. "Don't you know it's the Sabbath? You are breaking the Law by carrying your mat!"

¹¹The man answered, "But the one who healed me said, 'Pick up your mat and start walking.'"

¹²"What man told you it was all right to carry your mat?"

¹³The man who had been healed could not identify who it was, because Jesus had disappeared into the crowd.

[14]Later, Jesus found the man at the Temple. "Now that you are healthy, do not sin anymore, or something worse might happen."

[15]Then the man knew who had healed him and left to tell the Jewish leaders.

[16]The Jews became hostile toward Jesus and wanted him dead because he had ignored their Sabbath rules.

[17]Jesus offered this defense to the Jewish leaders who complained about his work on the Sabbath: "My father has always been at work doing good, and I must do the same."

[18]This response made the leaders even more determined to find a way to kill him. Not only had he broken their Sabbath law, but he called God his Father, claiming to be equal with God.

[19]"I assure you," Jesus said, "that the Son can do nothing by his own initiative but will only do what he sees the Father doing. Whatever the Father does, the Son will do likewise, [20]because the Father loves the Son and shows him everything he does. The Father will reveal in the Son even greater works than you have seen, so you will be amazed.

[21]"Just as the Father raises the dead and gives them life, the Son gives life where he chooses. [22]The Father does not judge anyone, but has given the Son authority to judge so people will honor the Son as much as the Father. [23]Those who do not respect the Son have no regard for the Father who sent him.

[24]"Listen. Those who hear what I am saying and believe on him who sent me have eternal life. They will avoid condemnation, passing from death to life. [25]Truly, the time has come for the dead to hear the voice of the Son of God, and those who hear will live. [26]Just as the Father has power to give life, he has made the Son to be the source of life.

[27]"He has given me authority to judge, because I am the Son of Man. [28]Do not be surprised, for the voice of the Son of Man will

soon be heard by those who are dead and buried, [29]and they will rise from their tombs, the righteous unto life and the evil unto damnation.

[30]"I can do nothing by my own initiative. I listen and judge rightly because I seek to please the Father, who sent me, not myself. [31]If I were to testify on my own behalf, you would have no proof that what I say is true. [32]But someone else supports me with his testimony, and what he says about me is true. [33]You sent men to inquire of John the Baptizer, and his testimony was true. [34]I do not need another man's testimony for my words to be true, but I point out the fact so you may believe and be saved. [35]John was a blazing, bright lamp, and for a while, you were happy with his light. [36]But I have a witness greater than John. The tasks my Father has given me to complete, the message and the miracles, prove he has sent me. [37]In this way, the Father has testified concerning me, although you have neither heard his voice nor seen his face.

[38]"You do not have God's message in your hearts, because you have not believed the one he has sent to you. [39]You search the scriptures, thinking you will find eternal life, but those words testify concerning me. [40]Still, you refuse to come and receive life from me.

[41]"I do not need your approval, [42]because I know God's love is nowhere in your hearts. [43]I have come representing my Father, and you have rejected me. But you will readily receive another man who comes representing himself. [44]How can you believe when you lavish praises upon one another but care nothing about seeking the highest honor that comes from God alone? [45]Even so, I am not the one who will accuse you before the Father. Moses will accuse you, because you say you put your trust in him. [46]If you really believed Moses, you would believe me, because he wrote about me. [47]Since you have not believed what Moses wrote, it's no wonder that you do not believe me either."

Chapter 6

¹Later, Jesus crossed the Sea of Galilee, also known as the Sea of Tiberias. ²A huge crowd followed because they had seen his miracles in healing the sick. ³Jesus went up on the hillside and sat there with his followers. ⁴It was almost time for the Jewish Passover feast.

⁵As Jesus looked over the multitude and saw how many there were, he said to Philip, "Where can we buy bread to feed all these people?" ⁶He already knew what he was going to do, but said this to test him.

⁷Philip answered, "Six months' wages would not be enough to give everyone a few bites."

⁸Andrew, Simon Peter's brother, said, ⁹"There is one boy who brought five barley loaves and two fish, but what good are they for this crowd?"

¹⁰"Have the people sit down."

There was a lot of grass where they were, so the men sat down, about five thousand, plus women and children.

¹¹Jesus took the five loaves and gave thanks. He broke the loaves and fish and handed them to his disciples, who distributed the pieces to the people. ¹²When they all had eaten as much as they wanted, he said to his disciples, "Gather everything left over so no food is wasted."

¹³The disciples gathered twelve baskets full of leftover bread and fish.

¹⁴People saw the miracle, how Jesus had fed the multitude with a few loaves and fish, and said, "Surely, this is the Prophet who is to come into the world."

¹⁵Jesus knew they were ready to force him to be their king, so he went high into the mountain to be alone.

[16]In the evening, the disciples went down to the sea, [17]got into their boat, and left for Capernaum. It was dark, and Jesus had not returned. [18]A strong wind came, making the seas rough.

[19]After they had rowed only three or four miles, they saw Jesus coming toward them, walking on the water. They were terrified, [20]but Jesus said, "It's all right. I am Jesus. You do not need to be afraid."

[21]They gladly welcomed him aboard. Immediately, the boat reached the shore where they were going.

[22]The day after five thousand men were fed with a few loaves and fish, the crowd that had been left on the opposite shore near Bethsaida realized that the disciples had taken the one boat and Jesus had not gone with them.

[23]Other boats from Tiberias came ashore near where Jesus had given thanks and the people ate bread. [24]Since Jesus and the disciples were obviously not on their side of the sea, they got into the boats and went to look for Jesus in Capernaum. [25]When they found him, they said, "Teacher, when did you arrive here?"

[26]"The truth is, you were not searching for me because of the miracles but because I filled your stomachs with bread. [27]Do not work for food that spoils. Spend your energy seeking the eternal life that the Son of Man can give you. God the Father has sent me for this purpose."

[28]They said, "What must we do to perform the works of God?"

[29]"What God wants from you is to believe the one he has sent."

[30]"Show us a miraculous sign so we may see and believe. What can you do? [31]Our ancestors ate manna in the wilderness. Scripture says Moses gave them bread from heaven to eat."

[32]"Moses did not give you bread from heaven. Actually, my Father did. [33]God's bread is the one who came down from heaven to give life to the world."

³⁴"Sir, give us that bread every day."

³⁵"I am the bread of life. Whoever comes to me will never be hungry. Whoever believes in me will never thirst. ³⁶You have seen me, but you have not believed me. ³⁷Everyone the Father gives to me will come, and I will never reject one who comes to me. ³⁸I came from heaven, not to do my will, but to do the will of the one who sent me.

³⁹"This is the will of my Father, who sent me: I will not lose any of those he has given me but will raise them up on the last day.

⁴⁰"This is the will of my Father, who sent me: all who see the Son and believe will have eternal life, and I will raise them up on the last day."

⁴¹The Jews criticized Jesus because he said he was the bread from heaven. ⁴²They said to one another, "Isn't this Jesus, the son of Joseph, whose father and mother we know? How can he say, 'I have come from heaven'?"

⁴³"Do not complain among yourselves," Jesus said. ⁴⁴"People cannot come to me unless the Father draws them, and I will raise them up on the last day. ⁴⁵In the prophets, it is written, *All your children will be taught by God.* Everyone who hears and understands the Father will come to me.

⁴⁶"Except for the one who is from God, no man has ever seen the Father. ⁴⁷I guarantee, everyone who believes in me will have eternal life. ⁴⁸I am the bread of life. ⁴⁹Your ancestors ate manna in the wilderness, and they all died. ⁵⁰Let me tell you about the bread from heaven that a man may eat and not die. ⁵¹I am the living bread from heaven. Those who eat this bread will live forever. This bread is my body that I willingly give for the life of the world."

⁵²The Jews argued among themselves, "How can he give us his flesh to eat?"

⁵³"I am telling you exactly the way it is," Jesus said. "Unless you commit your whole being to the Son of Man, as one who would eat his flesh and drink his blood, you cannot live. ⁵⁴Those who eat my flesh and drink my blood will have eternal life, and I will raise them up on the last day. ⁵⁵My flesh is real food and my blood is real drink. ⁵⁶Those who eat my flesh and drink my blood abide in me, and I abide in them.

⁵⁷"I live because of the living Father, who sent me. Therefore, anyone who feeds on me will live because I live. ⁵⁸I am not like the bread your ancestors ate. They died. I am the true bread from heaven that people may eat and live forever."

⁵⁹He said all these things while teaching in the Capernaum synagogue.

⁶⁰Many of his followers said, "This teaching is difficult to understand. Who can figure it out?"

⁶¹Aware of the murmuring among his disciples, Jesus said, "Is what I said bothering you? ⁶²What if you saw the Son of Man ascend to where he was before? ⁶³It is the Spirit, not the flesh, that gives life. The words I have spoken to you are spirit and life. ⁶⁴Yet some of you do not believe me."

From the beginning, Jesus knew who the nonbelievers were and who would betray him.

⁶⁵"That is why I said, 'Everyone the Father gives to me will come.'"

⁶⁶After hearing this, many of his followers walked away and did not follow him anymore.

⁶⁷Jesus turned to the twelve. "Are you going to leave too?"

⁶⁸Simon Peter answered, "Sir, where would we go? You alone have the words that give eternal life. ⁶⁹We are fully confident that you are the Anointed One, the son of the living God."

⁷⁰"I chose all twelve of you," Jesus said. "Yet one of you is a devil."

⁷¹He was referring to Judas Iscariot, son of Simon, because he knew which one would betray him.

Chapter 7

¹After this, Jesus ministered throughout Galilee, avoiding Judea because the Jewish leaders there sought to kill him. ²Near the time for the Jewish Feast of Tabernacles, ³Jesus' brothers said to him, "You should go to Judea, where more of your followers can witness your miracles. ⁴You cannot become well known by hiding what you do. You should let the whole world know."

⁵His own brothers did not believe in him.

⁶Jesus said to them, "My time has not yet come, but you can always go. ⁷The world cannot hate you, but it hates me because I expose the evil being done. ⁸You go on to the feast, because it is not yet time for me to go."

⁹So he remained in Galilee.

¹⁰Later, after his brothers had gone, he also left for the feast, in secret, to avoid being noticed.

¹¹At the feast, the Jews kept asking where Jesus was. ¹²Among the crowds, many argued about him, some saying, "He is a good man," while others said, "No, he deceives the people." ¹³However, for fear of the Jewish leaders, no one would openly defend Jesus.

¹⁴When the feast was half over, Jesus went to the Temple and began to teach.

¹⁵Astonished, the people asked, "How does this man know so much when he has never studied the Law?"

¹⁶"My message is not my own," Jesus said. "It comes from the one who sent me. ¹⁷Those who are doing what God wants will know whether my words are from him or me. ¹⁸A man who speaks on his own behalf seeks glory for himself, but he who honors the one who

sent him speaks truthfully, without deception. [19]You are not obeying the Law that Moses gave you, so why do you seek to kill me?"

[20]"An evil spirit has twisted your mind," the people said. "Who is trying to kill you?"

[21]"You could not believe me because I did one miracle on the Sabbath. [22]Moses commanded you to circumcise your sons, a practice begun by your ancestors. How is it that you circumcise a baby on the Sabbath? [23]If you circumcise on the Sabbath to avoid breaking the Law of Moses, why are you angry with me for making a man well? [24]Stop judging by social standards and judge by what is right."

[25]Some of those who lived in Jerusalem asked one another, "Isn't this the man they are trying to kill? [26]But here he is, speaking boldly, and no one is saying anything to him. Do our leaders believe he really is the Messiah? [27]How could that be? When the Messiah appears, no one will know where he's from, but we know where this man is from."

[28]Jesus shouted, "You know me and where I am from, but I am not here for myself but for the one who sent me. You do not know him, [29]but I know him because I came from him. He has sent me to you."

[30]After he had said this, the Jewish leaders wanted to arrest him. Yet no one laid a hand on him because his time had not yet come. [31]Many in the crowd believed in him, saying, "What miracles would a Messiah do that this man has not done?"

[32]The Pharisees overheard the people whispering their support of Jesus among themselves, so they and the chief priests sent Temple guards to arrest him.

[33]"Wait!" Jesus told the guards. "Only a little longer will I be with you. I must return to the one who sent me. [34]You will look but never find me because you cannot come to where I am going."

[35]The guards said to one another, "Where can he go that we cannot find him? Will he go to Jews in foreign lands or teach the Greeks? [36]What did he mean, 'You will never find me because you cannot come to where I am going'?"

[37]On the last and most celebrated day of the feast, Jesus stood and shouted, "Let anyone who is thirsty come to me and drink. [38]Rivers of living water will flow from the innermost being of those who believe on me, as the scripture has said."

[39]*Living water* referred to the Holy Spirit, whom believers were about to receive. Because Jesus had not yet ascended into glory, the flow of the Spirit had not been given.

[40]When the crowd heard this, some said, "This man really is the Prophet." [41]Others said, "He is the Messiah." But some objected, saying, "The Messiah cannot be from Galilee. [42]Don't scriptures say he will be a descendant of David, out of Bethlehem, where David lived?" [43]So a dissension rose among the people over who Jesus was. [44]Some wanted to arrest him, but no one laid a hand on him.

[45]The chief priests and Pharisees said to the returning guards, "Why didn't you bring him in?"

[46]"Never has anyone spoken the way he does," they answered.

[47]"Has he also deceived you? [48]Have any of us believed in him? No, not one Jewish leader or Pharisee. [49]These people are cursed because they do not know the Law."

[50]Nicodemus, the one who had earlier seen Jesus at night, said to them, [51]"Does the Law allow us to convict a man without a hearing, without first determining what he has done?"

[52]"You must be Galilean," they answered. "Search the scriptures for yourself. No prophet comes from Galilee."

[53]Everyone went home.

Chapter 8

¹Jesus returned to the Mount of Olives.

²At dawn, Jesus entered the Temple's outer court. After a crowd had gathered, he sat down and began to teach.

³Pharisees and teachers of the Law brought a woman who had been caught in adultery. While she stood before the people, ⁴they said, "Teacher, this woman was found with a man who is not her husband. Her guilt is certain because she was taken in the act. ⁵In the Law, Moses says we are to stone to death such women. What do you say?"

⁶Their question was intended to trap him into saying something against either the Law or public opinion.

Instead of answering, Jesus stooped down and wrote on the ground with his finger. ⁷They continued to ask until he stood and said, "Let the one among you who is without sin throw the first stone." ⁸Again, he stooped down and wrote on the ground.

⁹After hearing what he said, they were convicted by their own conscience and slipped away, one at a time, from oldest to youngest, until only Jesus was left with the woman before him.

¹⁰Jesus stood. "Woman, where are your accusers? Is there no one here to condemn you?"

¹¹"No one, sir."

"Neither do I condemn you. Go and sin no more."

¹²Later, Jesus said to the people, "I am the light of the world. Those who follow me will never walk in darkness, because they have the light of life."

¹³The Pharisees argued, "You cannot testify on your own behalf. Without verification, your words mean nothing."

¹⁴"Even though I speak for myself, my testimony is still true. You do not know where I came from or where I am going, but I know. ¹⁵You judge from a fleshly perspective, but I do not judge like

you. [16]My judgment is true because my decisions are made with the Father, who sent me. [17]By your own Law, the testimony of two witnesses verifies the truth. [18]I testify on my own behalf, and the Father, who sent me, is the second witness."

[19]"Where is this father of yours who will testify?"

Jesus answered, "If you do not know me, you cannot know my Father. If you knew me, you would also know my Father."

[20]He said this while teaching in the area where offerings were given in the Temple, but no one arrested him because it was not yet time for him to be taken.

[21]At another time, he said, "I am leaving. You will look for me but will die in your sins. You cannot come to where I am going."

[22]The Jewish authorities said, "Is he planning to commit suicide? Is that what he means by saying we cannot go where he is going?"

[23]"You are from below," Jesus told them. "I am from above. You belong to this world; I do not. [24]That is why I said you will die in your sins. If you do not believe I am who I am, you will surely die in your sins."

[25]"Who are you?"

"I am the one I have always claimed to be. [26]Concerning you, there is much I could say and judge, but I will speak to the world only the truth that I hear from the one who sent me."

[27]They still did not realize he was talking about the Father.

[28]So Jesus said, "When you lift up the Son of Man, you will know I am who I am. I do nothing on my own initiative. I say only what the Father instructs me to say. [29]The one who sent me is with me. Because I always do what pleases him, he has never left me on my own."

[30]As he said these things, many put their faith in him.

[31]To those who believed, Jesus said, "If you keep following what I say, you really are my disciples. [32]And you will know the truth, and the truth will set you free."

³³"We are Abraham's descendents," they said. "We have never been in bondage to anyone, so how can you say we will be free?"

³⁴"I tell you the absolute truth: everyone who sins is a slave to sin. ³⁵A slave has no rights as part of the family, but a son belongs forever. ³⁶So if the Son makes you free, you really are free. ³⁷I know you are Abraham's descendants, but you want to kill me because my message has no place in your hearts. ³⁸I declare what my Father has shown me, and you do what your father has shown you."

³⁹"Our father is Abraham."

"If you were Abraham's children, you would act like him. ⁴⁰Instead, you seek to kill me because I tell you the truth I heard from God. This is nothing like Abraham did. ⁴¹No, you are doing the works of your true father."

"We are not bastards. God is our true Father."

⁴²"If God were your Father, you would love me, because I came from him. I did not decide to come, but he sent me. ⁴³Why don't you understand what I say? I will tell you why. You do not want to hear my message. ⁴⁴You come from your father, the devil, and your desires are like his. From the beginning, he was a murderer and opposed the truth, because truth was not in his nature. When he lies, he speaks from his heart, because he is a liar and the father of lies. ⁴⁵So it is only natural, when I speak the truth, that you do not believe me.

⁴⁶"Can any of you prove I have told even one lie? No one. Since I am telling you the truth, why don't you believe me? ⁴⁷Those who belong to God hear his words. You do not hear because you are not his children."

⁴⁸The Jewish leaders said, "We were right all along in saying you were a Samaritan heretic, possessed by an evil spirit."

⁴⁹"I do not have an evil spirit. I honor my Father, while you dishonor me. ⁵⁰I am not trying to get honor for myself. But there is

one who does honor me, and he is the true judge. ⁵¹I assure you, whoever hears and follows my teachings will never die."

⁵²"Now we know you have an evil spirit. Abraham and the prophets are all dead, and you say those who follow your teachings will never die. ⁵³Are you greater than Abraham and the prophets who have died? Who do you think you are?"

⁵⁴Jesus answered, "Honor means nothing if I give it to myself. My Father, the one you say is your God, is the one who honors me. ⁵⁵You do not even know him, but I do. If I said I did not, I would be a liar like you. But I do know him, and I follow his instructions. ⁵⁶Your ancestor Abraham rejoiced as he looked forward to my coming. When he saw me, he was overjoyed."

⁵⁷"You are not even fifty years old," they said. "How can you say you have seen Abraham?"

⁵⁸"I assure you, before Abraham was born, I am."

⁵⁹They picked up stones to kill him, but Jesus disappeared from their midst and left the Temple area.

Chapter 9

¹As Jesus walked down the street, he saw a man who had been blind since birth.

²His disciples asked, "Teacher, why was this man born blind? Was his condition caused by the man's sin or the sin of his parents?"

³"Neither one. His blindness is not due to sin but was given so the works of God could be revealed in him. ⁴While we have daylight, we must do the work of the one who sent me, because the night will come when no one can work. ⁵For as long as I am here, I am the light of the world."

⁶After saying this, Jesus spat on the ground, made mud from the saliva, and smeared the ointment on the blind man's eyes. ⁷"Go wash in the Pool of Siloam," he said.

The meaning of the pool's name was *sent*.

The man washed his eyes and came back, able to see.

[8]His neighbors and others who knew him when he was blind asked, "Is this the same man we used to see sitting and begging?"

[9]Some said, "Yes," but others said, "No, he just looks like him."

But he said, "I am the man, all right."

[10]So they asked him, "How is it that you now can see?"

[11]"A man called Jesus made mud and anointed my eyes. He said, 'Go to the Pool of Siloam and wash.' So I did, and now I can see."

[12]"Where is this man?"

"I don't know," he answered.

[13]They took the formerly blind man to the Pharisees [14]because Jesus had made the mud and healed him on the Sabbath. [15]The Pharisees began their interrogation, asking how he had received his sight.

He detailed how Jesus had anointed his eyes with mud, sent him to wash, and then he could see.

[16]Some said, "This Jesus cannot be from God, because he violates the Sabbath." Others disagreed, saying, "How can a sinner do such miracles?" The controversy deepened. They could not reach an agreement about him.

[17]Again, they asked the man, "What do you have to say about the man who opened your eyes?"

"He is a prophet."

[18]The Jewish leaders did not believe the man had been blind until they heard the testimony of his parents. [19]"Is this your son?" they asked. "Do you affirm that he was born blind? Then how does he now see?"

[20]"Yes, he is our son. He was born blind. [21]But we do not know how he can now see. We do not know who gave him his sight. He is of legal age, so ask him. He can speak for himself."

²²They answered in this way because the Jewish leaders had made it known that they would put out of the synagogue anyone who said Jesus was the Messiah. ²³That's why they said, "He is of age, so ask him."

²⁴For the second time, the Jewish leaders called the formerly blind man to appear before them. "Give God the glory for this miracle," they said, "because we know this man Jesus is a sinner."

²⁵"I do not know whether he is a sinner or not," the man said. "Of one thing I am sure. I used to be blind. Now I can see!"

²⁶They said to him, "What did he do to you? How did he open your eyes?"

²⁷"I already told you. Weren't you listening? Why do you want to hear it all over again? Are you interested in becoming his disciples?"

²⁸They cursed and ridiculed him. "You are his disciple, but we are disciples of Moses. ²⁹We know God spoke to Moses. As for this man, we do not even know where he came from."

³⁰"This is amazing. You do not know where he came from, but he healed my blind eyes. ³¹We know God does not listen to sinners. He listens to a man who worships him and does his will. ³²Never in the world's history has anyone heard of a man healing someone who was born blind. ³³If this man did not come from God, he could do nothing."

³⁴"You were born a sinner," they said. "Who are you to lecture us?" And they threw him out of the synagogue.

³⁵After hearing what had happened, Jesus found the man. "Do you believe in the Son of Man?"

³⁶"Tell me who he is, sir, and I will believe in him."

³⁷"You have already seen him," Jesus said. "He is the one talking with you."

³⁸He knelt before Jesus. "Yes, I do believe, sir."

³⁹Jesus said, "I came to this world to bring people to a point of decision, to give sight to the blind and blindness to those who think they see."

⁴⁰Some Pharisees overheard him. "Are you saying we are blind?"

⁴¹"If you were blind," Jesus said, "you would be blameless. But because you say you can see, you remain blind."

Chapter 10

¹"Without a doubt," Jesus said, "the man who avoids the gate to the sheep pen, but slips in some other way, is a thief and a robber. ²The shepherd of the sheep always enters through the gate. ³He is the one the gatekeeper welcomes. The sheep recognize his voice as he calls them by name and leads them out. ⁴When he has brought out all his sheep, he goes before them. They follow him because they know his voice. ⁵They will not follow a stranger but will scatter before the sound of strange voices."

⁶Jesus used this analogy, but the people did not understand what he was saying, ⁷so he explained what he meant. "I tell you the truth, I am the gate for the sheep. ⁸Those who came by another way were thieves and robbers, but my sheep did not listen to them. ⁹I am the gate through which people may be saved from destruction, where they can freely come and go and be satisfied. ¹⁰The thief comes with one purpose: to steal, kill, and destroy. I came to bring the fullness of life.

¹¹"I am the good shepherd and will sacrifice my life for the sake of the sheep.

¹²"When the hired hand sees a wolf coming, he will abandon the sheep, because he is not their shepherd and the sheep do not belong to him. So the wolf will attack and scatter the flock. ¹³The man will flee because he works for the money and cares nothing for the sheep.

¹⁴"I am the good shepherd. I know my sheep and my sheep know me, ¹⁵just as the Father knows me and I know the Father. I will sacrifice my life for the sake of my sheep. ¹⁶In another fold, I have more sheep and must also bring them. They will hear my voice, and there will be one flock with one shepherd.

¹⁷"The Father loves me because I will sacrifice my life and take it back again. ¹⁸No one will take my life from me. I choose to give it up. I have the power to lay it down and to take it up again, because this is what my Father has commanded."

¹⁹After hearing these words, the Jewish leaders were divided in their opinions about Jesus. ²⁰Many said, "An evil spirit has made him crazy. You should pay no attention to him." ²¹Others disagreed, saying, "Can an evil spirit open blind eyes? These are not the words of someone possessed."

²²At the time of Hanukkah, the Feast of Dedication, in the winter, ²³Jesus was in the Temple, walking in the area called Solomon's Porch. ²⁴Some of the Jewish leaders gathered around him and asked, "How long are you going to keep us wondering? If you really are the Messiah, then say so."

²⁵"I have already told you," Jesus said, "but you did not believe me. The miracles I do in my Father's name prove who I am, ²⁶but you do not believe, because you are not my sheep. ²⁷My sheep recognize my voice. I know them, and they follow me. ²⁸I give them everlasting life, so they will never die. No thief can take them from me, ²⁹because my Father has placed them in my care. He is more powerful than anyone else, so no one can snatch them from his protection.

³⁰"My Father and I are one."

³¹The Jews picked up stones to throw at him.

³²Jesus said, "Under the authority of my Father, I have done many good works. For which of those do you want to stone me?"

³³They answered, "We are not stoning you for any good work, but for blasphemy, because you are just a man but claim to be God."

³⁴"Don't your own scriptures say, *You are gods?* ³⁵We know the scripture is as true now as it was then. If God called those people gods, ³⁶why do you call it blasphemy when the one whom the Father has anointed and sent into the world says, 'I am the Son of God'? ³⁷If I am not doing the works of my Father, then don't believe me. ³⁸But if I am, and you cannot believe me, then believe the miracles and know that the Father is in me and I am in him."

³⁹Once again, they tried to seize him, but he escaped from their grasp.

⁴⁰He went beyond the Jordan River and stayed near the place where John had first baptized. ⁴¹People came to him, saying, "John did not do any miracles, but everything John said about this man is true."

⁴²Many from that area believed Jesus was the Messiah.

Chapter 11

¹A man named Lazarus lived in Bethany, where his sisters, Mary and Martha, lived. He was sick. ²This is the same Mary who later anointed Jesus with expensive perfume and wiped his feet with her hair. ³The two sisters sent word to Jesus, saying, "Sir, your dear friend Lazarus is sick."

⁴When Jesus received the message, he said, "The purpose of his sickness is not to cause his death but to bring God glory, that the Son of God may be exalted."

⁵Although he loved Martha, Mary, and Lazarus, ⁶and had heard that Lazarus was sick, he stayed where he was for two more days. ⁷After that, he said to his disciples, "Let's go back to Judea."

⁸"Why?" they protested. "Not long ago, the Jewish leaders tried to stone you, and you want to go there again?"

⁹"Aren't there twelve hours of daylight? If a man walks during the day, he can walk safely because he has the sunlight. ¹⁰But if he walks at night, he stumbles because there is no light with which to see. ¹¹Our friend Lazarus is asleep, and I must go to wake him."

¹²The disciples said, "Sir, if he is sleeping, he will soon get better." ¹³They thought Lazarus was resting comfortably.

But Jesus meant he had died, ¹⁴so he had to tell them plainly, "Lazarus is dead. ¹⁵I am glad I was not there. This is good for your sake, so you will believe. Let's go to him."

¹⁶Thomas, the one called Twin, said to the others, "Sure, let's go too. We can all die with him."

¹⁷At Bethany, Jesus learned that Lazarus had been in the tomb four days.

¹⁸They were only a couple of miles from Jerusalem, ¹⁹so many of the Jewish leaders had come to the house of Martha and Mary to comfort them concerning their brother.

²⁰When Martha heard that Jesus was coming, she ran to meet him, but Mary stayed at the house. ²¹"Sir," Martha said, "if you had been here, my brother would not have died, ²²but nevertheless, I know God will give you whatever you ask of him."

²³"Your brother will rise to life."

²⁴"Yes, I know," she said. "He will rise to life in the resurrection at the last day."

²⁵Jesus said, "I am the resurrection and the life. Those who believe in me will live, even if they have died, ²⁶and those who are living and believe in me will never die. Do you believe this?"

²⁷"Yes, sir. I know you are the Messiah, the son of God, who was to come into the world."

²⁸Martha went home and talked to her sister privately. "The Teacher is coming, and he is asking for you!"

²⁹Immediately Mary went to him.

³⁰Jesus had not yet entered the town, but was waiting at the same place where Martha had met him.

³¹In the house, the Jewish leaders who had come to provide comfort saw Mary rush out, and they followed. They assumed that she was headed to the tomb to mourn.

³²When Mary arrived, she fell at Jesus' feet. "Sir, if you had been here, my brother would not have died."

³³As Jesus saw her crying and saw the Jews also crying, he was deeply distressed in his spirit. ³⁴"Where have you laid him?"

"Sir, come and see," they replied.

³⁵Jesus started crying.

³⁶Seeing him, the Jewish leaders said, "My, how much he loved him!" ³⁷Some of them said, "He healed the blind man. Surely he could have kept this man from dying."

³⁸Again deeply moved, Jesus came to the tomb, a cave with a stone covering the entrance. ³⁹"Take away the stone."

"But sir," Martha said, "he has been dead four days. By now, his body stinks from decay."

⁴⁰"Didn't I say, if you believed, you would see the glory of God?"

⁴¹When they removed the stone from the entrance, Jesus looked toward the sky and said, "Father, thank you for hearing me. ⁴²You always hear me, but I say this so others around me may believe you have sent me." ⁴³With a booming voice, he cried, "Lazarus, come out!"

⁴⁴The dead man came out, his hands and feet bound with grave clothes, a cloth around his face.

Jesus said to them, "Unwrap him and let him go."

⁴⁵Many of the Jewish leaders believed because they had been with Mary and saw what Jesus did, ⁴⁶but some of them went to tell the Pharisees what had happened.

⁴⁷The chief priests and Pharisees called a meeting of the council. "What shall we do?" they asked. "This man is performing many miracles. ⁴⁸If we allow him to continue, everyone will believe in him. The Romans will take away our authority and destroy our nation."

⁴⁹Caiaphas, the high priest, said, "You do not understand what must happen, ⁵⁰for God is saying one man must die for the people so the whole nation will not be destroyed." ⁵¹He spoke, not as a man, but as the high priest, prophesying that Jesus would die for the nation, ⁵²not just for those in Israel, but for the gathering of all God's children scattered abroad.

⁵³From that day on, the council planned to kill Jesus.

⁵⁴Therefore, Jesus no longer appeared publicly among the Jews but went to a desolate town called Ephraim, where he stayed with his disciples.

⁵⁵With the Jewish feast time approaching, many people from around the country went up to Jerusalem before Passover to purify themselves. ⁵⁶Looking for Jesus, they stood in the Temple and asked one another, "Do you think he will show up or not?"

⁵⁷The chief priests and Pharisees had given orders for anyone who saw Jesus to let them know. Then they could arrest him.

Chapter 12

¹Six days before Passover, Jesus came to Bethany, the town where he had raised Lazarus from the dead. ²A dinner was prepared for him. Martha served and Lazarus was one of those who sat at the table.

³Mary brought a jar of very expensive perfume. She anointed Jesus' feet and wiped them with her hair until the house was filled with the fragrance.

⁴Judas Iscariot, son of Simon, the one who later betrayed Jesus, said, ⁵"That perfume was worth a year's wages. Why wasn't it sold and the money given to the poor?" ⁶He said this, not because he cared for the poor, but because he was a thief. He carried the moneybag and could take some for himself.

⁷"Leave her alone," Jesus said. "She has prepared my body for burial. ⁸You will always have the poor with you, but you will not always have me."

⁹Word spread among the Jewish leaders that Jesus was there, and many came, not just to see Jesus, but also Lazarus, whom he had raised from the dead. ¹⁰Therefore, the chief priests planned to kill Lazarus ¹¹as well as Jesus because he had swayed many Jews to believe.

¹²The next day, many who had come to Jerusalem for Passover heard that Jesus was coming. ¹³People cut branches from palm trees and went to meet him, shouting, "Hail to the King! Blessed is the one who comes in God's name."

¹⁴Jesus found a young donkey and sat on it, fulfilling the words of the prophet: ¹⁵*Have no fear, people of Zion. Look! The king is coming, riding upon a colt, a donkey's foal.*

¹⁶At the time, the disciples did not understand that prophecy was being fulfilled. After Jesus had risen from the dead and ascended into heaven, they remembered the scriptures and saw how what had happened matched what had been predicted.

¹⁷Those who had been with Jesus at the raising of Lazarus from the dead had spread the word about what they had seen. ¹⁸Some went out to meet Jesus because they had heard about the miracle.

¹⁹The Pharisees said to one another, "Look! The whole world is following him, and there is nothing we can do about it."

²⁰Some Greeks were among those who had come to worship during Passover. ²¹They went to Philip with their request. "Sir, we want to meet with Jesus."

²²Philip told Andrew, and the two of them asked Jesus if he would meet with the Greeks.

²³"The time has come," Jesus said, "for the Son of Man to be glorified. ²⁴I tell you the truth, until a grain of wheat is put into the ground and dies, it lives alone. But if it dies, it produces a great harvest. ²⁵A man who loves life in this world will lose it, but he who hates life here will live forever. ²⁶If you want to serve me, you must follow me and be wherever I am. If you serve me, you will be rewarded by my Father.

²⁷"Right now, my soul is troubled. Should I say, 'Father, save me from what I am about to face'? No. This is why I came. ²⁸Father, bring glory to your name."

A voice from heaven said, "I have already glorified my name and will do so again."

²⁹Many bystanders heard only a sound they thought was thunder. Others said, "An angel has spoken to him."

³⁰Jesus said, "That voice was for your benefit, not mine. ³¹Now is the time for the prince of this world to be judged and cast out. ³²When I am lifted up from the earth, I will draw everyone to me." ³³In saying this, he predicted how he would die.

³⁴The crowd said, "Scriptures say the Messiah will live forever. How can you say the Son of Man must be crucified? Who is this Son of Man?"

³⁵"For only a little longer," Jesus said, "my light will be with you. Walk in that light while you can so you will not be caught in the darkness. Those who walk in darkness do not know where they are going. ³⁶Trust the light while there is still time, and you will become children of light." After saying these things, Jesus left and hid from the people.

³⁷Despite all the miracles he had done, the people still did not believe in him, ³⁸fulfilling what the prophet Isaiah wrote: *Who would*

have believed what we have prophesied? Who can see the Lord's hand at work?

³⁹They had no faith, as Isaiah wrote elsewhere: ⁴⁰*Harden the hearts of these people and close their ears and cover their eyes so they will not see with their eyes, hear with their ears, and understand with their hearts and be forced to turn to me and be healed.* ⁴¹Because he had seen the Messiah's glory, Isaiah said these things about him.

⁴²Even so, many people did believe in Jesus, including some of the Jewish leaders. Fearing the Pharisees who would put them out of the synagogue, they did not openly confess their faith. ⁴³They were more concerned about human approval than pleasing God.

⁴⁴With a loud voice, Jesus told them, "Those who believe in me are also believing in the one who sent me. ⁴⁵Those who see me are also seeing the one who sent me. ⁴⁶I come as light into the world so those who believe in me will not remain in the dark. ⁴⁷I am not the judge of those who hear but will not believe. I came, not to judge, but to save the world. ⁴⁸Those who reject me and will not hear my message will face the Day of Judgment, when the words I have spoken will judge them. ⁴⁹My teaching is not my own, but the Father, who sent me, has determined the lessons and dictated the words. ⁵⁰I know that his commandment leads to eternal life, so I will only say what he tells me to say."

Chapter 13

¹Before the Passover feast, Jesus knew it was time to leave the earth and go to the Father. He had loved his disciples and would love them until the end.

²As the meal progressed, Judas Iscariot, son of Simon, assembled his devilish thoughts on how he would betray Jesus.

³Jesus was fully aware of who he was and that the Father had given him complete power. He had come from God and would return

to God. ⁴He rose from the table, set aside his outer garment, and wrapped a towel around his waist. ⁵After pouring water into a basin, he washed each disciple's feet and dried them with the towel—⁶until he reached Simon Peter.

"Master," Peter said, "are you going to wash my feet?"

⁷"Right now, you do not understand what I am doing, but you will."

⁸"You are not going to wash my feet."

"If I do not," Jesus said, "we cannot be together."

⁹"In that case, do not stop with my feet. Wash my hands and my head as well."

¹⁰"Those who have bathed need only wash their feet to be clean. You are clean, but not everyone." ¹¹Because he knew who would betray him, he said, "Not everyone."

¹²After he had washed everyone's feet, he dressed and returned to his place at the table. "Do you understand what I have done? ¹³You do well to call me Teacher and Master, for that is who I am. ¹⁴Since I am your teacher and master and I have served you, you should serve one another. ¹⁵I have given you an example, so you should do for others as I have done for you. ¹⁶I cannot overemphasize this truth: the servant is not greater than his master. The messenger is not greater than the one who sent the message. ¹⁷Knowing the truth is not enough. You must do the serving to experience true happiness.

¹⁸"I am not talking about all of you. I know those I have chosen, but the scripture must be fulfilled: *My trusted friend who ate bread with me has turned against me.* ¹⁹I tell you this beforehand so after it comes to pass you will believe who I am. ²⁰You can be sure that anyone who receives the one I send also receives me, and anyone who receives me also receives the one who sent me."

²¹Troubled in spirit, Jesus declared, "I tell you the truth. One of you will turn against me."

²²They looked at one another, wondering who the man was. ²³One disciple whom Jesus loved sat next to Jesus. ²⁴With gestures, Simon Peter asked him to find out who the betrayer was. ²⁵So the disciple leaned closer to Jesus and asked, "Sir, who is it?"

²⁶"I will dip this piece of bread in the sauce and give it to him." He dipped the bread and offered it to Judas Iscariot, son of Simon.

²⁷When Judas took the bread, he saw this as the opportune moment for his devilish scheme.

Jesus said, "Hurry and do what you must do."

²⁸No one else at the table understood what Jesus meant. ²⁹Since Judas had the moneybag, some thought Jesus wanted him to either buy something for the feast or give money to the poor.

³⁰Still holding the piece of bread, Judas rushed out into the night.

³¹With Judas gone, Jesus turned to the disciples. "The time has come for the Son of Man to be glorified. And God will be glorified in him. ³²If God is glorified in him, he will not delay his plan to glorify the Son of Man.

³³"My students," Jesus said, "I cannot be with you much longer. I must tell you what I told the Jewish leaders: you will look but not find me because you cannot come to where I am going. ³⁴I give you a new commandment: love one another in the same way that I have loved you. ³⁵If you love one other, people will know you are my disciples."

³⁶Simon Peter asked, "Sir, where are you going?"

"Where I go, you cannot follow. But you will, later."

³⁷"Why can't I follow you now? I would die for you."

³⁸"Die for me? I guarantee," Jesus said, "before the rooster crows tonight, you will deny me three times."

Chapter 14

¹"Don't be distressed," Jesus said. "You trust God. Trust me as well. ²There are many places where you can stay in my Father's house. I would have told you if that were not true. I must go to make the place ready for you. ³After I have prepared for your arrival, I will come back for you so we can be there together. ⁴You know where I am going, and you know the way."

⁵"No, we don't," Thomas said. "Sir, we don't know where you are going, so how can we know the way?"

⁶"I am the way, the truth, and the life," Jesus said. "Everyone who reaches the Father goes through me. ⁷If you really knew me, you would also know my Father. From now on, you will know him, because you have seen him."

⁸Philip said, "Master, show us the Father and that will satisfy our needs."

⁹"Philip! Have I been with you so long and you still do not recognize who I am? Anyone who has seen me has seen the Father. So why do you ask me to show him to you? ¹⁰Don't you know that I am in the Father and the Father is in me? The words I speak are not due to my own initiative. The Father lives within me and does his work through me. ¹¹Believe me when I say I am in the Father and the Father is in me. If you struggle with that, consider the miracles I have done that only God can do. ¹²I guarantee, those who believe in me will do the work I have been doing. They will do even greater work because I go to the Father.

¹³"To reveal the Father's glory in the Son, ¹⁴I will do whatever you ask under my direction and authority. ¹⁵If you love me, you will do what I tell you to do. ¹⁶I will ask the Father, and he will give you another Guide, one who will always be with you, ¹⁷the Spirit of Truth. The world cannot receive him, because it neither sees him

nor knows who he is. But you know, because he lives with you and shall be in you. [18]I will not leave you as orphans. I will come.

[19]"In a little while, the world will not see me anymore, but you will. Because I live, you will also live. [20]On that day, you will know that I am in my Father. You will know that you are in me and I am in you. [21]Those who receive and obey my instructions are the ones who love me. My Father loves those who love me, and I will love and reveal myself to them."

[22]Judas (not Iscariot) asked, "Sir, why would you reveal yourself to us and not to the world?"

[23]"People must love me enough to do what I say. Then my Father will love them, and we will come to live with them. [24]Anyone who does not love me will not obey my teaching. Remember that my words are not from my own initiative but from the Father, who sent me. [25]I can tell you these things because I am with you.

[26]"Under my direction and authority, the Father will send the Holy Spirit, your new Guide, to teach you all things and cause you to remember everything I have told you. [27]I give you peace that is nothing like what the world has to offer. Because of me, you do not have to worry or fear. [28]You heard me say I was leaving and will return. If you love me, you will be happy that I am going to the Father, because he is greater than I am.

[29]"I have told you this beforehand so when it happens, you will believe. [30]I cannot speak to you much longer, because the prince of this world is coming. He has no power over me, [31]but I will show the world that I love the Father and will do all that he has commanded. Come. It is time for us to go."

Chapter 15

[1]"I am the true vine, and my Father is the gardener. [2]He cuts off every branch of mine that does not produce fruit. He prunes the branches that bear fruit so they will produce more.

[3]"You are pruned by the words I have spoken to you. [4]Remain attached to me, and I will live in you. As the branch must be on the vine to bear fruit, so must you stay joined to me.

[5]"I am the vine, and you are the branches. You will bear much fruit if you remain in me and I live in you, but without me you can do nothing. [6]Anyone who does not remain in me is like a withered branch to be thrown away. Such branches are gathered, cast into the fire, and burned. [7]If you remain in me and my words direct your life, whatever you ask will be done for you.

[8]"When you bear much fruit, you glorify my Father and show that you are my disciples.

[9]"I have loved you like my Father has loved me. Remain in my love. [10]If you obey my commandments, you will remain in my love, just as I have obeyed my Father's commandments and remain in his love. [11]I have told you these things so you may have the joy I have, full and overflowing.

[12]"This is my commandment: love others as I have loved you. [13]There is no greater love than for a man to sacrifice his life for his friends. [14]You are my friends if you do all that I instruct you to do. [15]I have called you servants, but no longer, because servants do not know their master's business. Because you are my friends, I have told you everything that I have heard from my Father.

[16]"You did not choose me. I chose you. I appointed you to bear fruit that has a lasting impact. Whatever you ask the Father under my direction and authority, he will give you.

[17]"This is my commandment: love one another.

[18]"If the world hates you, remember that it first hated me. [19]If you belonged to the world, its people would love you as one of their own. Because you do not belong to the world but I have chosen you, its people will hate you. [20]Remember what I said before. The servant is not greater than his master. If they have persecuted me, they will

persecute you. If they had listened to me, they would listen to you. [21]They will treat you the same way they treated me, because they do not know the one who sent me. [22]If I had not spoken to them, they would not have had their sin exposed, but now they have no excuse.

[23]"Anyone who hates me also hates my Father. [24]If I had not done miracles that no man has ever done, they would not be to blame. But they saw my deeds and hated both me and my Father. [25]This fulfills what the scripture says: *They hated me for no reason.* [26]When I send the Guide from my Father, the Spirit of Truth, he will speak about me.

[27]"You also will be my witnesses, because you have been with me from the beginning."

Chapter 16

[1]"I tell you these things so your faith will not be shaken. [2]People will put you out of their synagogues. In fact, there will be a time when they will kill you and think they have pleased God. [3]They will do those things because they do not know the Father or me. [4]I am telling you this now so when the time comes, you will remember what I said and not be alarmed. I did not tell you earlier, because I was going to be with you for a while.

[5]"Now that I am going to the one who sent me, none of you have asked, 'Where are you going?' [6]That is because you are filled with grief over what I have said. [7]Even so, I tell you the truth. I must go, or the Guide will not come. But if I go, I will send him to you.

[8]"When he comes, he will reveal to the world the truth about sin, righteousness, and judgment. [9]About sin because they do not believe in me. [10]About righteousness because I go to my Father, and you will no longer see me. [11]About judgment because the prince of this world is condemned. [12]I have much more to tell you, but you cannot handle it right now. [13]But when the Spirit of Truth comes, he

will guide you into all truth. He will not speak on his own authority but will say only what he hears. He will reveal to you things to come. [14]He will glorify me by hearing my words and revealing them to you.

[15]"All that belongs to the Father belongs to me. That is why I can say he will receive my message and deliver it to you. [16]Soon, you will not see me anymore, but soon after that, you will see me again."

[17]Some of the disciples asked one another, "What does he mean, 'Soon, you will not see me anymore, but soon after that, you will see me again' and 'I go to my Father'? [18]What does he mean by 'soon'? What is he talking about?"

[19]Jesus saw that they had questions they wanted to ask. "Are you asking one another what I meant when I said, 'Soon, you will not see me anymore, but soon after that, you will see me again'? [20]Certainly, you will cry and mourn, but the world will rejoice. You will grieve, but your grief will turn to joy. [21]A woman who is about to give birth is in great pain when the moment comes. But afterward, she forgets the pain because of the joy that a child has been born. [22]Right now, you have sorrow. But when I see you again, you will rejoice, and no one will be able to take that joy away. [23]Then you will have no questions. I assure you, whatever you ask the Father under my direction and authority, he will give you. [24]Before now, you have not asked anything under my authority. If you ask, you will receive and experience fullness of joy.

[25]"I have spoken to you figuratively, but the time will come when I will speak to you plainly about the Father. [26]At that time, you can ask the Father under my authority, and I will not need to speak to him on your behalf, [27]for the Father himself loves you, because you love me and believe I came from God.

[28]"I came from the Father and entered the world. Now I must leave the world and go to the Father."

²⁹"Now you are speaking plainly," the disciples said, "without the confusing figures of speech. ³⁰We can see that you know all things, and we do not have to ask more questions to know that you came from God."

³¹"Do you believe now? ³²Listen, the time is coming—in fact, it is already here—when you will scatter to your own homes and abandon me. Yet I am not alone, because the Father is with me. ³³I have told you these things so you will have peace because of me. In this world, you will suffer, but cheer up. I have overcome the world."

Chapter 17

¹After Jesus finished speaking, he looked toward heaven. "Father, the time has come. Glorify your son so he can glorify you. ²For you have given him authority over all people, to give eternal life to those you have given him. ³Eternal life comes by knowing you, the only true God, and the one you have sent, Jesus Christ. ⁴I have glorified you on earth by completing the work you gave me to do. ⁵Now, Father, restore to me the glory I had with you before the world existed.

⁶"I have revealed you to those you gave me out of the world. They belonged to you, and you entrusted them to me. They have obeyed your word, ⁷and now they know that everything I have comes from you. ⁸They have received the message that you gave to me and are convinced that you sent me. ⁹I pray for them, not the world. I pray for those you have entrusted to me, because they belong to you. ¹⁰All these who are mine belong to you, and all who are yours belong to me, so they bring me glory.

¹¹"I am leaving the world to come to you, but they must remain here. Holy Father, protect them by the direction and authority you gave me so they may be of one spirit, as we are. ¹²While I was with them, I protected them by the authority you gave to me. Not one

of those you gave me has been lost except the one destined for destruction so scripture might be fulfilled.

[13]"Now I am coming to you. I have said these things while still with them in the world so their lives may be filled with my joy. [14]I have delivered your message to them. The world hates them because they do not belong to this world, just as I do not belong. [15]I do not pray for you to take them out of the world but that you would protect them from that which is evil. [16]They do not belong to the world any more than I do. [17]Let the truth of your word dedicate them to your service.

[18]"Just as you sent me, I send them into the world. [19]I dedicate myself to meet their needs so they also may be dedicated to true service.

[20]"I pray, not only for these disciples, but also for those who will believe in me because of their message. [21]Let them be of one spirit, as we are. Let them be one with us so the world will believe you sent me. [22]I have given them the glory that you gave me so they may be of one spirit, as we are. [23]Because I am in them and you are in me, they will be in perfect unity. Then the world will know you have sent me and that you love them as much as you love me.

[24]"Father, I want those you have given to me to be with me where I am, to see the glory you gave to me because you loved me before the creation of the world.

[25]"Righteous Father, the world does not know you, but I do. And these disciples know you have sent me. [26]I have shown them who you are and will continue to make you known so your love for me will be in them, and I will be in them."

Chapter 18

[1]After praying, Jesus went across the Kidron Valley with his disciples and entered the garden there.

²Judas, the traitor, knew the place where Jesus often retired with his disciples. ³He was followed by a mob of men, including guards from the chief priests and Pharisees, carrying lamps, torches, and swords.

⁴Jesus was fully aware of all that would happen to him and stepped forward to greet the men. "Who are you looking for?"

⁵"Jesus of Nazareth."

"I am he."

Judas, the traitor, stood there with the mob. ⁶The moment Jesus said, "I am he," the mob backed away and fell to the ground.

⁷Jesus again asked, "Who are you looking for?"

"Jesus of Nazareth."

⁸"I have already told you who I am. Since I am the one you want, let these others go." ⁹This fulfilled what he had said earlier: *None of those you gave me has been lost.*

¹⁰Simon Peter drew a sword and cut off the right ear of Malchus, the high priest's servant.

¹¹Jesus said to Peter, "Put your sword back. Shall I not drink the cup of suffering that my Father has given to me?"

¹²The mob leader and Jewish guards grabbed and bound Jesus. ¹³They took him to Annas, the father-in-law of Caiaphas, who was the high priest at that time. ¹⁴Caiaphas was the one who had told the Jewish leaders, "One man must die for the people so the whole nation will not be destroyed."

¹⁵Simon Peter followed Jesus.

Another disciple also followed, who was known to the high priest. He was allowed to enter the high priest's courtyard with Jesus.

¹⁶Peter waited outside near the gate until the other disciple spoke to the servant girl at the door and brought him in.

¹⁷The girl at the door asked Peter, "Are you one of this man's disciples too?"

Peter answered, "No, I am not."

¹⁸The servants and guards had made a fire and gathered to warm themselves. Peter stood with them and warmed himself.

¹⁹Annas asked Jesus about his disciples and what he had been teaching.

²⁰"I have spoken openly before everyone," Jesus said. "I have taught in the synagogues and in the Temple, wherever the people gather. I have said nothing in secret, ²¹so why question me? Ask those who were there and heard me speak. They know what I said."

²²One of the guards slapped Jesus. "That is not the way you should answer the high priest."

²³"If I said something wrong," Jesus said, "testify against me. But if I have spoken the truth, why do you strike me?"

²⁴Annas had sent Jesus, his hands still tied, to Caiaphas, the high priest.

²⁵While Simon Peter was standing there, warming himself, someone asked, "Aren't you one of his disciples?"

He denied it, saying, "No, I am not."

²⁶One of the high priest's servants, a relative of the one whose ear Peter had cut off, said, "Didn't I see you in the garden with him?"

²⁷Again, Peter denied any connection with Jesus.

Immediately, a rooster crowed.

²⁸Early in the morning, guards led Jesus from Caiaphas to the headquarters of the Roman governor. They stayed outside to keep from being defiled, which would prevent them from eating the Passover meal.

²⁹Pilate walked out to them. "What charges do you bring against this man?"

³⁰"If he were not a criminal, we would not have brought him to you."

³¹"You take him and judge him according to your own law."

"But it is not lawful for us to put anyone to death," the Jews replied. [32](This happened so the way Jesus had said he would die would come to pass.)

[33]Pilate went inside and summoned Jesus. "Are you the king of the Jews?"

[34]"Is that your own question, or have others told you about me?"

[35]"Am I a Jew? Your own people and your chief priests delivered you to me. What have you done?"

[36]"My Kingdom is not of this world," Jesus said. "If it were, my disciples would have fought to prevent my arrest by the Jews. No, my Kingdom is not from here."

[37]"Are you a king, then?"

Jesus answered, "Yes, you could say that. For that reason, I was born. I came into this world to testify to the truth. Everyone who wants the truth hears my voice."

[38]"What is truth?" Pilate asked. He went back out to the Jews. "I do not find this man guilty of any crime.

[39]"Each year at Passover," Pilate said to the crowd, "you customarily ask me to release a prisoner. Shall I release to you the king of the Jews?"

[40]"No, not this man. We want Barabbas," they shouted. Barabbas was a criminal.

Chapter 19

[1]Pilate ordered Jesus to be flogged. [2]Soldiers wove a crown out of thorns, put it on his head, and gave him a kingly purple robe. [3]"Hail! King of the Jews," they mocked as they slapped him with their hands.

[4]Again, Pilate went out to the people. "Look, I am bringing Jesus before you to declare that I find him not guilty."

⁵When Jesus came out, wearing the crown of thorns and purple robe, Pilate said, "Behold the man."

⁶As soon as the chief priests and guards saw Jesus, they shouted, "Crucify him. Crucify him!"

"You crucify him, then," Pilate said. "I find him not guilty."

⁷The Jewish leaders said, "By our law, he must die because he claimed to be the Son of God."

⁸When Pilate heard this, he became more fearful. ⁹He went back inside and asked Jesus, "Who are you?"

Jesus said nothing.

¹⁰"Why won't you answer? Don't you know I have the authority to either release or crucify you?"

¹¹"You would have no authority over me at all if it had not been given to you from above. Therefore, those who delivered me to you are guilty of the greater wrong."

¹²After they had talked, Pilate sought to release Jesus, but the Jewish leaders shouted, "If you release this man, you are no friend of Caesar. Anyone who claims to be a king opposes Caesar."

¹³At these words, Pilate brought Jesus out and sat in the judgment seat, a mosaic called the Platform, Gabbatha in Hebrew. ¹⁴It was about noon on the preparation day of Passover. He said to the Jews, "Behold your king!"

¹⁵"Away with him," the people shouted. "Away with him! Crucify him!"

"Shall I crucify your king?" Pilate asked.

The chief priests answered, "We have no king except Caesar."

¹⁶Then Pilate gave the order for Jesus to be crucified, and the soldiers took him away, ¹⁷bearing his cross, to a place called the "skull," which is called Golgotha in Hebrew.

¹⁸The soldiers nailed Jesus to the cross, and two others with him, one on the right, the other on the left.

¹⁹Pilate ordered the posting of a sign on the cross that said, "Jesus of Nazareth, the king of the Jews."

²⁰Many of the Jews read the sign, because the crucifixion took place near Jerusalem and the message was written in Hebrew, Greek, and Latin. ²¹The chief priests protested to Pilate, "You should not have written, 'The king of the Jews,' but rather, 'He claimed to be king of the Jews.' "

²²Pilate answered, "What I have written, I have written."

²³After the soldiers had crucified Jesus, they divided his garments among the four of them. The tunic was a single woven piece, without seams. ²⁴Rather than rip it, they decided to gamble to determine its rightful owner. This fulfilled the scripture that says, *They divided my clothes and threw dice for my garment.*

²⁵Jesus' mother, his mother's sister, Mary Magdalene, and Mary the wife of Clopas stood near the cross. ²⁶When Jesus saw his mother standing next to his beloved disciple, he said, "Woman, he is your son." ²⁷To the disciple, he said, "She is your mother." From that moment, the disciple took her to live in his own home.

²⁸Later, after everything was finished, he said, "I am thirsty," so the scripture would be fulfilled. ²⁹Someone filled a sponge from a nearby jug of sour wine, put the sponge on a hyssop branch, and held it to Jesus' mouth. ³⁰After Jesus had received the wine, he said, "It is finished." He bowed his head and quit breathing.

³¹On the day of preparation, the Jews asked Pilate to break the legs of the crucified so they would die and could be taken down before the Sabbath, a special day because of Passover.

³²So the soldiers broke the legs of the two who were crucified with Jesus. ³³But when they came to Jesus and saw that he was already dead, they did not break his legs.

³⁴One of the soldiers pierced his side with a spear, and bloody water gushed out.

³⁵An eyewitness has given this true testimony so you will believe. ³⁶These things happened to fulfill the scripture: *He protects his bones so none are broken.* ³⁷And another scripture: *They will look upon the one whom they have pierced.*

³⁸Soon afterward, Joseph from Arimathea, disciple of Jesus in secret because of his fear of the Jews, asked Pilate for the body of Jesus. Given permission, he took the body down from the cross. ³⁹Nicodemus, the one who had come to Jesus by night, went with Joseph and carried about seventy-five pounds of a mixture of myrrh and aloes. ⁴⁰According to Jewish burial custom, they wrapped the body in linen, with the spices.

⁴¹Not far from the crucifixion was a garden with an unused tomb. ⁴²They buried Jesus there because it was near the end of the day of preparation, and the tomb was nearby.

Chapter 20

¹Early on Sunday, the first day of the week, while it was still dark, Mary Magdalene went to the tomb and saw that the stone had been rolled back from the entrance. ²She ran to find Simon Peter and John. "They have stolen Jesus from the tomb," she said, "and we do not know where they have put him."

³Peter and John left for the tomb. ⁴They ran together, but John ran faster and reached the tomb first. ⁵He stooped and looked inside, saw the linen pieces lying there, but did not go in.

⁶When Peter arrived, he went in and saw the linen cloth. ⁷The piece that had been around Jesus' head was folded in place, separate from the other linen.

⁸John went in, saw the evidence, and believed his body had been stolen.

⁹As yet, they still did not understand from scripture that Jesus must rise from the dead, ¹⁰so the disciples went back home.

[11]Mary stood outside the tomb, crying. As she cried, she stooped to look inside [12]and saw two angels dressed in white, seated where Jesus' body had been, one at the head, the other at the feet. [13]"Woman, why are you crying?" they asked.

"Because they have stolen my master's body, and I do not know where they have put him." [14]She turned and saw someone standing by her but did not know it was Jesus.

[15]"Woman, why are you crying?" Jesus asked. "Who are you looking for?"

She assumed he was the gardener. "Sir, if you have taken his body, tell me where you have put him, and I will take him away."

[16]"Mary!" Jesus said.

She turned and said to him in Hebrew, "*Rabboni*," which means "Teacher."

[17]"You do not have to cling to me," Jesus said, "because I am not going to my Father yet. But go to my brothers and tell them I will soon ascend to my Father and your Father, to my God and your God."

[18]Mary Magdalene found the disciples, told them she had seen Jesus, and delivered the message.

[19]That Sunday evening, the disciples met behind closed doors because they were afraid of the Jewish leaders.

Jesus appeared and stood among them. "Peace be with you." [20]After he showed them the wounds in his hands and side, they realized it was Jesus and rejoiced.

[21]"Peace be with you," Jesus said. "As the Father has sent me, I send you." [22]After saying this, he breathed on them. "Receive the Holy Spirit. [23]The sins you forgive will be forgiven, and the sins you do not forgive will not be forgiven."

[24]Thomas, one of the twelve, who was called the Twin, was not with the rest of them when Jesus came.

²⁵They told him, "We have seen Jesus."

But he said, "Unless I see the scars in his hands, put my finger where the nails were driven, and place my hand on his wounded side, I will not believe."

²⁶Eight days later, the disciples were again gathered behind closed doors, and Thomas was with them.

Jesus appeared and stood among them. "Peace be with you." ²⁷He said to Thomas, "Look at the scars in my hands, and put your finger where the nails were driven. Put your hand on my side. Do not doubt anymore. Believe."

²⁸Thomas cried, "My Lord and my God!"

²⁹"Because you have seen me, Thomas, you have believed. Blessed are those who have not seen me, yet believe."

³⁰The disciples saw Jesus do many other miracles that have not been recorded, ³¹but these are written so you will believe that Jesus is the Messiah, the Son of God. By believing, you will have life through his name.

Chapter 21

¹Sometime later, Jesus again revealed himself to the disciples.

²Simon Peter, Thomas called the Twin, Nathanael of Cana in Galilee, the sons of Zebedee, and two other disciples had gone to the Sea of Galilee.

³"I am going fishing," Simon Peter said.

The others said, "We will go too."

They went out in the boat, fished all night, and caught nothing.

⁴At dawn, Jesus stood on the shore, but the disciples did not know who he was. ⁵"Young men," Jesus said, "have you caught anything?"

"Nothing," they answered.

⁶"Cast your net on the right side of the boat, and you will catch plenty."

When they did, they caught so many fish they could not pull the net back into the boat.

⁷John said to Peter, "It's Jesus!"

When Simon Peter realized who it was, he grabbed his clothes, jumped into the water, and headed toward shore. ⁸Only a hundred yards from shore, the rest of the disciples followed in the boat, dragging the net full of fish. ⁹When they reached shore, they saw a fire already prepared, a fish lying on the coals, and bread.

¹⁰Jesus said, "Bring some of the fish you caught."

¹¹Simon Peter went out and pulled the net to shore. There were 153 fish, yet the net was not torn.

¹²"Come and eat," Jesus said.

None of the disciples dared ask, "Who are you?" They all knew he was Jesus.

¹³Jesus took the bread, broke it, and gave it to them. He did the same with the fish. ¹⁴This was the third time Jesus appeared to his disciples after he was raised from the dead.

¹⁵After they had eaten, Jesus said, "Simon, son of Jonah, do you love me more than the others?"

"Yes, sir, you know I do."

Jesus said to him, "Take care of my lambs."

¹⁶Again, Jesus said, "Simon, son of Jonah, do you love me?"

"Yes, sir, you know I do."

Jesus said to him, "Take care of my sheep."

¹⁷A third time, Jesus said, "Simon, son of Jonah, do you love me?"

Peter was offended that his love had been questioned for a third time.

"Sir, you know everything. You know that I love you."

"Take care of my sheep," Jesus said. [18]"I tell you the truth. When you were young, you dressed and went wherever you wanted. But when you are old, you will put out your hands, and someone else will dress you and take you where you do not want to go." [19]He said this to indicate the kind of death by which Peter would glorify God. Jesus said to him, "Follow me."

[20]Peter looked back to the disciple whom Jesus loved, the one who had leaned against Jesus at the supper and asked who would betray him. [21]"Sir, what about him? How will he die?"

[22]"If I want him to live until I return, that is not your concern. You must follow me."

[23]A rumor spread that this disciple would not die, but that is not what Jesus said. He only said, "If I want him to live until I return, that is not your concern."

[24]This disciple is the eyewitness who recorded the events, so we know his testimony is true. [25]If all that Jesus did were told, the whole world could not contain all the books that should be written.

References to Prophecy Fulfilled

E

Exodus 12:46—He protects his bones so none are broken. ... 236

H

Hosea 11:1—I called my son out of Egypt............................3

I

Isaiah 6:9–10—You listen but do not understand. You see but have no recognition. Harden the hearts of these people and close their ears and cover their eyes so they will not see with their eyes, hear with their ears, and understand with their hearts and be forced to turn to me and be healed. 26, 221

Isaiah 7:14—Watch for this! A virgin will become pregnant and give birth to a son named Immanuel. 2

Isaiah 8:3–5—Clear a path in the wilderness, because the Lord our God is coming. 4, 69, 120, 188

Isaiah 9:1–2—Darkness will not last forever. The insignificant land of Zebulun and Naphtali, between the Jordan River and the Mediterranean Sea, will be a glory to the nation. People who walk in darkness will see a bright light. Upon those who live under dark shadows of death, the light will shine..5

Isaiah 11:1—He will be called a Nazarene. 3

Isaiah 29:13—These people express love with their mouths and their lips offer praise, but their hearts are

somewhere else. Their reverence for me is nothing
but a ritual.. 32

Isaiah 40:3–5—Listen! Someone is shouting, Clear a path
in the wilderness, for the Lord our God is coming. Fill
the valleys and flatten the mountains. Straighten the
curves and smooth the rough places. The glory of the
Lord will appear for all to see. God has spoken. It will
surely come to pass..................................... 4, 69, 120

Isaiah 42:1–4—Here is my chosen servant, my beloved in
whom I am well pleased. I have put my Spirit upon
him to bring justice to the people. He will not argue
or raise his voice in the streets. He will not break off
a weakened reed or put out a flickering lamp but will
judge in truth. He will not quit until he has established
justice throughout the earth. Distant lands will place
their hope in him. 23

Isaiah 53:1—Who would have believed what we have
prophesied? Who can see the Lord's hand at work? 220

Isaiah 53:4—Truly, he has taken our infirmities and carried
our pain. 14

Isaiah 53:9—Behold, a true Israelite in whom is no deceit..... 189

Isaiah 53:12—He was treated as one of the criminals........... 176

Isaiah 54:13—All your children will be taught by God......... 202

J

Jeremiah 31:15—A cry is heard in Ramah, mourning and
wailing. Rachel weeps for her children and will not be
comforted, because they are gone. 3

John 6:39—None of those you gave me has been lost. 231

L

Luke 22:34—Before the rooster crows twice, you will
deny me three times. 178

M

Malachi 3:1—See, I will send my messenger to prepare the way before me. 21, 69, 132

Mark 14:30—Before the rooster crows twice, you will deny me three times. 107

Matthew 26:34—Before the rooster crows twice, you will deny me three times. 63

Micah 5:2—But you, Bethlehem near Ephrath, are only a small village among the people of Judah. Yet out of you will come one who will rule Israel, whose origin is from ancient times. 2

P

Psalm 8:2—From the mouth of infants and children, you have raised up a strong voice to refute your enemies, silencing the adverse words of all who oppose you. 46

Psalm 22:18—They divide my clothes and throw dice for my garment... 235

Psalm 34:20—He protects his bones so none are broken. 236

Psalm 41:9—My trusted friend who ate bread with me has turned against me. 222

Psalm 69:4—They hated me for no reason. 227

Psalm 69:9—Passion for your house burns like fire within me because those who offend you have offended me....... 191

Psalm 78:2—I will open my mouth with a parable and explain mysteries kept secret from the beginning............. 28

Psalm 91:11–12—God will command his angels to protect you wherever you go. They will hold you in their hands lest you strike your foot against a stone.................... 5, 122

Psalm 118:22–23—The stone that the builders rejected has become the cornerstone. God has done this, and it's a wonderful sight to behold. 47, 98, 170

Z

Zechariah 9:9—Have no fear. People of Zion, rejoice. Shout for joy, people of Jerusalem. Look! The king is coming, righteous and victorious savior, yet humble, riding upon a colt, a donkey's foal.........................45, 219

Zechariah 11:12–13—They took the thirty pieces of silver, the value that Israel's people placed on him, and bought the potter's field as God commanded. 64

Zechariah 12:10—They will look upon the one whom they have pierced. 236

Zechariah 13:7—Strike the shepherd, and the sheep will be scattered..60, 105

Chronology of Events

Eyewitnesses begin their amazing testimony.   Mark 1:1; Luke 1:1–4; John 1:1–18
The ancestry of Jesus is recorded.   Matthew 1:1–17; Luke 3:23b–38
An angel meets Zechariah in the Temple.   Luke 1:5–25
A child is miraculously conceived.   Matthew 1:18–25; Luke 1:26–38
Mary visits her aunt Elizabeth.   Luke 1:39–56
John, son of Zechariah, is born.   Luke 1:57–80
Shepherds hear news about a baby in a manger.   Luke 2:1–38
Wise men search for the new king of the Jews.   Matthew 2:1–18
Jesus grows up in Nazareth.   Matthew 2:19–23; Luke 2:39–52
John, son of Zechariah, becomes John the Baptizer.   Matthew 3:1–12; Mark 1:2–8; Luke 3:1–18
John baptizes Jesus.   Matthew 3:13–17; Mark 1:9–11; Luke 3:21–23a
The Holy Spirit leads Jesus to an encounter with Satan.   Matthew 4:1–11; Mark 1:12–13; Luke 4:1–13
John the Baptizer recognizes Jesus as the Lamb of God.   John 1:19–34

Disciples of John the Baptizer meet Jesus for the first time.   John 1:35–51
The wedding feast continues after Jesus changes water into wine.   John 2:1–12

The merchants are driven out of the Temple.
        Matthew 21:12–13; Mark 11:15–18; Luke 19:45–48;
    John 2:13–22

Nicodemus learns about spiritual birth.   John 2:23–25; 3:1–21
Jesus and his disciples baptize many in Judea.   Matthew 4:12; Luke 3:19–20; John 3:22–36; 4:1–3
A Samaritan woman comes for water and finds life.   John 4:4–44

A government official seeks healing for his sick son.
        Matthew 4:17; Mark 1:14–15; Luke 4:14–15;
    John 4:45–54

At his boyhood home, Jesus is rejected.   Luke 4:16–30
Jesus invites some men to follow him.   Matthew 4:13–16, 18–22; Mark 1:16–20; Luke 4:31
A man possessed by an evil spirit is delivered.   Mark 1:21–28; Luke 4:31–37
Peter's mother-in-law is healed.   Matthew 8:14–15; Mark 1:29–31; Luke 4:38–39
Jesus works after sunset.   Matthew 8:16–17; Mark 1:32–39; Luke 4:40–44
Fishermen are taught about fishing.   Luke 5:1–11
A leper is cleansed.   Matthew 8:2–4; Mark 1:40–45; Luke 5:12–16

A paralyzed man is lowered through the roof to see Jesus. Matthew 9:1–8; Mark 2:1–12; Luke 5:17–26
Matthew is invited to follow Jesus. Matthew 9:9–13; Mark 2:13–17; Luke 5:27–32
The disciples don't follow religious tradition. Matthew 9:14–17; 12:1–8; Mark 2:18–28; Luke 5:33–39; 6:1–5
A man with a shriveled hand is healed on the Sabbath. Matthew 12:9–14; Mark 3:1–6; Luke 6:6–11
Jesus teaches a large crowd at the Galilean seashore. Matthew 12:15–21; Mark 3:7–12
Jesus selects twelve apostles out of his group of followers. Mark 3:13–19; Luke 6:12–16
Jesus teaches about blessings that follow tough times. Matthew 5:1–12; Luke 6:17–26
God's people are to let their light shine. Matthew 5:13–16
God seeks righteous behavior that is more than the Law required. Matthew 5:17–37
People are to show kindness to even their enemies. Matthew 5:38–48; Luke 6:27–36
Jesus teaches about prayer. Matthew 6:1–8, 14–18
What you treasure needs to have lasting value. Matthew 6:19–34
Jesus teaches the principles of God's Kingdom. Matthew 7:1–29; Luke 6:37–49
A Roman officer recognizes Jesus as a man under God's command. Matthew 8:5–13; Luke 7:2–10

A widow's son at Nain is raised from the dead.   Luke 7:11–17
Jesus gives testimony about John the Baptizer.   Matthew 11:2–15; Luke 7:18–30
People are rebuked for not believing.   Matthew 11:16–30; Luke 7:31–35
A Pharisee invites Jesus to dinner and learns about forgiveness.   Luke 7:36–50; 8:1–3
Jesus is accused of using satanic power when he casts out evil spirits.   Matthew 12:22–45; Mark 3:20–30
Jesus identifies his true family.   Matthew 12:46–50; Mark 3:31–35; Luke 8:19–21
Jesus uses a farming illustration to teach about hearing God's word.   Matthew 13:1–23; Mark 4:1–20; Luke 8:4–15
Jesus describes what the Kingdom of God is like.   Matthew 13:24–53; Mark 4:21–34; Luke 8:16–18
Jesus calms a violent storm.   Matthew 8:18, 23–27; Mark 4:35–41; Luke 8:22–25
Jesus delivers a man who was possessed by many evil spirits.   Matthew 8:28–34; Mark 5:1–20; Luke 8:26–39
Jairus's daughter is raised from the dead.   Matthew 9:18–34; Mark 5:21–43; Luke 8:40–56
Jesus is like the prophet who isn't appreciated in his own country.   Matthew 13:54–58; Mark 6:1–6a

Jesus sends workers into the fields.
    Matthew 9:35–38; 10:1–42; 11:1; Mark 6:6b–13;
    Luke 9:1–6

A lame man at the Bethesda pool is healed.   John 5:1–16
Jesus claims equality with God.   John 5:17–47
Herod thinks John the Baptizer has returned from the dead.   Matthew 14:1–12; Mark 6:14–29; Luke 9:7 9

With five loaves, Jesus feeds five thousand men.
    Matthew 14:13–21; Mark 6:30–44; Luke 9:10–17;
    John 6:1–13

Jesus walks with Peter on the water.   Matthew 14:22–33; Mark 6:45–52; John 6:14–21
Jesus is the bread of life.   John 6:22–71; 7:1
Traditions of men don't make people right with God.   Matthew 14:34–36; 15:1–20; Mark 6:53–56; 7:1–23
A Greek woman begs help for her daughter.   Matthew 15:21–28; Mark 7:24–30
Jesus does spectacular miracles.   Matthew 15:29–31; Mark 7:31–37
With seven loaves, Jesus feeds four thousand men.   Matthew 15:32–38; Mark 8:1–9
Religious leaders ask for undeniable proof.   Matthew 15:39; 16:1–4; Mark 8:10–13
Jesus warns of danger in religious teachings.   Matthew 16:5–12; Mark 8:14–21
A man sees trees that walk.   Mark 8:22–26
Peter recognizes Jesus as the Messiah sent from God.   Matthew 16:13–28; Mark 8:27–38; 9:1; Luke 9:18–27
Three disciples see Jesus talk with Moses and Elijah.   Matthew 17:1–13; Mark 9:2–13; Luke 9:28–36

Jesus delivers when the disciples can't.   Matthew 17:14–21; Mark 9:14–29; Luke 9:37–43a

The disciples receive private tutoring.
    Matthew 17:22–27; 18:1–35; Mark 9:30–50;
    Luke 9:43b–50

Jesus goes to Jerusalem unannounced.
    Matthew 8:19–22; 19:1–2; Mark 10:1; Luke 9:51–62;
    John 7:2–13

Guards are sent to arrest Jesus.   John 7:14–53; 8:1
Jesus forgives a woman who was caught in adultery.   John 8:2–11
Jesus teaches in the Temple.   John 8:12–59

Jesus sends another seventy-two disciples into the fields of
    ministry.
    Luke 10:1–24

A good Samaritan helping a Jew shows how to love others.   Luke 10:25–37
Jesus heals a man who was born blind.   John 9:1–41
The good shepherd cares for his sheep.   John 10:1–21
Martha becomes frustrated with her sister's behavior.   Luke 10:38–42
The disciples learn more about how to pray.   Matthew 6:9–13; Luke 11:1–13
Freed from an evil spirit, a man is able to speak.   Luke 11:14–36
A Pharisee asks Jesus to dinner.   Luke 11:37–54

Jesus warns against religious hypocrisy.   Luke 12:1–12
A rich man shows how greed is never satisfied.   Luke 12:13–34
The Lord's coming requires constant readiness.   Luke 12:35–59
Jesus stresses the importance of bearing fruit.   Luke 13:1–21
The Kingdom demands a wholehearted effort.   Luke 13:22–30
People start to stone Jesus for blasphemy.   John 10:22–42
Pharisees reveal a threat on Jesus' life.   Matthew 23:37–39; Luke 13:31–35
Jesus teaches about the banquet table.   Luke 14:1–24
A builder must count the cost.   Luke 14:25–35
That which is lost is especially important.   Luke 15:1–32
Jesus teaches on faithfulness.   Luke 16:1–17
Jesus teaches about divorce.   Matthew 19:3–12; Mark 10:2–12; Luke 16:18
A dead man wants to tell his brothers about his eternal torment.   Luke 16:19–31
Servants must be faithful to their duties.   Luke 17:1–10
Lazarus is raised from the dead.   John 11:1–54

One of ten lepers thanks Jesus.   Luke 17:11–19
Jesus tells about the day of his return.   Luke 17:20–37
Jesus teaches about prayer.   Luke 18:1–14
The value of children is stressed.   Matthew 19:13–15; Mark 10:13–16; Luke 18:15–17

People should recognize the value of eternal rewards.
    Matthew 19:16–30; 20:1–16; Mark 10:17–31;
    Luke 18:18–30

The disciples are told that Jesus must suffer and die.   Matthew 20:17–19; Mark 10:32–34; Luke 18:31–34
Two disciples seek the highest honor.   Matthew 20:20–28; Mark 10:35–45
Zacchaeus climbs a tree to see Jesus.   Luke 19:1–28
Two blind men want to see.   Matthew 20:29–34; Mark 10:46–52; Luke 18:35–43
Mary anoints Jesus with expensive perfume.   Matthew 26:6–13; Mark 14:3–9; John 11:55–57; 12:1–11

People cheer as Jesus rides into Jerusalem on a donkey.
    Matthew 21:1–9; Mark 11:1–10; Luke 19:29–44;
    John 12:12–19

Some Greek men want to see Jesus.   Mark 11:10–11; John 12:20–50
Jesus curses a fig tree.   Matthew 21:14–22; Mark 11:12–14, 19–26
Religious leaders question Jesus' authority.   Matthew 21:23–32; Mark 11:27–33; Luke 20:1–8

Sharecroppers kill the landowner's son.
Matthew 21:33–46; Mark 12:1–12; Luke 20:9–19
Jesus compares the Kingdom to a wedding feast.
Matthew 22:1–14
Religious leaders seek to trap Jesus with a question about taxes.
Matthew 22:15–22; Mark 12:13–17; Luke 20:20–26
Jesus teaches about life after death.
Matthew 22:23–33; Mark 12:18–27; Luke 20:27–40
A man asks what is the most important commandment.
Matthew 22:34–40; Mark 12:28–34
Jesus answers a question about the Messiah.
Matthew 22:41–46; Mark 12:35–37; Luke 20:41–44
Jesus condemns the religious leaders.
Matthew 23:1–36; Mark 12:38–40; Luke 20:45–47
A widow gives everything to God.
Matthew 24:1–2; Mark 12:41–44; 13:1–2; Luke 21:1–6
Jesus reveals what will happen before his return.
Matthew 24:3–42; Mark 13:3–37; Luke 21:7–36
A good servant works without supervision.
Matthew 24:43–51
A story about ten virgins shows the importance of being ready.
Matthew 25:1–13
People have a responsibility to use what they have been given.
Matthew 25:14–30
Jesus compares God's judgment to the separation of sheep and goats.
Matthew 25:31–46
Judas agrees to betray Jesus.
Matthew 26:1–5, 14–16; Mark 14:1–2, 10–11; Luke 21:37–38; 22:1–6

Two disciples prepare for Passover.
    Matthew 26:17–19; Mark 14:12–16; Luke 22:7–13;
    John 13:1

Jesus celebrates Passover with the disciples.
    Matthew 26:20, 26–29; Mark 14:17, 22–25;
    Luke 22:14–20; John 13:2

Jesus washes the disciples' feet.   Luke 22:24–27; John 13:3–17

Jesus predicts his betrayal.
    Matthew 26:21–25; Mark 14:18–21; Luke 22:21–23;
    John 13:18–32

Peter declares his loyalty, but Jesus predicts denial.
    Matthew 26:31–35; Mark 14:27–31; Luke 22:28–38;
    John 13:33–38

Jesus gives final words to his disciples.   Matthew 26:30; Mark 14:26; Luke 22:39; John 14:1–31
On the way to Gethsemane, Jesus teaches his disciples.   John 15:1–27; 16:1–33
Jesus gives an intercessory prayer.   John 17:1–26

Jesus prays at Gethsemane.
    Matthew 26:36–46; Mark 14:32–42; Luke 22:40–46;
    John 18:1

Religious leaders arrest Jesus.
    Matthew 26:47–56; Mark 14:43–52; Luke 22:47–53;
    John 11:50; 17:12; 18:2–14, 19–23

Jesus is tried before Caiaphas.
    Matthew 26:34, 57–75; Mark 14:30, 53–72;
    Luke 22:34, 54–65; John 13:38; 18:15–18, 24–27

The ruling council gives Jesus the death sentence.   Matthew 27:1; Mark 15:1; Luke 22:66–71

Judas commits suicide.   Matthew 27:3–10

Jesus stands before Pilate.
    Matthew 27:2, 11–14; Mark 15:1b–5; Luke 23:1–5;
    John 18:28–38

Pilate sends Jesus to Herod Antipas.   Luke 23:6–12

Pilate pacifies the mob by ordering Jesus to be crucified.
    Matthew 27:15–26; Mark 15:6–15; Luke 23:13–25;
    John 18:39–40; 19:1–16

On the way to crucifixion, Simon of Cyrene is forced to carry
    Jesus' cross.
    Matthew 27:27–34; Mark 15:16–23; Luke 23:26–32;
    John 19:16–17

Jesus is nailed to the cross and dies.
    Matthew 27:35–56; Mark 15:24–31; Luke 23:33–49;
    John 19:18–30

Joseph of Arimathea and Nicodemus give Jesus a hasty burial
    before sundown.
    Matthew 27:57–66; Mark 15:42–47; Luke 23:50–56;
    John 19:31–42

The tomb is opened, and people can't find Jesus' body.
    Matthew 28:1–15; Mark 16:1–11; Luke 24:1–12;
    John 20:1–18

Jesus appears to two of his followers on the way to Emmaus.   Mark 16:12–13; Luke 24:13–35
Jesus appears to his disciples for the first time.   Mark 16:14; Luke 24:36–43; John 20:19–31; 21:1–23

The disciples watch Jesus ascend into the clouds.
    Matthew 28:16–20; Mark 16:15–20; Luke 24:44–53;
    John 21:24–25

Comments on Difficult Passages

- **Matthew 2:1–18—We have seen the star signaling his birth and have come to worship him.**

Some scholars believe the wise men's search for the new king of the Jews is a fairy tale, and for good reason. A star doesn't travel through the sky, so it can't be followed, neither could it disappear, leaving the wise men to search in Jerusalem. Nor could it reappear on their way to Bethlehem. In addition, King Herod was so fearful of anyone who threatened his rule that he killed members of his own family. He would never send strangers to find the infant king. Or would he?

Although stars don't appear, disappear, and reappear, comets do. When the "star" first appeared, the wise men understood its significance and began their months-long journey to Jerusalem. By the time they were on their way to Bethlehem, the comet had orbited around the sun and reappeared. When they arrived at the house where the child lived, the comet was directly in front of them.

Suppose Herod, in his cunning, realized that searching with his own men would lead to hiding the child, but townspeople wouldn't fear foreigners coming with gifts. All he had to do was have someone follow the wise men and report the location of the house. How angry he would have been when his subsequent dispatch of soldiers found the house empty.

All this is speculation, of course, but it's sufficient to show a plausible way in which the event did happen. It wasn't a fairy tale.

- **Matthew 2:19–23; Luke 2:39–52—When Jesus was twelve, the family went to Jerusalem to celebrate the Passover festival, according to Jewish custom.**

Some translations might lead us to believe that all Jews went to Jerusalem to celebrate Passover every year. If that were true, the rest of the nation would be without inhabitants and enemies would take over the land. When returning from Egypt, because of the threat of King Herod's son, Joseph was warned in a dream and settled in Nazareth instead of the Jerusalem area.[1] We can be sure that Joseph didn't celebrate Passover in Jerusalem while Archelaus was in power.

The family's trip to Jerusalem when Jesus was twelve, soon after the death of Archelaus, was probably their first time to visit the Temple after Jesus was consecrated there as a baby.

- **Matthew 4:1–11; Mark 1:12–13; Luke 4:1–13—Satan took [Jesus] to the Temple in Jerusalem and stood him on a high place, towering above the Kidron valley. "Since you are the Son of God, jump."**

The temptations of Jesus present a number of difficulties until we understand the level of their contention. Satan knew who Jesus was, and Jesus knew who Satan was. If deception were possible, it would have to be of the highest order, like one chess master playing another. A blatant lie would never work. Satan's best ploys would be misapplications of the truth. We should expect no less from the "father of lies," who always works to present his truth of pride and independence as if it were in our best interest to make that choice.[2]

---

[1] Matthew 2:16.
[2] John 8:44.

Begin with an understanding that Jesus would break no law if he were to take stones and make them bread. During forty days of fasting, Satan never tempted Jesus to make bread, not even in the early days when hunger pangs strike their hardest. He waited until after the fast was over, and there was no compelling of the Holy Spirit not to eat. Satan would checkmate Jesus if he could get him to do something of his own human will, independent of God's direction. But Jesus saw through the deception and set the standard by which he lived—to do nothing of his own initiative. [3]

We must now ask how anyone could be tempted to take a flying leap off a thirty-story building. Who would want to jump from an airplane without a parachute and become a grease spot on the ground? Satan's enticement to jump doesn't sound like the deception of a master player until we recognize the truth of his words: "God will command his angels to protect you wherever you go. They will hold you in their hands lest you strike your foot against a stone." We might doubt those words, but Jesus knew they were true. In an instant, the angels would be there, and that is why it was a viable temptation. Again, Jesus had the ability to be independent but chose not to act on his own initiative.

- **Matthew 21:12; Mark 11:15; Luke 19:45; John 2:15—In the Temple's outer court, Jesus threw out the merchants who were buying and selling there.**

John places this event at the beginning of Jesus' ministry while other gospels place it nearer to the crucifixion. When did it happen, or did it happen more than once?

Ancient writers did not have the need for chronological accuracy that we have today. Events were recorded in the order they came to mind, not necessarily in their relative place in time. Because

---

[3] John 8:28.

John is chronological, associating events with the feasts, such as Passover, we know the merchants were thrown out when Jesus and his disciples first visited the Temple. The only remaining question is whether a similar event occurred later, as we might assume from where it is placed in the other gospels.

We need to understand the conditions under which the merchants did business. The selling of animals for sacrifice and the exchange of foreign coins for the half-shekel Temple tax was a service approved by the Jewish leaders. If Jesus had been the only man upsetting the tables, he would have quickly been subdued and arrested by the Temple guards.

The disciples didn't stand aside and watch. They were also upsetting cages and tearing down animal pens. Even so, a dozen men would not have been sufficient to end a practice established by the council unless public opinion had changed. The Bible records only a few of the words from Jesus' passionate message that must have gathered a mob against the Temple enterprise.

In his zeal for his Father's house, he shouted sufficient arguments for the people to understand the need to change Temple worship. "The scriptures say the Temple will be called a house of prayer for all nations, but you have turned it into a hangout for robbers."[4]

This helps explain much of the Jewish leaders' hatred of Jesus from the beginning.

- **Matthew 4:19; Mark 1:17—Come, follow me, and I will make you fishers of men.**

Because the Bible gives only a summary of what happens, we might think the disciples were, at the first sight of Jesus, mysteriously drawn away from their homes and businesses. Actually, before they were called to be with him all the time, they were with

---

[4] Matthew 21:13; Mark 11:17; Luke 19:46.

Jesus in many different places, heard him speak, and witnessed his miracles.

Before the disciples were called to be fishers of men, John the Baptizer pointed out Jesus to John and Andrew. Afterward, John and Andrew brought their brothers, James and Peter, to see Jesus, and they were joined by Philip and Nathanael as they went through Capernaum and Cana in Galilee. Over a period of weeks, perhaps months, of being with Jesus at various times, they developed a confidence that made them willing to forsake everything at the final call and go wherever Jesus went.

• **Matthew 10:16—Listen, I am sending you like lambs into a pack of wolves. Therefore, you must be wise as snakes . . . harmless as doves.**

People in the first century understood the analogy, but we need an explanation because snakes don't usually slip into our houses without invitation. Certainly, Jesus was not telling his disciples to bite people like venomous snakes or to fly like birds. What was his point?

In ancient times, houses had cracks through which snakes could slip in unnoticed. The disciples were to enter cities without fanfare, quietly slipping in like any other stranger. At the first sign of contention, they were to flee, which is exactly what doves do when their nests are threatened. In summary, what Jesus meant was "You must be wise as snakes, slipping in unnoticed, and harmless as doves, fleeing when threatened."

• **Matthew 8:5–13; Luke 7:2–10—A Roman officer sent respected Jewish leaders to Jesus, pleading for help.**

The story in Matthew is usually given as the Roman officer talking directly to Jesus. From Luke, who is prone to give more details, we know the communication was in messages sent through emissaries, the method we should expect from an official who had the highest respect for Jesus, one whom he regarded as a superior under God's authority.

- **Matthew 11:28–30—Take my yoke upon you. The load is light.**

Today, we don't see enough teams of oxen pulling plows to understand Jesus' analogy. In a team of two oxen yoked together, one ox takes the lead while the other follows. Jesus is saying, if we will pull with him, the load will seem light because his strength will bear most of the burden.

- **Matthew 12:26–28; Luke 17:20—If Beelzebub is my power over evil spirits, by whom do your followers cast them out?**

To avoid acknowledging Jesus as one under God's authority, religious leaders often told the people that Satan was Jesus' source of power. Jesus was quick to point out that any kingdom working against itself is soon destroyed. He then pointed to the fact that the leaders' own followers cast out evil spirits. The original text is missing the words necessary to give that fact any relevance. In what way did the action of the followers validate the authority of Jesus?

Jesus had already pointed out the absurdity of Satan casting out his own evil spirits. That left only God with both the ability and desire to see people delivered. The Jewish leaders believed their followers cast out evil spirits by the power of God. For them to see the work of Jesus differently, they had to use a double standard of judgment. In both cases, they observed the same evidence but chose to reach opposite conclusions.

- **Matthew 9:18–34; Mark 5:21–43; Luke 8:40–56—My little daughter is dying, but if you will come lay your hand on her, she will live.**

Matthew is usually rendered to say the daughter was already dead. While that was true, Jairus didn't know until later. Mark and Luke tell us that Jairus learned of that fact on the way to his house.

- **Matthew 10:5—Do not go among the Gentiles or into any Samaritan city.**

There is no reason to instruct people to do something they would never consider doing. Earlier, the disciples had received an overwhelming welcome at Sychar in Samaria. This success was followed by great failure. People in Galilee, especially those in Nazareth, refused to believe. Since people have a tendency to build on past successes and avoid anything that has failed, the disciples were naturally inclined to seek converts among Gentiles and Samaritans, who were not steeped in Jewish prejudice. Therefore, Jesus needed to instruct them to go to places in Israel where they had not been before.

- **Matthew 15:21–28; Mark 7:24–30—I was only sent to the lost sheep of Israel.**

We know Jesus was being sarcastic, because he had already stirred a huge revival in Samaria, among a people the Jews detested.[5] He had quickly agreed to heal a Roman officer's son.[6] His preaching about God's favor upon foreigners stirred the men of Nazareth to try to kill him.[7]

By adopting the view of the narrow-minded Jews who were present, Jesus demonstrated the absurdity of their bias.

---

[5] John 4:4–44.
[6] Matthew 8:5–13; Luke 7:2–10.
[7] Luke 4:25–29.

- **Matthew 17:14–21; Mark 9:14–29; Luke 9:37–43—If you had real faith the size of a mustard seed, you could tell this mountain to move and it could not stand still.**

Frustrated disciples came to Jesus because they had been unable to cast out an evil spirit. Earlier, Jesus had sent them to the Judean countryside to preach the kingdom, heal the sick, cast out evil spirits, and raise the dead.[8] Afterward, they rejoiced that even the devils were subject to them.[9] Why was this evil spirit any different?

If a hundred tons of TNT failed to move a mountain, we would look for bigger, more powerful explosives. In contrast, Jesus used the example of a mustard seed to show that the tiniest amount of true faith was sufficient. The disciples didn't need to believe harder. They needed a better connection with God, and that's why prayer and fasting was important.

- **John 8:2–11—Their question was intended to trap [Jesus] into saying something against either the Law or public opinion.**

Because the Law called for those guilty of adultery to be put to death, some scholars believe Jewish women in the first century were stoned for this sin. If that were true, there would have been no trap in asking Jesus to give judgment. The Jewish leaders thought they had a question that would hurt Jesus no matter how he answered. If he said, "Let the woman live," he openly advocated breaking the Law and could be arrested. If he said, "Obey the Law and stone the woman," he went against public opinion and would lose the respect of the people.

---

[8] Matthew 10:5–8.
[9] Luke 10:17.

- **Matthew 6:9–13; Luke 11:1–13—"When you pray," Jesus said, "say something like this."**

The section of Matthew that we commonly call "the sermon on the mount" is a compilation summary of many messages. On many days, Jesus taught from high on the grassy hillsides. Some of his points were often repeated, in different ways at different times, as we would expect from any evangelist.

In the synagogues, people recited numerous prayers. A pattern of prayer was nothing new. We might say, "All Jews knew how to pray," but if that is true, how is it that John the Baptizer taught his disciples to pray?[10] Since people don't need to be taught what they already know, John must have taught something new. What was it? Perhaps they learned to pray spontaneously, to form their own words that were not part of an established liturgy.

In Luke's gospel, the disciples—men who already knew synagogue prayers and had been taught by John the Baptizer—saw Jesus praying and asked him to teach them.[11] What did Jesus teach about prayer that people didn't already know? They may have learned more about praying from the heart. The apostle Paul says we don't know how to pray but need the help of the Holy Spirit.[12] Whatever the focus of Jesus' teaching was, we can be sure it involved the principles of prayer offered from the heart, not the pattern contained in the words.

- **Luke 11:9—Ask and you will receive, seek and you will find, knock and the door will be opened for you.**

Many times, Jesus said, "You have heard it said . . . But I say . . ." He used expressions that people already believed were true and gave

---

[10] Luke 11:1.
[11] Luke 11:1.
[12] Romans 8:26.

them deeper meaning and better application. The Jews believed in the law of reaping and sowing. They believed persistent, hard effort always produced its reward. However, evidence does not support that perception. Business owners go bankrupt through no fault of their own. People often ask but never receive. They seek and never find. They knock, but the door never opens. Why would Jesus say something that isn't always true?

Jesus gave the common belief so he could point to the conditions that make it always true. When we ask, seek, and knock on anyone's door other than God's, we may be disappointed, but if we remain at God's door, we can trust him to always give us what we need.[13]

- **Matthew 23:37–39; Luke 13:34–35—I have wanted to gather you to myself like a hen brings her chicks under her wings.**

Jesus expressed the longing of God's heart that no one should perish.[14] Nothing can separate people from his love[15] other than their own choice to join many others who take the broad way to destruction.[16] Matthew's gospel places Jesus' words after his triumphant entry into Jerusalem, but Luke, with his better attention to details, places it correctly, prior to entering the city.

- **Matthew 19:24–26; Mark 10:25–27; Luke 18:25–27—Jesus said, "Those who trust in riches will have a very difficult time entering the Kingdom." [The disciples said,] "If that is true, who can be saved?"**

Common Jewish belief said that God rewards the righteous and afflicts the sinners. Therefore, except for the traitorous tax

---

[13] Matthew 6:8; Luke 11:13.

[14] 2 Peter 3:9.

[15] Romans 8:38–39.

[16] Matthew 7:13.

collectors, all the rich Jews must be righteous, since they were obviously blessed by God. Supposedly, the sickly and those living in poverty suffered because of sin. That's why Jewish leaders told the man who had been born blind that he was "born a sinner."[17] People already believed that all the poor people weren't saved. If the rich people couldn't be saved either, who was left? Jesus had to explain that, with God, all things are possible. He is able to save anyone who is willing to lose his life for his sake.[18]

- **Matthew 20:1–16; 22:1–14—Many are called, and few are chosen.**

  More than once, Jesus says, "Many are called, and few are chosen." Why isn't everyone chosen? If we're not careful, we miss his point and risk thinking God is not being fair. In one of his stories, workers slaved all day and thought they were unfairly treated when they received the same pay as those who worked only an hour. At another time, Jesus talked about a wedding feast in which people didn't deserve the honor of an invitation. Because the people didn't come, the place was filled with different, willing guests.

  Without the power of choice, people would be robots, and love would have no meaning. The distinction between the "called" and the "chosen" is who does the work for which they were called. Because God is not willing that any should perish,[19] we know we all have an opportunity to fulfill his purpose for our lives. However, not everyone is willing to answer the call and be counted among the "chosen." To enter the Kingdom of Heaven, it is not enough to say Jesus is our master.[20] If he really is our master, we must do the will of our heavenly Father.[21]

---

[17] John 9:34.
[18] Luke 9:24.
[19] 2 Peter 3:9.
[20] Matthew 7:21.
[21] James 2:20–26.

- **Matthew 20:20–28; Mark 10:35–45—In your glorious kingdom . . . award the seats of honor on your right and left.**

Mark says James and John asked Jesus for the seats of honor in the Kingdom. Matthew says it was their mother. Which was it?

Both reports show a different and important insight about the same event. James and John were present to participate in the request at their mother's prodding.

- **Luke 19:1–9—Sir, I will give half my wealth to the poor. If I have defrauded anyone, I will pay back four times the amount.**

Because Jesus responded positively, we can be sure this was a valid offer from Zacchaeus to make restitution to anyone he had defrauded. The Jews regarded all tax collectors as crooks, but simple math says Zacchaeus had to have been relatively honest in his dealings. Otherwise, the half that he had left after giving to the poor would not be sufficient to compensate the cheated parties with four times the amount.

- **Matthew 20:29–34; Mark 10:46–52; Luke 18:35–43—Two blind men, including one named Bartimaeus (son of Timaeus), sat by the side of the road, begging.**

Matthew says there were two men. Mark and Luke mention only one man. Who is right? The answer is, both are. The fact that there were two men doesn't mean that both men did the talking. From Mark's record, we know that Bartimaeus was the more aggressive of the two and spoke for both of them.

- **John 15:1–8—Whatever you ask will be done.**

A self-centered, materialistic culture wants to be in control. Its people would love to believe in a God who functions like a cosmic genie and does whatever they perceive is good or desirable. When the words "whatever you ask will be done" are considered by themselves, they seem to prove our ability to command mountains to move. If we allow ourselves to be caught in that misconception, we will not be able to explain why we have believed and commanded, but the mountain remains.

Jesus' illustration of our being a branch attached to the vine explains that we don't decide what God should do. We depend upon God to tell us what we should do. We must be and do whatever God commands. Because we are under his authority, we cannot act independently. Our prayer has power only while we remain attached to him, doing his will, not ours.

- **Matthew 27:3–10—[Judas] flung the silver across the Temple floor, left, and hanged himself.**

Matthew says Judas hanged himself. In the book of Acts, Luke tells us that he fell to his death, his body split open, and his intestines spilled out.[22] Which was it? Did he hang himself or fall to his death? It doesn't have to be one or the other. Both can be true. Judas hanged himself, and when the rope came loose or was cut, he fell upon the rocks below. His body split open, and his intestines spilled out.

- **Matthew 27:46; Mark 15:34—My God, my God, for this I was born.**

Ancient translators were unsure what the Aramaic *Eloi, Eloi, lema sabachthani* meant, so they included those words next to the Greek interpretation: "My God, my God, why have you forsaken me?" That rendering cannot be correct, because the Father, Son, and Holy Spirit, being one, cannot be separated. Some scholars compound

---

[22] Acts 1:18.

the error by providing a reason for the separation, saying the Father could not look upon sin. If that were true, then Satan could not have appeared before the throne of God concerning Job,[23] and the Son had no additional redemptive price available to ever reunite with the Father. There must be another explanation.

In *Idioms in the Bible Explained*,[24] George Lamsa presents conclusive arguments from his knowledge of the ancient eastern texts to resolve the incorrect rendering in the Greek. Those near the cross misunderstood what Jesus said, thinking he had called for Elijah. For centuries, translators have missed the meaning of the Aramaic. Now we know that Jesus neither called for Elijah nor wondered where his Father was.

Before entering Jerusalem, Jesus revealed the purpose for which he had come, that he must be lifted up so all men would be drawn to him.[25] He looked forward to his suffering on the cross and felt pressed to complete it.[26] After saying the anticipated moment had come with "For this I was born," he concluded with "It is finished," bowed his head, and quit breathing.[27]

- **Matthew 28:1–15; Mark 16:1–11; Luke 24:1–12; John 20:1–18—Mary Magdalene . . . was the first to see Jesus after he rose from the dead.**

Mary Magdalene was among the women who went to the tomb early in the morning.[28] When the women left the tomb, Jesus appeared to them.[29] Later, after telling Peter and John that the tomb

---

[23] Job 1:6.

[24] George M. Lamsa, *Idioms in the Bible Explained and A Key to the Original Gospels* (New York, NY: HarperCollins Publishers, 1985).

[25] John 12:32.

[26] Luke 12:50.

[27] John 19:20.

[28] Matthew 28:1; Mark 16:1–2.

[29] Matthew 28:9–10.

was empty,[30] Mary Magdalene was at the tomb crying when the man she assumed was the gardener made himself known, and she discovered that Jesus had risen from the dead.[31] At first glance, it seems impossible that Mary could see Jesus in the morning and later recognize him for the first time. How are these facts reconciled?

At sundown that concluded the Sabbath, the women bought spices to anoint Jesus' body.[32] Early the next morning, while it was still dark, they took the spices they had prepared but wondered who would roll away the stone.[33] When they discovered the empty tomb and talked to the angels, they were more mystified than amazed. Despite what they had seen and heard, they couldn't get past their reality that Jesus was dead. Their interpretation of "raised from the dead" was spiritual, not physical, which explains why the disciples could see Jesus, look at the nail prints in his hands, and not believe.[34] They thought he was a ghost until he ate with them. Therefore, the body had obviously been stolen,[35] a terrible tragedy that left people running everywhere to tell the news while others came to investigate.

Although Mary Magdalene was with the women who left the tomb and was the first to see Jesus, she was already running to tell Peter and John that the tomb was empty. At the time, she didn't realize who he was.

• **Mark 16:12–13; Luke 24:13–35—Two of Jesus' followers left for Emmaus.**

Who were the two people who didn't recognize Jesus as he walked with them to Emmaus? One name is given. Cleopas asked Jesus,

---

[30] John 20:1–2.
[31] John 20:13–17.
[32] Mark 16:1.
[33] Matthew 28:1; Mark 16:2–3; Luke 24:1.
[34] Luke 24:41.
[35] John 20:13.

"Are you the only visitor to Jerusalem who does not know what has happened in the last few days?"[36] The other person is less obvious until we consider what Cleopas said to convince the eleven disciples that he had seen Jesus. "The Lord Jesus has risen. It's not my word alone. Simon was with me, and he saw him too."[37] Simon is a common name. In the Gospels, we have Simon who was called Peter, Simon the Zealot, one of the twelve disciples, Simon of Cyrene, who carried Jesus' cross, Simon the Pharisee, who invited Jesus to dinner, Simon the brother of Jesus, Simon the father of Judas Iscariot, and Simon the leper whom Jesus healed. We can be sure that Simon, the follower who walked with Jesus to Emmaus, was a different person from the other Simons; otherwise, Luke, who had an interest in details, would have said so.

- **John 20:21–23—The sins you forgive will be forgiven, and the sins you do not forgive will not be forgiven.**

People have no power to forgive an offense done to someone else. Only God can forgive a sin committed against him. The Jews were angered when Jesus said, "Your sins are forgiven," because he assumed an authority that belonged to God.[38] The disciples were only able to forgive (or not forgive) sins when they acted under the direction of the Holy Spirit.

---

[36] Luke 24:18.
[37] Luke 24:34.
[38] Matthew 9:2–6.

eyewitness
OTHER TOOLS

Besides *Eyewitness*, other tools refresh, encourage, and explain the sacrifice God made so people could enjoy abundant life.

Eyewitness Stories: Four Reports on the Life of Christ
- A contemporary English translation of the four Gospels that is the source text for the *Eyewitness* chronological story
- Sections on chronology, fulfilled prophecy, and comments on difficult passages
- Perfect for seekers, new believers, or those wanting an enjoyable yet accurate modern translation

Eyewitness Audio Book
- A dramatized audio presentation with Dallas Holm, renowned singer-songwriter of Christian music, as the voice of Jesus
- Enjoy a smooth and seamless telling of the gospel story as it happened, in chronological order

Eyewitness Disciple Bible Study Series (first book to be released in 2009)
- Bible studies that enlighten and minister to those who want to learn more about the life of Christ. Great for individuals or small groups.
- Adds insight and application from the life of the most important man who ever lived

Eyewitness Inspiration: Contemporary Vignettes for Life
- Devotionals to encourage trust in God.

Visit your local bookstore, go online to www.winepressbooks.com, or call 1-877-421 READ (7323).